A MAN OF TWO FACES

Also by Viet Thanh Nguyen

Fiction

The Committed

The Refugees

The Sympathizer

Nonfiction

The Displaced:
Refugee Writers on Refugee Lives (editor)

Nothing Ever Dies:
Vietnam and the Memory of War

Transpacific Studies:
Framing an Emerging Field
(coedited with Janet Hoskins)

Race and Resistance:
Literature and Politics in Asian America

Children's Literature

Chicken of the Sea
(with Ellison Nguyen, Thi Bui, and Hien Bui-Stafford)

A MAN OF TWO FACES

A MEMOIR, A HISTORY, A MEMORIAL

VIET THANH NGUYEN

Grove Press
New York

FIRST EDITION

Published simultaneously in Canada
Printed in the United States of America

First Grove Atlantic hardcover edition: October 2023

Library of Congress Cataloging-in-Publication data is available for this title.

ISBN 978-0-8021-6050-8
eISBN 978-0-8021-6051-5

Grove Press
an imprint of Grove Atlantic
154 West 14th Street
New York, NY 10011

Distributed by Publishers Group West

groveatlantic.com

23 24 25 26   10 9 8 7 6 5 4 3 2 1

for Mẹ
for Má
for Linda Kim Nguyen
for Nguyễn Thị Bảy
for my mother

1937–2018

contents

CONTENTS

part three

A MAN OF
TWO FACES

part one

How can the word "I" be put into the plural . . .
how can I speak of an I other than my own?

Maurice Merleau-Ponty,
Phenomenology of Perception

do you know the way to san josé?

When does memory begin?
What memory is it that I seek?
And where, on the thin border between
history and memory, can I re
member myself?

Memory begins with Ba Má, their images like photographs, their story
like a movie, the kind found in the black box of a VHS tape, in an era
when I have long ago gotten rid of my VCR.

All our parents should have movies made of their lives. Or at least my
parents should. Their epic journey deserves star treatment, even if only
in an independent, low-budget film. Beautiful Joan Chen in her prime
would play my mother; the young heartthrob Russell Wong, my father.

So what if neither actor is Vietnamese?
We're all Asians here.

Joan Chen did play a Vietnamese mother in the big-budget *Heaven
and Earth*, Oliver Stone's biopic about Le Ly Hayslip, a Vietnamese
peasant girl caught in the whirlwind of a terrible war. Sexy Russell,
with his chiseled cheeks and pouty lips, could have been a movie star
if Hollywood ever cast Asian American men as romantic leads. His
slicked-back hair reminds me of my father's in a black-and-white head-
shot from the 1950s, his hair agleam. I, whose unending obsession
with the styling and maintenance of my hair begins at sixteen, should
have asked Ba, when he could still remember, what hair product he
used. I could try to fix my own hair in that same fashion, the way I
tried on my mother's gray sweatshirt after she died and discovered
that I could fit inside its void.

In this movie flickering in my mind's musty theater, the songs are
composed by the legend Trịnh Công Sơn and sung by his equally

legendary muse with the smoky voice, Khánh Ly. Their collabora-
tions constitute the soundtrack of nostalgia and loss for Vietnamese
exiles and refugees, played on cassette tapes at forty-five minutes a
side, filtered through a haze of cigarette smoke and accompanied by
Hennessy VSOP cognac. Wong Kar-wai directs in his typically moody,
seductive way. The lighting? Dim. The mood? Romantic. The color
scheme? Faded Polaroid.

And the actor who plays me? A cute little boy with big black eyes.

> After the movie comes and goes,
> he is never heard from again.
> No one remembers his name.

Perhaps Wong Kar-wai and his cinematographer Christopher Doyle
could cast their cinematic spell on our house by the freeway in San José,
stained a dark brown perhaps meant to evoke tree bark, built from wood
and shingle, stucco and silence, memory and forgetting.

Imagine the realtor's shock when my parents, refugees not fluent in
English, paid in full with cash.

For most refugees and immigrants, life is rented rooms or rented homes,
overcrowded apartments or overstuffed houses, extended families and
necessary tenants. Cluttered rooms. Bare lives. This is how Fae Myenne
Ng describes immigrant living in her novel *Bone*. Her setting is an
unexotic Chinatown, but at least it's in coastal San Francisco. Who has
ever written about provincial San José, an hour's drive away, or shined
the light of cinema on it? At least Dionne Warwick celebrated the city
with a song: "Do You Know the Way to San José?"

> Of course it's not as good as the songs about San Francisco.

Our street didn't even possess a name, like the Mango Street of Sandra Cisneros. Just a direction and a number, South Tenth, black iron bars on the windows. Our countrymen from the old world must have installed those bars, since they could not be opened from inside, trapping us in the event of fire. I blame our countrymen, always taking the shortcut. When some of them pour a cement patio for us, they forget to smooth it, leaving a surface with the texture of the moon.

With a classic San José flourish, the people who buy the house from us later pave the lawn for more parking. My mother used to recline on that lawn, posing to have her picture taken by my father. Our American photos are almost always in color, unlike most of our Vietnamese photos, where a glamorous haze illuminates my parents. My mother, on a grassy slope by a church, is resplendent in one of her many áo dài. My father, slim as one of today's Korean pop stars, leans with his hip against his Toyota sedan.

His sunglasses have disappeared, dust blown away in all the lost detritus of our past. I could wear them now, be just as fashionable on Sunset Boulevard as he was with his automobile.

Most people owned only motorbikes, if they had even that much. Even today in the place where I come from, more people drive motorbikes than cars. As one joke puts it:

> What do you call a Vietnamese minivan?
> A motorbike.

In a black-and-white Nick Ut photograph on my living room wall—not the one of Phan Thị Kim Phúc, burned by napalm, running and screaming— a man drives a motorbike, fleeing a battle, two boys in front of him, wife behind clutching another boy, two more boys behind her, staring at Nick Ut's camera.

In a flickering single frame of memory, a family employee drives me to preschool on a motorbike. You stood in front of him on his Vespa 50, my father told me a few years ago. I wish I had a photograph of me with the wind in my hair, a perfect shot for Wong Kar-wai to capture as we zoom past sun-browned men pedaling their xích-lô or driving three-wheeled Lambretta taxis. Seat belt? Car seat? Helmets? Ha! This was Việt Nam!

If I were to ask Ba now if he remembered this memory, I'm afraid he would say no. So I stay silent.

Ba is the family documentarian. His camera recorded our first house in a middle-class suburb of Harrisburg, where we lived for our first three years in the United States, but he did not memorialize our second house on a busy two-lane road in the middle of the city: redbrick with renters upstairs, white parents whose little girl plays with me on the couch the previous owner abandoned in the yard. My brother and I share a room, him listening to seventies hits like "Hotel California," which Vietnamese males of his generation were required to memorize. I call the kitchen the "chicken," making my father laugh during that brief interval when his English was better than mine.

South Tenth was the third house, another step toward the blinking red neon sign of the AMERICAN DREAM™ beckoning us forward across the dark plains of this republic. My parents crossed those plains by jet after hearing about San José, California, from their good friend Bác Quý, who had fled with my mother from our hometown. Warmer weather, better opportunities, many more of our countrymen. So, in 1978, we moved.

Thank God.

Just kidding, Harrisburg.
I don't even believe in God.

No, I really am just kidding, Harrisburg. I was happy with
you—state capital of Pennsylvania!—but a seven-year-old,
so long as someone loves him, can be happy anywhere,
even if it is only fifteen miles from Three Mile Island,
site of the worst nuclear disaster in the United States,
the meltdown occurring a year after we left.

And so what if San José has a song and you don't, Harrisburg?
No one needs directions to San Francisco.

Dionne Warwick herself admitted, It's a dumb song and I didn't want
to sing it. Still, her song won a Grammy, sold millions, was a global
top ten hit in 1968. While people sang along to their home hi-fis or in
the comfort of wood-paneled station wagons, American soldiers commanded by a Mexican American captain murdered 504 Vietnamese
civilians in Mỹ Lai, three years before my birth.

My country continues killing innocents.
On the day I first revise these words, the

> "Pentagon Admits to
> Civilian Casualties
> in Somalia for Third Time."

The victim is Nurto Kusow Omar Abukar, dead
five months earlier in the town of Jilib, in a strike

> targeting members of the Shabab, an
> extremist group linked to Al Qaeda.

Nurto Kusow Omar Abukar, eighteen-year-old
girl, initially reported as a

> terrorist

by AFRICOM, killed by a GBU-69/B small glide
munition manufactured by Dynetics, which

> provides responsive, cost-effective
> engineering, scientific and IT solutions to the
> national security, cybersecurity, space, and
> critical infrastructure security sectors.

My brother says he knew one of the children, a
former classmate.

Years later I visit Sơn My, as the Vietnamese call the
village of the massacre. Cement pathways wind
through the village, marked with trails of footprints
symbolizing the absent dead, the living ghosts. I am
careful not to walk in their footprints.

A decade after Dionne Warwick's song climbs the charts, I arrive in
San José, watch a public service announcement about the city accompanied by her song, and think, This is so not cool, even if I myself was
definitely so not cool.

Those who find their way to San José may drive through East Santa
Clara Street, the digestive tract running through the city's potbelly of
a downtown. On a small, shady appendix of a side street, Bác Quý has
opened the first Vietnamese grocery store, Bác Quý who never mar-
ries, who never has children, and who bestows on me hundred-dollar
bills for Tết. Má helps her for several months while Ba works on an
assembly line. Then Ba Má open the city's second Vietnamese grocery
store . . . two blocks away.

That must be the definition of friendly competition.

Located on East Santa Clara Street, the store is the belly button of the
city's potbelly. My parents call it the SàiGòn Mới, fusing the westernized
"Saigon" and the original "Sài Gòn." Not translating SàiGòn Mới must
be an assertion that *we are here because you were there*. Not translating
might even be a sign of defiance, but I do not understand this yet. I
simply accept that this store is for us, for people who need no translation, yet who must exist only in translation every time they meet the
Americans surrounding them.

When my brother graduates as valedictorian of San José High, the *San José Mercury* of 1982 profiles him and describes Ba Má's SàiGòn Mới as a

> miniature department store overflowing with
> bolts of silk and Vietnamese books in
> addition to Indochinese groceries
> and American junk food.

A miniature department store!
Why did I never imagine this humble
enterprise of my parents in this manner?

Creaking accordion gates protect the storefront, protesting every time they are opened and closed. Long tongues of sticky yellow paper dangle from the ceiling, studded with dead flies. White rice in fifty-pound sacks is stacked to the rafters. In the back, a butcher hacks at fish and meat while I stamp prices in purple ink on cans of grass jelly and lychees in syrup. Soy sauce, oyster sauce, nước mắm, and mắm ruốc in a sickly shade of purple. Coco Rico coconut soda in green cans. A machine for grinding coffee, whose aroma mixes with the rice. JVC stereos with cassette players in boxes behind the counter, which my parents send home to our relatives, who sell them for cash.

Why do they need cash?
And why can we not just
send cash if they need it?
My life with Ba Má
defined by questions
I never ask.

Under the glass counter are Chinese martial arts paperback novels, translated into Vietnamese, which my brother can read but I can't (and never will). I am eight. I can (and do) eat all the Chinese doughnuts and fried sesame seed balls I want, as well as Danish butter cookies in blue tins and sugary ladyfingers and chocolate-covered cherries that pop and ooze in my mouth.

I have not tasted any of them again since the
days of the SàiGòn Mới. What would
happen if I ate a chocolate-covered
cherry now? Would I remember
all I have forgotten or
tried to forget?

I have everything I need but almost nothing I want. I don't want Catholicism, but my parents enroll me in Saint Patrick School a few blocks south, a Vietnamese boy wearing Irish-green corduroys and an Irish-green cardigan with a shamrock on its pocket.

I have never worn corduroy or Irish green since.

Every morning, after the Pledge of Allegiance, we recite a Hail Mary and the Lord's Prayer. I know the Lord's Prayer by heart and never imagine I can forget it, though as I try to recite it now, I realize I can get only so far as

> forgive us our trespasses as we
> forgive those who trespass against us.

I have forgotten the second half.

In another Polaroid of memory, I receive First Communion in Harrisburg. All children look cute receiving this sacrament, the little boys with clip-on ties, the little girls in white frocks. I must have been pretty adorable, walking solemnly down the aisle, cupped hands extended to the priest for the sacred Styrofoam, eager to wash down that morsel of Christ's Body with my first sip of Christ's syrupy Blood.

> The red wine
> fails to seduce.
> I turn out an atheist.

> Don't tell my father, who
> gifts me a bottle of monk-made
> sacramental wine every Christmas.

Ba's Catholic name is Joseph, same as mine. My mother's, Maria. Like many other immigrants and refugees before them, Ba Má become human sacrifices, throwing themselves onto barbed wire so I can walk across their backs into this strange new world. They work relentlessly, almost every waking hour, almost every day of the year except for Easter, Tết, and Christmas.

> Every day their own
> station of the cross.

One way I know, now, that they loved my brother and me is that they only occasionally made us work at the SàiGòn Mới. This is why, one

Christmas Eve circa 1980, when I am nine, my parents are at the SàiGòn Mói while my brother and I stay home.

At the SàiGòn Mói, Ba would be dressed in shirt and slacks; Má, in blouse and slacks or knee-length skirt, perhaps with a matching jacket. In the world outside our home, they are always neat, presentable, semi-formal, with no trace of their rural origins. Superheroes in disguise as parents, they are saving us, not with the Hollywood derring-do of helicopters and fast cars and supposedly witty repartee, but from a secret headquarters disguised as the SàiGòn Mói.

Soon they will come home, to a kitchen with a dishwasher they never use and a dining room with a linoleum floor and a chandelier with six glass shades for lights, one of which I break on the first night we move into the house because I am so excited I run around the house screaming and bump into the low-slung fixture. My brother sweeps up the broken glass, and my exasperated father berates me. Tonight my brother and I wait for my parents in a house that had been perfect and new until I broke that shade. I am watching television.

> Through the windows of my sandcastle of memory,
> I can hear the ocean of amnesia, perpetual, invincible.

When Ba Má come home, exhausted but perhaps pleased that they are, once again, their own bosses, they will prepare dinner for their waiting children. In later years, my father describes my otherwise dutiful brother as a picky eater, in contrast to me, who eats everything my parents make. Perhaps being a picky eater is my otherwise responsible elder brother's way of resisting his obligations. Perhaps I intuit that to prepare a meal is to show love without ever saying I love you.

If they return home in the blue cargo van that Ba uses to fetch goods for the SàiGòn Mói and that he parks in the driveway, they will enter through the front door. If they return in the white Ford sedan with its burgundy top and trim, they park in the garage and enter through the garage door. They take off their shoes at the door and change into their casual clothes, a white T-shirt and shorts for Ba, a nightgown for Má. Too tired to care what they look like, too pressed to have the time to shop for tracksuits or sweatpants or whatever else American working parents are supposed to wear at home. Their sons are the only eyewitnesses to their vulnerability, to their flesh, to their occasional short tempers.

Ba Má will share the kitchen with its Formica countertop and fluorescent lights. Ba is unusual for a Vietnamese man, doing half the housework and cooking, as well as the mending, sewing, and alterations, having once been a tailor. He makes the curtains and hems my jeans, while Má irons creases into them. My classmates tease me for being so fresh off the boat as to wear creased jeans.

Ba deserves credit for doing much more than most Vietnamese men while also declining their vices—smoking, billiards, alcohol, mistresses, whiling away time with male buddies in homosocial cafés where the patrons suck on both cigarettes and nostalgia. But Má deserves even more credit just for doing what is expected of her as a Vietnamese woman, the triple shift of working outside the home, doing the chores, and bearing the children.

Má is not a great cook, but it is not for lack of talent, just lack of time. In her retirement, she masters a few elaborate dishes, like the jumbo shrimp in garlic sauce that appears every time I visit for dinner. But at the end of 1980, her repertoire, and my father's, is simple. The meal they would have made that Christmas Eve would have had three courses, as always: a vegetable side, like stir-fried rau muống or sliced cucumbers in a vinaigrette; a simple soup, most likely canh cà chua, the tomatoes blistered by the hot broth, flavored by a handful of tiny dried shrimp;

and a meat dish, oftentimes the boiled organ meat of cows and chickens, served with a weak dipping sauce of nước mắm, diluted by water, or salt and pepper floating in a puddle of lemon juice.

I chew and chew without protest, perhaps because I know no better, but I probably do. I can see the meat loaf and roast beef and casseroles that white people eat on TV. I chew and chew because I love my parents and know no other way to repay them than to eat what they cook and to attempt to be what they say I must be at nearly every meal: good, obedient, respectful. I interpret these commands to mean: Do as I am told. Be quiet. Ask no questions.

When Ba Má have the time, they will fry a half dozen or more pork chops in caramelized soy sauce and sugar, my favorite. My father makes sure I eat two or three or four, more than he takes for himself. The centerpiece of the meal and table is the squat, capacious National one-button rice cooker that does only one thing, make white rice, unlike the fancy Zojirushi I own now that also makes sushi rice and porridge. The cute Zojirushi with its smart chip belongs in an anime cartoon and breaks down easily. The analog National endures like everything else Ba Má own. Like Ba Má themselves.

Perhaps, because it's Christmas Eve, Ba Má will bring home a bottle of $3.99 Cook's Champagne from the Lucky supermarket a couple of blocks from the SàiGòn Mới. The Champagne gives me a headache and makes me think for decades that I do not like Champagne. But Christmas Eve dinner never arrives. Instead of the pop of the Champagne bottle, the phone rings in the kitchen, and my brother leaves me where I am, watching cartoons in the living room. I am laughing when my brother reappears.

Ba Má have been shot, my brother says.

                                        Perhaps I laugh the way my
                                        nine-year-old son does now
                                        when watching cartoons:
                                        uproariously,
                                        enraptured.

Ba Má have been shot, he says again.

                                                                    I

    What's the matter with you?

                                                              stop

        Why don't you say anything?

                                                        laughing.

        Don't you *feel* anything?

                                        Honestly, no.
                                        Is numbness
                                        a feeling?

        Your brother, seven years older, is crying.

                                        You keep your gaze fixed
                                        on the television, saying
                                        nothing, which you
                                        will excel at.

You have no memory of how you sleep that night, or of how or when
Ba Má return from the hospital the next day, but you know they soon

go back to work. Mere flesh wounds cannot stop them, or so you think at the time. Ba Má are inevitable. Ba Má are immortal.

> Easier to think of them in this way, or not to
> think of them at all, than to imagine them lying
> on their queen-sized bed on their return home,
> nursing wounds, maybe even weeping, terrified
> of the next day and night at the SàiGòn Mói.

Your family never speaks of this incident, just as you will never speak of so many things, just as you never cry for the stigmata you do not ask to see and Ba Má do not show, wounds awash in the red neon light of the movie of their lives that no one will make.

Too bad you become a writer instead of a filmmaker.
Now you live in Los Angeles. When you
tell people you're a writer

no one cares.

hello, hollywood?

You are refugees, not exiles.
You are refugees, not expats.
You are refugees, not migrants.
You are refugees, not immigrants.
You are many, not few.
You are many, not one.
But though you are
a horde, you are also
nothing. You
refugees.

Perhaps some of the refugees of World War II received the Hollywood treatment, but very few Hollywood movies feature you, the refugees of the last few decades, though your lives have everything Hollywood desires: Drama! Tragedy! War! Romance! Separated lovers! Orphaned children! Divided families! Impossible odds! Heartwarming stories of reunion and success! (Ignore the ones not reunited, the ones not successful).

BUT—
and this is a big

BUT

—you refugees lack one crucial
element Hollywood needs:

You. Are. Not. White.

You own a house or rent an apartment. You live with your family or by yourself. You wake in the morning and drink your coffee or tea. You drive a car or a motorbike, or perhaps you take the bus. You go to work and turn on your computer. You go out at night and flirt and date. You watch movies and television shows and fantasize about seeing yourself on-screen. You live in a small town or big city, or maybe in the countryside. You have hopes, dreams, expectations. You take your humanity for granted. You still believe you are human when catastrophe renders you homeless. Smoke and fire shroud your town or city or countryside. You drive, run, walk, or catch a bus to the border or the sea. Only then, having fled, hoping to leave, or making it across the border or the sea, on foot, on boat, on raft, on truck, do you understand that those who are not refugees see you refugees as the zombies of the world, the undead rising from dying states to march or swim toward the borders of the living in endless frightening waves.

> Those on the other side do
> not see you as human at all.

This is the dread experience of joining the world's 103 million forcibly displaced people, as the United Nations High Commissioner for Refugees calls them. The refugees from Russia's invasion of Ukraine receive a more hospitable welcome because they are a rarity: they are white. Perhaps Hollywood might even make a movie about the odyssey of Ukrainian refugees fleeing to Mexico and claiming asylum at the U.S. border, starring Angelina Jolie as a bedraggled but still beautiful refugee. But Hollywood will probably not make a movie about the African refugees fleeing from Ukraine, abused at the Polish border, or the Central American refugees kept waiting at the U.S. border while white Ukrainians pass on through.

The nation of the displaced looms larger than New Zealand or Ireland, Norway or Denmark, Singapore or Hong Kong, Switzerland or Austria, Portugal or Greece, Belgium or the Netherlands, Taiwan or Australia, South Korea or the United Kingdom, Saudi Arabia or Spain, Italy or France, Cambodia or Thailand, Germany or Iran.

Why even compare yourself to a nation?
People hate you, define themselves against
you, no longer part of a nation, reminder
of the fragility of homes and nations,
a threat to the existence of nations.
Even if they do not hate you,
they see you as a crisis.

You refugees.

This nation of displaced persons is a little larger than Việt Nam, ninety-seven million people, the world's fifteenth-largest nation. Despite their demure appearance, your people really enjoy procreating! But as much as they might be driven by Eros, perhaps Thanatos also haunts them, shadowed as they are by three million war deaths and the hundreds of thousands or maybe millions of dead who preceded them from the other conflicts, famine, and colonization of the previous hundred years. You are proud of your lustful, fertile people, you who were one of them until you were

Dis-placed.
        Dis place.
            Dys-place.
                This place that is no place that is still your place.

The forcibly displaced include the internally displaced and asylum seekers, as well as 32.5 million refugees (as a nation, larger than Malaysia, smaller than Angola). The countries sending forth or forcing out the most refugees are the Syrian Arab Republic, Venezuela, Ukraine, Afghanistan, and South Sudan. Force and violence beat refugees into existence. Fear and terror shape refugees. Things are done to refugees before they do things like flee. Escape. Say please. And thank you.

As for the European Jews who survived the Holocaust and became refugees, Hannah Arendt wrote:

> We were told to forget; and we forgot
> quicker than anybody ever could imagine.

You have done your best to
forget. You have become very good at
forgetting. And now it is difficult, having
forgotten so many parts of yourself and those you
love, to re member your many disremembered pieces.

The countries hosting the most refugees are Turkey, Colombia, Germany, Pakistan, and Uganda. Until the Russian invasion of Ukraine in 2022, the West had not welcomed most of the world's refugees since World War II, despite the cries of some Westerners that too much is asked of the generous, liberal, cosmopolitan West, which has, among other civilized accomplishments, invented the fork—so much easier to use than chopsticks, so much cleaner than one's hand—as well as the napalm dropped on Phan Thị Kim Phúc, the camera and the film that recorded her burned and naked, and the entire apparatus of mechanical reproduction that etched her into people's memories all over the world, to the point that her face and body now stand in for Việt Nam, country of war, country of victims, deserving of pity from the West and most of the rest.

> Are you a Westerner?
> You must be a Westerner.
> San José is in the West, and
> you know the way to San José.

You were born in Ban Mê Thuột, now spelled Buôn Mê Thuột or Buôn Ma Thuột, its name changed by the victors, along with many other things. Get rid of French influences, restore some Sinicized roots, or just rename after new heroes. Sài Gòn becomes Hồ Chí Minh City, and if you land at the airport and call it phi trường instead of sân bay, or if you call a bank nhà băng instead of ngân hàng, people will know you left in 1975. As for your hometown, Buôn Ma Thuột is closer to Buôn Ama Thuột, the name used by the people who first lived there, the Ê Đê.

You remember nothing of what the *New York Times* called a

> sleepy, charming highlands town

where the last emperor, Bảo Đại, once had hunting lodges. By the time you are born, American military advisers occupy those lodges. American-made jeeps and trucks rumble through paved two-lane roads and streets, driven by southern soldiers. Ban Mê Thuột has changed, for when President Ngô Đình Diệm visited in 1957, around the time Ba Má moved there, the town was little more than a village with dirt roads, known for its coffee, its waterfalls, and its ethnic minorities, including the Rade who

> padded barefoot through its streets
> or rode on hulking elephants.

The Rade are now the Ê Đê. You, an ethnic minority in the United States, are the majority, the Kinh, in Việt Nam.

> The Kinh are an imperial, warlike people, who marched
> south from China to seize the lands of the Cham, the
> Cambodians, and dozens of Indigenous highlander
> peoples whom the French called Montagnards.
> You called them Mọi. "Savage." You, the
> colonizer now colonized by the

French, staff the French
colonial bureaucracy,
almost white but
not quite.

If a movie was made of your family's epic refugee journey, most likely a low-budget passion project by a Vietnamese filmmaker with a diasporic history like yourself, it would begin with a quiet prelude in early March 1975, when your handsome father boards a plane for Sài Gòn on business. He carries a briefcase with gold and cash to buy a house in Sài Gòn. The plan is for you and your brother to be educated there instead of your provincial hometown.

Perhaps Má takes you to the Phụng Dực airport with its burnt-orange control tower and small terminal the length of two or three railroad cars. Perhaps Ba hugs you in farewell, for you have just turned four and are still in need of hugs. Perhaps you wave bye-bye and watch his plane take off from the red earth runway, soaring past the military helicopters and transport planes. You return to your home to the west of the airport on Ama Trang Long street. Your family's quarters are above the family business. This one sells jewelry and auto parts and evolved from the original business with which Ba Má began their ascent: a one-stop shop where Má sold cloth and Ba did the tailoring, a first-of-its-kind innovation in the local economy.

You are unaware that you are about to enter History. Not far away, the communist army is assembling nineteen divisions to launch its decisive surprise invasion of the south. Its first target: Ban Mê Thuột.

You are grateful for all those things you do not remember. You do not remember the artillery barrage that begins at 3:00 A.M. on March 9, the sapper attacks on the Phụng Dực airport, the gun battles between northern and southern troops, the latter armed with M16s and protected by American helmets. The sounds of war would be familiar to Má, parts of town having been burned down almost exactly seven years before in February 1968, during the Tết Offensive.

Decades later, at a stranger's suburban party in San Gabriel Valley, California, the host pulls out an AK-47 and shoots into the ground to ring in the New Year. The clamor is deafening. You can feel the impact of the bullets on the ground as the gunner empties his magazine. Multiply by a thousand to generate the volume and the velocity of flying metal and the fear your mother felt. You leave the party as fast as you can after the twentysomething host walks around with the AK-47, shaking hands. Your friends tell you he frowns as you leave, but you don't care. You're a coward. You intend to stay that way.

An image of northern soldiers in olive-green uniforms and pith helmets sitting on tanks flashes out of your ocean of amnesia, but no picture of your mother, frantic as she is unable to call your father, all lines of communication cut. Má makes a decision. She flees with Bác Quý, your ten-year-old brother, and you, leaving behind your sixteen-year-old (adopted) sister to guard the family property. Your mother believes your family will return. The war has gone back and forth for years. Why would it end now?

When you are sixteen, you are a high school student working your first job, at Great America amusement park. Your major concern: finding a girlfriend. Your sixteen-year-old (adopted) sister faces a different coming of age. She watches her mother and brothers abandon her. Was it daylight? Most likely it was the dark of night, to evade communist patrols. She shuts the door, locks it. Her heart beats fast. She cries alone. A child facing an immense and terrifying future.

You do not know that any of this happened, but what else could have happened? You do not know whether you cry when you leave her, but you hope so, giving her a sign that she would be loved and missed.

You do not remember this moment or your (adopted) sister at all. Your parents will not see her again for nearly twenty years. You will not see her again for nearly thirty years.

This is a war story.

Your brother remembers dead paratroopers hanging from the trees, although you do not. You also do not remember whether you walked the entire 184 kilometers to Nha Trang, or whether your mother carried you, or whether you got a ride on the cars, trucks, carts, motorbikes, and bicycles clogging the road. Perhaps she does remember, but you never ask about the exodus, about the tens of thousands of civilian refugees and fleeing soldiers, the desperate scramble to get on a boat in Nha Trang, some of the soldiers shooting civilians to clear their way, using American M16s rather than AK-47s.

Má hired strangers to carry you, your brother says.
Má strapped gold to your brother's legs, your father says.
But forty-five years later, Ba also says,
I really don't know what your mother underwent.

You do not remember the weather, but in the months of March and April it must have been good, not too hot, not too wet. You do not remember finding your father in Sài Gòn, or how you waited another month until the communist army attacked the city, or how terrified your parents must have been, or how their days were spent trying to find ways to leave the city, and how, on the last day before the city's capture—or liberation, depending on one's point of view—you tried to get into the airport, then the American embassy, then somehow fought through crowds at the docks to reach a boat, how your father became separated from the rest of you but decided to jump on a boat by himself anyway, how your mother did the same, both trusting themselves to God but also, as always, taking their lives into their own hands, and then how you were reunited on a larger ship, how you floated for three days, how your family is a part of THE FALL OF SAIGON with the picture of the helicopter on a roof, a line of human beings who are becoming refugees climbing up a ladder.

> Are you a witness to history
> because you were there?
> Can you be a witness to history
> if you do not remember it?

You remember a kind man sharing milk with your mother for you, or perhaps you just remember Má telling you this story. Perhaps the milk is rotten. Or perhaps, even if the milk is good, you associate its taste with a crowded boat, frightened people, a sea you have never seen before. In the future, Má mixes sugar into milk to get you to drink it, but you never overcome your distaste of milk and cheese, gagging even at the soft, bland wedges of Laughing Cow that Ba likes to eat with bites of banana. You think you might have been six feet tall if it weren't for your allergy to dairy, one minor consequence of being a refugee embedded into your taste buds and your body.

> Or perhaps you're just lactose intolerant.

You remember the blue sea. You remember soldiers on your boat opening fire on a smaller boat of refugees trying to approach.

> Your brother says, That never happened.

> What if he is wrong?

New Life—this is the name of the haphazard American operation to rescue American allies from the Republic of Việt Nam, a country that no longer exists except in the imagination of its global refugee diaspora of more than five million people, a country most of the world remembers as South Việt Nam. After a war that kills three million Vietnamese people; several hundred thousand Laotians, Cambodians, and Hmong; more than fifty-eight thousand Americans; some five thousand South Koreans; and hundreds more from other countries, perhaps this is an appropriate name.

Or is it?
AMERICA™,
a pro-life nation,
indivisible, under God,
has watered its dark fields
with blood spilled from
colonization,
genocide,
slavery
& war.

Born in the Year of the Pig as Nguyễn Thanh Việt, reborn in AMERICA™ as Viet Thanh Nguyen. History performs your caesarean, as it does for all refugees to AMERICA™, delivering you as that mythological subject, the amnesiac, rootless, synthetic New American.

Contrary to sentiment and compliment, newborn
babies—purple, slimy, and screaming, eyes
screwed shut against the alien light—
are generally kind of ugly.
You are no exception.

The sandcastle of your memory really begins to rise after your stops at a chain of American military bases in the Philippines, Guam, and, finally, Pennsylvania. From bases in the Philippines and Guam—as well as Thailand and Japan—the United States launched bombing strikes on Việt Nam, Laos, and Cambodia with B-52 Stratofortresses manufactured by Boeing, the same company that makes most of the airplanes you now fly on as you jet around the world. But by the time you stumble onto those bases, confused and dazed, they have taken a pause from death-dealing to giving New Life to refugees fleeing from countries once colonized by the imperial French. You are escaping to

AMERICA™

(Cue song of the same title by Neil Diamond,
son of Jewish immigrants from Poland and Russia,
whose birth name really is Diamond and
whose lyrics you cannot afford to reprint.)

America the Great!
America the Exceptional!
A country
fundamentally
opposed to
imperialism and
colonialism!

Except when AMERICA™ colonized the Philippines, Guam, Hawai'i, Puerto Rico, Samoa, the Virgin Islands, the Thirteen Colonies, and pretty much the western three-quarters of what is now the United States of America, which did buy 828,000

square miles for $15 million from a French dude,
the world historical equivalent of you buying a
really cheap, brand-new Sony PlayStation
from the trunk of some guy in
a parking lot who says,
It's all legit, bro.

From the bases of the American empire in the Pacific, 130,000 of
you are flown, probably on Boeing planes, to temporary digs in Fort
Chaffee, Arkansas; Eglin Air Force Base, Florida; Camp Pendleton,
California; and Fort Indiantown Gap, Pennsylvania. From these do-
mestic military bases, the apparatus of government and charities dis-
perses you throughout the country, diluting your refugee intensity so
the American body politic can more easily swallow your strangeness
and bitterness. The Hmong, fellow refugees from Laos, land in the
wintry states of Minnesota and Wisconsin as well as sunny California.
Your family arrives in Pennsylvania. You refugees, who say Cali for
California and Los with a long *oh* for Los Angeles and *Chick-ah-go* for
Chicago, must have looked at the name of Ben Franklin's state and
sighed one long, long sigh.

Your parents, Joseph and Maria? Refugees twice.
Joseph and Mary of the Bible? Refugees once.

You and 22,000 other Vietnamese and Cambodian refugees get to the
unpronounceable state in early summer 1975. Instead of the stable
that Joseph and Mary found, you are housed in one of the fort's many
two-story barracks, marked *T* for "temporary" though they were built
in the 1930s.

Each barracks can house sixty soldiers or ninety-six refugees in bunk
beds. Seventy-two square feet per soldier, forty square feet per refugee.
No partitions for privacy. The one common bathroom features a row

of exposed toilets and a cramped, dark shower room with no windows or stalls. You see these details when you return for a tour forty-seven years later, but you remember nothing of the camp, certainly not the lessons in pronunciation and vocabulary that the comedian Richard Pryor says are taught there:

> You got all the Vietnamese in the army
> camps and shit, takin' tests and stuff,
> learnin' how to say "nigger,"
> so they can become
> good citizens.

Your people are good at taking tests. Have you passed this one?

Pryor isn't wrong, except that some refugees already know the difference between Black and white. Your Americanization starts in Việt Nam, where the Americans exported everything, including their racism, like the French before them. This is why so many Vietnamese despise the Amerasian or Eurasian children of Black fathers much more than the Amerasian or Eurasian children of white fathers.

Although you are semi-Americanized, you need American sponsors to leave the camp. Families and churches throughout the country take in refugee families. No one wants your entire family. One sponsor takes your parents, another your brother. A third comes for you. You are four.

> Go where it hurts,
> the writer Bharati Mukherjee, your teacher, once told you.
> Cut to the bone.

> This . . . is where it hurts.

memory's beginning

That classic Nietzsche line you quote over and over because it is true:

If something is to stay in the memory it must be burned in:
only that which never ceases to hurt stays in the memory.

A handful of bad memories can be more indelible than a lifetime of good memories or mediocre ones. We notice the scar, not the skin. Being taken away from your parents is burned in between your shoulder blades, a brand you do not usually see until you examine yourself with the mirrors of your own writing.

You do not remember being taken away the first time, but your sponsor brings you to see Ba Má one night, then inevitably pulls you away again.

You howl and scream. You are four.
You think Má is crying, too, but perhaps
you are only hoping she cried.

You remember the howling and not the room or house or apartment in which it took place, nor the sponsor who brought you there and took you away. You are the physical sound and feeling, the essence of yourself, a scream, the reverse of Munch's famous painting, so that instead of seeing the silent scream you can only hear it. The sound makes you grateful you cannot remember the journey out of Ban Mê Thuột, Nha Trang, and Sài Gòn. But if you *did* remember . . .

. . . that would be incredible for your writing!

Think about it—
if only you could remember enough, you could be
A VOICE FOR THE VOICELESS.

The writer's dilemma:
be scarred enough to be a good writer,
but not so scarred as to be truly fucked up.
You have achieved the magic balance!
Congratulations!!!

Your first sponsors are a young couple. By couple, you mean man and woman. By man and woman, you mean white man and woman. They live in a trailer or mobile home. They seem kind, but your stay is short. Maybe you are not that cute, unlike the orphans of Operation Babylift, not all of whom are actually orphans, seventy-eight of whom die when their transport plane crashes in Sài Gòn. But the survivors must have been supercute, as Richard Pryor implies:

> It was funny, man, pleadin' for the orphans and shit.
> [mimicking white woman] *God, we've got to do something. The little orphans, oh my goodness.* Bitch almost had me goin' gettin' an orphan. People in Mississippi, white folks in Georgia and shit, adoptin' babies. Shit gonna last about a year. And that racism gonna come out. [mimicking white man] *Goddamn. What in the hell we got here, Margot? Ain't your eyes ever gonna round out? Look like one of 'em neighborhood coons.* And I'm for orphans, now, you know, don't get me wrong. I like orphans, but shit, they got ten million niggers here need to be adopted.
> [applause]

You are unaware of receiving your first benefit in not being Black. You lucky poor Asian child, total strangers willing to take you in! Your second sponsor family has children, at least one around your age, glowing with blondness. This family is also kind, but they unintentionally embarrass you by asking you to teach them to use chopsticks, which must have been quite exotic in 1970s Pennsylvania. You sit at a dining table, looking back at their kind, expectant faces, the father and the mother, the curious and skeptical children wondering who this strange kid is in their house, taking away the attention of their parents, requiring them to fondle these sticks. Did the parents order Chinese food to go with the chopsticks? Where else would they have found chopsticks other than from a Chinese restaurant? You are four years old. This is a lot of pressure. And, unfortunately, you have no idea how to use chopsticks. None too smart, you are already—gasp!—*losing your roots.*

> Oddly, you do not remember when
> you eventually learned to use chopsticks,
> presumably thanks to your parents.
> Do Americans remember
> when they learned to
> wield a fork?

You cannot recall their house, what room you slept in, whether you shared it, what strange foods you ate—cereal? mac 'n' cheese? potato salad? casseroles? tuna fish sandwiches?—or how you communicated with them when you did not know a word of English. If you talked at all.

> Wouldn't it have been sitcom hilarious if the
> only English you did know was GI number one!
> and Hey, GI! You want boom-boom?
> like the little kids in the movies?
> Cue the canned laughter.

Cute or not, you must have been a difficult guest. Four years old, separated from your parents.

> Are you supposed to be grateful?

You also have no memory of one Joseph H. Windish, a veteran of the Korean War who sponsored your father and mother. When your father searched for a job, Mr. Windish wrote a letter of recommendation, now framed in the cabinet of your father's living room that holds wineglasses, a crystal bowl, and a picture of your brother with President Obama, whose charismatic smile radiates even through the photograph. In the letter, Mr. Windish describes your father as

> trustworthy and stable, a family man, having
> a wife and two children who he has
> obviously taken care of well.

This is the first description of you in English, a testament to Ba Má.

You are a minority as refugees and as Asians, but so was Mr. Windish, who shares a name with your father (and you). Unlike Mr. Windish, the majority of Americans do not want to accept refugees from Southeast Asia. Some of the majority's fears are realized. Some of you refugees commit crimes, including murder, for which a family acquaintance in Pennsylvania goes to prison. Some of you depend on welfare. But some of you become doctors, lawyers, engineers, soldiers, sailors. One of you even invents one of the deadliest weapons ever made:

> It's a terrifying device. The thermobaric bomb crushes caves
> with a super-hot blast that can destroy internal organs as far as a
> quarter-mile away. Its explosion is designed to tunnel through
> convoluted caves and pulverize anyone hiding as deep as
> 1,100 feet inside, and then incinerate whatever remains.

From being bombed to inventing bombs—the AMERICAN DREAM™!

And don't forget when Tippi Hedren visits fellow actor and friend Kiều Chinh (who could also play your mother in the movie of her life) at Camp Pendleton and takes such pity on the refugees that she asks her manicurist to train some of these women.

And this is how, nearly fifty years later,
you Vietnamese make up 58 percent of the
nail salon industry in this country.

Your failures—and successes—happen not necessarily because you
are refugees or Southeast Asian, but because you are human. At four
years of age, you do not know that some people do not perceive you as
human, but as a refugee, a Vietnamese, a victim to be pitied or scorned,
rescued or rejected. But the first blow has been dealt. Being taken away
shows you your vulnerability and the powerlessness of your parents.
For most of your life you recall this moment only as a fact, not a wound.

That is not true.

You begin to re member yourself when your son turns four in 2017. You
have named your son Ellison in homage to the novelist Ralph, whose
Invisible Man impressed you deeply when you read it in college. Ralph's
middle name is Waldo, after the philosopher Emerson, whose essays
you also read in college. Consistency is the hobgoblin of little minds,
your inconsistent self likes to tell itself.

Naming your son after Ralph Ellison places him in a Black and white
American genealogy of thinkers and writers who have grappled with
the question of whom AMERICA™ includes and excludes, whom it
idolizes and demonizes, whom it sanctifies and sacrifices. You want
your son to understand that the language of these writers and thinkers is his home, too, as much as AMERICA™ is. You want Ellison to
understand, eventually, that to be an American—

and he is an American, born and bred,
eligible to be the president!

—is to be squeezed in the vise between these binaries of memorializa-
tion and murder, to waver dialectically so long as AMERICA™ exists,

because AMERICA™ itself is and will always be a contradiction. When Ralph Ellison describes his narrator as being caught between invisibility and hypervisibility, you understand that this also describes your existential situation, your being and becoming, in AMERICA™.

Meanwhile, your poor son just wants to play *Minecraft*.

When Ellison turns four, ███████████ has been elected president of the United States. He pledges to stop what he calls the American carnage and promises that

You will never be ignored again.

This "you" obviously does not include you,
invisible under an indivisible God,
and probably doesn't include
your son either.

In ███ country, you, as an Asian, are the Other, nobody and nothing, unseen until you are seen everywhere. But you are not yet in the front rank of Others for ███ and his followers. Your turn will come soon enough, but bullies and demagogues begin with the weakest, the undocumented immigrants coming north from the other American countries overshadowed by AMERICA™. They, too, are invisible until they become, now, hypervisible. To deter these immigrants, ███ severs parents from their children and warehouses them in cages.

Brutalizing select immigrants and refugees,
meaning darker-skinned ones, is done by both
Democratic and Republican presidents, although
███ insists on turning bureaucratic cruelty into
political, theatrical spectacle.

Seeing your son at four makes you think of yourself at that age, when your brief separation from your parents seemed eternal. What you tried not to think about for decades resurges. A force more powerful than your parents took you away to give your father and mother time to become self-sufficient. But a child only understands the powerlessness, the abandonment, the sound of his screaming.

The solution is for the parents to return.

The parents do not return.

The other solution: stop feeling.

The children in the camps and the parents separated from them will never forget. Their separation is not benevolent. Their separation will burn.

Their separation may never end.

You never think of what your parents experience when they are forced to give you up. But when your son turns four, you finally see Ba Má as they were then, younger than you when you at last became a father, their bodies vital, their future old age an abstraction, their missing children the reality.

Your separation from your parents eventually ends. No photo exists of your reunion with your parents. Your family photos record only the good times afterward. In one Pennsylvania photo, you pose cheerfully in shorts and sandals, somewhere woodsy. You especially like the photo of yourself in a puffy snowsuit, standing in the snow with your mother. This must be the winter of 1975 or 1976, your parents transported from the tropics to a white Christmas, less than a year after Armed Forces Radio in Việt Nam plays "White Christmas" to alert the remaining Americans to flee.

In this photo, as in all photos, Má smiles and looks fashionable. Ba Má bought the house they are standing in front of, their first in this country, with some of the gold they carried with them to AMERICA™. They lost most of their wealth, but they did not arrive poor. Despite the gold, their first jobs are in the laundry of a nursing home. Your parents did not become wealthy by being lavish. When Ba is fired for being too slow, he finds work with Olivetti, the typewriter manufacturer. Má quits because the work is too hard. Her English is not as good as your father's. She does not get another job.

In Ban Mê Thuột, Nguyễn Thị Bảy was a self-made woman who worked all her life and could drive the Toyota. In Harrisburg, Bay Thi Nguyen's name becomes as flattened as her life as a housewife, stuck at home, alone and eventually unemployed.

With you.

Má walks you to the bus stop in the morning. Her hair is long and black, and you know she loves you because she has packed you lunch in a tin lunch box with a cartoon character on the lid—you forget who—which you think is very American. The thermos contains 7UP, not milk, for which the kids make fun of you because they think the soda is water. You have no idea what Má does at home while you are gone, because for you Má only exists to take care of you.

You love your young children, but when you become trapped at home with them for months during the plague that kills millions while you write these words, you understand your mother's situation. Work gives her life meaning. Work comes second only to God—or, blasphemously, perhaps work is just as important.

One day, Má disappears.

You vaguely remember sitting on steps, perhaps at the back of your house, with your father and brother. Something is being explained, but you do not understand it, this foreshadowing of what will come. One can see a foreshadow only from the future.

Your mother comes back, but
you do not remember her return.
Má is simply present again.

Despite her short, or maybe long, absence, you enjoy life in Harrisburg, ignorant of your parents' struggle. You go to an amusement park for a day sponsored by Ba's company and learn how to play bingo. Ba or Má wins. They task your brother with claiming the prize. Because he is slow to do so—he must be only eleven or twelve years old, already in the role of the translator he will be for the rest of his life—the bingo master tells your brother he doesn't get the prize. Someone else already claimed it. You snooze, you lose—another American lesson.

It's easier to remember the
deprivation than the joy.
One burns. The
other fades.

Try to re member the joy. But since all happy families are alike, as Tolstoy wrote, unhappiness is more interesting to write and read about. Your happiness is mundane: a big brother who shares your room, plays Monopoly with you, protects you from neighborhood bullies who steal your Halloween candy. The picnics and vacations your parents can take you on because they are not yet overworked. New York is dirty and noisy, but you can still see the view from the top of the Statue of Liberty and the Empire State Building.

For years afterward, a miniature Empire State Building that doubles as a thermometer stands on the living room bookshelf, next to an uncanny ginger-haired, blue-eyed, pink-skinned doll that your mother loves and that freaks you out with its permanently pursed lips and open eyes. The sparsely decorated bookshelf, which your parents curate, has no books.

Is there anything sadder?

Perhaps this: Years before, Ba Má sit in an office in a refugee camp at Fort Indiantown Gap on a day in late summer or early fall and receive the news that they will be separated from their children. Your father is forty-two, your mother is thirty-eight. Adults with full authority over their lives and their children. Until now. Because they are refugees.

You are probably outside, running and playing. Your brother remembers this as a good time, compared to Guam, where you had to wait an hour in line for food. The food lines are short here. Barracks are crowded but better than tents. Lots of daylight for games, lots of fireflies. Distracted parents too busy figuring out their next move to worry too much about their children. An idyll. A summer camp. For children.

Perhaps Ba Má wear clothes they brought from Việt Nam, perhaps they wear clothes donated by kindly Americans. Someone—a military officer, an aid worker, a church volunteer—is telling them in English what will happen. Perhaps they have already been prepared for the eventuality by reading *Đất Lành*, the mimeographed camp newsletter started by fellow refugees in both English and Vietnamese. *Đất Lành* announces weddings, reunions, sports events, visits by Christians and the circus, lessons in American culture like

Home is a barracks now

which informs the refugees that no one can enter their home without permission, for

A man's home is his castle

although

today we might say,
A person's home is his or her castle.

Someone is telling Ba Má that their best option is to break up the family. Someone is telling them *something*. To send their sons away with strangers. *Somethingsomethingsomething.* Má's English is limited; Ba's English is good enough to do business, so perhaps he completely understands what is being said, or perhaps he understands most of what is being said. It is what he cannot understand, the missing 10 or 20 percent, that confuses. *Somethingsomethingsomething.* Did Ba just hear right? Did this person say what he is thinking they said? Ba Má nod, showing they are listening if not fully understanding. *Somethingsomethingsomething.* Perhaps a fellow refugee translates, or perhaps the translator is one of those Vietnamese international students already in the United States who has volunteered to help.

It takes minutes, perhaps hours, for the reality to be absorbed into the mind and the flesh. Perhaps Ba Má argue. Perhaps one is for it, one against it. Perhaps both are against it. You cannot imagine both agreeing to the separation. But in the end they do. Perhaps the sympathetic person helping them tells them that this is their best, first opportunity to leave the camp. If they don't take it, they might be stuck here for much longer. Ba Má weigh the costs and benefits of staying in the camp with their sons, of leaving the camp without them. They rationalize the emotional damage that will be done, to their sons, to themselves. Má remembers how she left her mother behind and all her many sisters. Má recalls your (adopted) sister, all alone. What is her (adopted) daughter doing now? Ba thinks about how he left his father, brothers, and sister behind in 1954 the first time he became a refugee. He has not seen them since. And he turned out all right. Didn't he?

This is a war story.

You imagine, but you do not feel, what Ba Má suffered, because while you can imagine being separated from your son, you cannot feel what that feels like. The gap between imagining an emotion and feeling it is the distance between empathy and experience. The divide both writer and reader face as empathy brings them closer to others but cannot make them into those others. Empathy cannot turn a son into his father and mother, even if the son is also a father. You do not have to make the decision that Ba Má must. And in the end, you turn out all right. Don't you?

Even branded between the shoulder blades with this mark of the Other, you are the lucky one, separated for only a few months from parents who you feel are a part of you. Your brother, seven years older, doesn't come home for two years.

And that,
your brother says,
is how we know
Mom and Dad
love you more.

the only kind of model
you will ever be

Your brother is joking. You think. But a joke that perhaps holds some truth, as many jokes do.

Like you, anh Tùng is driven by being a refugee, by watching Ba Má suffer and sacrifice. But he finds his motivation earlier than you. Seven years after coming to the United States at ten years of age with no English, he graduates from one of the worst public high schools in San José and goes to Harvard.

So don't feel too bad for him.

Ba Má send you to the most elite private high school in San José. You repay them by being rejected by every college you apply to except one. Your first night at your last-choice university, your new classmates gather, look glumly at one another, and ask what you each did wrong.

Basically, you fucked up.

"Fuckup" is a relative term.

You had a B+ average!

Otherwise known as an Asian F.

F is for "fuckup." A is for "Asian."

The model minority stereotype is still true for your family and the types of Asians you know. A bête noire so powerful that even as you mock its inaccuracy, you often nevertheless behave like a model minority—quiet, polite, studious, hardworking, status conscious.

Sometimes you rock the boat, but mostly you row it, diligently.

Model minorities, the scholar erin Khuê Ninh argues, fear shaming themselves and their parents by being or appearing less than perfect. Burdened by emotional debt and filial piety, stricken with guilt over possibly wasting the legendary parental sacrifice, model minorities gear themselves to be little cogs in the capitalist machine, running smoothly until, perhaps, the day when they can run no more.

The slick fear of your own failure is the lubricant you need. You swear to work as hard as necessary to go to your dream school. You transfer to UCLA the next year, but stay only for the fall of 1989, until you are finally accepted in the spring of 1990 at your dream school, the University of Communists at Berkeley.

Another joke! Communists are somewhat socially acceptable at the school, but those who try to convert you as you walk through Sproul Plaza are more likely to be Evangelical Christians.

Visiting Berkeley with your high school girlfriend, J, you fall in love with the university at first sight. From Telegraph Avenue to campus and Sproul Plaza, where the Free Speech Movement of the 1960s had gathered in enormous numbers, you feel that this is where you have always wanted to be. Something is in the air, and it is not just marijuana.

Not that you have yet even seen actual marijuana. You are not saved by being rebellious or cool, like your fellow Berkeley students who wear black and Doc Martens and smoke cigarettes on the steps of Sproul Hall and publish art magazines for women and men of color with the titles *smell this* and *in your face*. You want to be a goth or a mod, but you are just a dweeb. You started wearing glasses in the second grade, your eyes the casualties of too much reading in the dark. You still want to be a great student, not just a good one.

And you are proud of your brother, anh Tùng. He plays football in high school and edits the school newspaper. The local television station lauds him, while the *San José Mercury* titles its profile of him:

"Vietnamese student excels despite barriers."

Years later at Berkeley, an Asian American student tells you, My mother showed me that article and said I should be like your brother.

Where's the movie about your brother's extraordinary life? Although if Hollywood made that movie, it would be about the white teacher who calls your brother "Tongue Win" and turns him on to the AMERICAN DREAM™.

People like your brother and you don't star in Hollywood movies, just television specials about the model minority.

Being admired by others may be good, but calling oneself a role model? Self-importance. Someone more powerful calling you a role model? Insidious.

The so-called majority hoists Asian Americans onto a pedestal, where this good minority either shows bad minorities how to be successful or shames them for their failures. Some Asian Americans enjoy the view from the pedestal. You know the type.

Work hard. Study hard. Rely on yourself. Do not depend on welfare. Do not blame the past or society for one's problems. Respect teachers. Consider the police your friend. Believe the law is on your side. Stress how you came here legally. Obey the law and don't mention any relatives, friends, parents, or grandparents who skirt the law, or your own skirt-ing of the law. ("Skirting the law" is what respectable people call their breaking of the law). Don't disagree too vocally. Maybe don't disagree at all. Be calm if passed over for promotion. Hold yourself responsible. Stay quiet. Keep your head down. Be a good follower. Internalize your own domination, subordination, repression. Distrust your anger and resentment at the racism, at the way the so-called majority marginalizes you and condescends to you. Take out your rage on the other so-called minorities. On wife, husband, lover, children. In public, under the white gaze, suppress your feelings. Call them, the poet and essayist Cathy Park Hong says, minor feelings.

Was embarrassment about being given
chopsticks by your white sponsors a minor feeling?

Was bewilderment when white kids stole your
Halloween candy in Harrisburg a minor feeling?

Was screaming and howling as you were taken
away from your parents a minor feeling?

If someone shoots Ba Má in a robbery and they return
to work the next day, who are you to feel anything?

Then this episode in the chronicle of minor feelings:

Ten or eleven years old, early 1980s,
not far from the SàiGòn Mới,
walking by yourself,
you spot a sign in
a shop window:

ANOTHER AMERICAN
DRIVEN OUT OF BUSINESS
BY THE VIETNAMESE

Printed or handwritten? You can't recall.

The type of business? You don't notice.

Who is American? The question never strikes you.

You cannot yet articulate what you have seen, although you understand that the sign points to people like your parents. Maybe you even thought of Ba Má, who dare to give their store a name with no translation. This person does not see your parents as Americans. Fair enough. When Ba Má say Americans, they refer to others, not themselves.

But are Ba Má dangerous? Ba Má, who take no vacations? Ba Má, who attend Mass every Sunday and pray the Rosary every night? Ba Má, who send money home to all the relatives so they won't starve? These deeds would prove the heroism and humanity of white people. These same deeds, done by Ba Má, prove a fanatical, inhuman will to work that terrifies and enrages some Americans.

How can one work too hard
in a country whose capitalism
and mythology exalt
working too hard?

Ba Má comfort themselves with a microwave; a wood-paneled stereo console with built-in speakers, a cassette deck, and an 8-track player; a wood-paneled television with an enormous twenty-five-inch screen that serves as your personal Americanization device; and a sleek, ultramodern VCR. Videocassette recorder. Cutting-edge technology for its day, as the gramophone once was. You insert a small black box into a large silver box in order to play exactly one movie.

You rent these movies from a dark, narrow Vietnamese video store near the SàiGòn Mới, past the Vietnamese beauty salon, the Vietnamese café, the Vietnamese sandwich shop, the Vietnamese restaurant, their alienness to non-Vietnamese people occasionally softened by French names: the Paris Beauty Salon, Les Amis Café.

You have taken over downtown San José.

And made it better.

Ba walks you from the SàiGòn Mới to the video store. A fellow country-man with a thin mustache greets you. Behind the counter, a wall with VHS movies in black boxes. You select movies from binders with titles on sheets. Your unsuspecting father pays, unaware that your selections might contain things children should not see.

This leads to trouble.
This helps make you a writer.

After you watch *Star Wars* a dozen times, you watch *Enter the Dragon* and *Return of the Dragon* with Bruce Lee. His mastery of martial arts impresses you, but he cannot be a role model for a nerdy, uncoordinated weakling such as yourself. Then—

—you watch *Apocalypse Now*.

You love war movies. You have watched John Wayne fighting Japs in *Sands of Iwo Jima* and Audie Murphy, the most decorated soldier of

World War II, fighting Krauts in *To Hell and Back*. You possess a fan's knowledge of battles, weapons, uniforms, campaigns, and slang, but all you know of *Apocalypse Now* is that it concerns the war that delivered you here.

It is the weekend. If it is Sunday, you have gone to Vietnamese-language Mass at Saint Patrick with Ba Má in the morning, bored on a hard wooden bench as you listen to a sermon you cannot understand. After Mass, you drive a few blocks north to the SàiGòn Mới with Ba Má, who give you a few dollars for the Winchell's Donuts House across the street. You buy the Sunday edition of the *Mercury* and a dozen doughnuts, all for you. Then Ba drives you home. You are left alone as always on the weekends, with the newspaper, doughnuts, your books, and a freezer full of Hungry-Man TV dinners and gallons of Neapolitan or mint chip ice cream. A freezer full of love. Ba, when he hits on something he thinks you like, makes sure you have a never-ending supply of it. Every weekend, you eat a rotating assortment of Salisbury steak and meat loaf, tater tots and mashed potatoes, apple pie and peach cobbler, as well as ice cream straight from the carton. Either you are in paradise or you are lonely. You are eleven.

After you read the newspaper cover to cover, after you eat a few dough-nuts and heat a TV dinner for lunch, you pop the videocassette into the VCR. You settle down on the carpet in front of the TV, or perhaps on the red velour couch. The house is quiet even though the living room window faces a street always busy with traffic. San José is not a city where people honk.

The movie starts. A weird song called "The End" by the Doors plays. Later you find out that the father of the lead singer, Jim Morrison, was a navy admiral who commanded Operation New Life. Fighter jets zoom over jungle treetops. Napalm blossoms. This is cool.

Martin Sheen, whom you have seen in *The Execution of Private Slovik* on television, plays Captain Willard. He stumbles around in a bedroom, nearly naked as he performs clumsy martial arts. He smashes a mirror with his hand and lies weeping on the floor in his own blood. You are confused.

Despite its strangeness, the movie fascinates you. I love the smell of napalm in the morning! Colonel Kilgore bellows. His helicopter squadron raids a Việt Cộng village to the tune of Wagner's "Ride of the Valkyries." You hear the song again years later when you see white-hooded Ku Klux Klan riding to rescue white women from Black men in the white supremacist blockbuster *The Birth of a Nation* (the *Star Wars* of its day, the movie is based on a novel called *The Clansman*, written by a friend of President Woodrow Wilson, who in 1915 screens the movie in the White House). The helicopters kill many Vietnamese and the Việt Cộng kill some Americans, but this is war and war is hell, except with more vulgarities and psychedelia than in World War II movies. World War II movies don't feature Playboy Playmates dressed up as half-naked cowboys and Indians, who add to the allure, at least for certain kinds of viewers like you. Some people think *Apocalypse Now* is an anti-war movie, but the U.S. Marine Corps shows the movie to its recruits to rev them up for combat. War movies cannot be anti-war stories when they excite young men with the spectacle of gun battles and sexy weaponry.

What is an anti-war story?
What about the unexciting stories of Ba Má,
your (adopted) sister, and all the thousands of
other refugees and civilians caught up in
wars not of their making or choice?

Then a navy patrol boat intercepts a sampan full of civilians. A woman dashes to protect a basket as a sailor tries to open it. The frightened, angry young sailors, both Black and white, open fire and massacre the jabbering, incomprehensible Vietnamese. The sailor opens the basket. It contains a very cute puppy.

Besides the puppy, the only other survivor is the woman, half dead.

The navy skipper wants to bring her to a hospital, but this will delay Willard's mission to find and terminate the rogue American colonel Kurtz. Willard takes out his pistol, fires a bullet into the woman's chest

and

splits

you

in

two

Are you the Americans killing?   Or the Vietnamese being killed?

Until this point,
stories saved you.
Now you encounter
the power of stories
to dismember you.

You watch the movie all the way to its bewildering conclusion, set in Cambodia with Marlon Brando as Kurtz, the white man who has gone native. Savage. Even as a savage, he is still a white man. The king of the natives. He rubs his bald head and mutters, The horror, the horror, before Willard hacks him to death with a machete. As Kurtz dies, the Cambodian tribesmen, played by the Igorot people of the Philippines, where the movie was shot, butcher a water buffalo. Like, really slaughter a poor buffalo! Authentic as *fuck*, that machete carving away chunks of buffalo flesh. They don't make movies like this anymore. Blame the liberal animal-huggers.

When a bloody Willard leaves with the machete in one hand and Kurtz's diary under his arm, the crowd of Cambodians/Igorots/natives/savages parts before him and kneels.

In retrospect, you understand that this is white fantasy. Only the white man/son can kill the white man/father, while the savages await their white man/god.

The Kānaka Maoli of Hawai'i did not share this fantasy when they killed Captain Cook on the beach in 1779.

You finish the movie and will not watch it again for decades, although you never forget it. But the shock of being split in two is too much, and you seal away your minor feelings until Berkeley, when the professor of an Asian American film class asks you to recount a movie scene that impacted you.

You stand before the classroom full of Asian American students and understand that they, of anyone, will understand what you feel. You begin describing the sampan massacre. Your trembling voice startles you.

The seal is broken.
You shake with rage and anger.
Major feelings.

Your emotional reaction is testimony to the power of *Apocalypse Now*, to director Francis Ford Coppola's artistic vision and commitment. Stories are not just there to entertain, to make you feel good, to reflect a positive image of yourself. Stories are also there to shake you, unnerve you, make you see yourself anew. *Apocalypse Now* is an unsettling cinematic masterpiece, one in which the Vietnamese, Cambodians, and Igorots serve as excuses for white spectacle. No doubt the movie condemns the murderous violence of Willard and Kurtz as well as the anti-Asian racism of their American army, as when a helicopter gunner shooting down a Vietnamese civilian who has blown up an American helicopter with a hand grenade says:

> Holy Christ!
> She's a savage!
> I'm gonna get that dink bitch.

But a work of art that condemns racism can also be racist at the same time, as Chinua Achebe argued about Joseph Conrad's *Heart of Darkness*, an inspiration for *Apocalypse Now*. A drama that foregrounds and centers white racism and violence while simultaneously silencing, distorting, exploiting, or erasing Others, with no hint of their subjectivities, is, implicitly, racist.

The white male actor who plays the nameless helicopter gunner gets a credit. So do the actors playing "MP Sergeant #2" and "Injured Soldier" and "Machine Gunner." The young Vietnamese woman with the hand grenade, who gets to say a few words before dying, is not credited. None of the Vietnamese are, despite the dozens of Vietnamese people killed in the movie, all of whom happen to be refugees from Việt Nam living in refugee camps in the Philippines.

> Neither do the names of Vietnamese, Cambodian, Laotian, or Hmong appear on the Vietnam Veterans Memorial in Washington, D.C., which memorializes all the American soldiers killed during the war. Southeast Asians, even if they are also Vietnam veterans, are only extras in a mostly white and occasionally Black American drama.

Your sense that Southeast Asians as extras are little more than props is reinforced when, decades later, you visit Coppola's winery in Geyserville, California. You mosey up to the wine bar, check out the selection, then notice an exhibit next to the bar. The patrons buzz happily around you as you step closer to the exhibit's glass case. It features costumes from *Apocalypse Now*, stills from the movie, the cameras of the photographer played by Dennis Hopper. And a stack of human skulls.

These skulls presumably decorated the fatal grounds of Kurtz's camp, testimony to his going native among the savage natives. But a stack of human skulls, from a movie set in Cambodia, recalls the stacks and stacks of human skulls that you saw in Cambodia at some of the places where the Khmer Rouge massacred their victims. The skulls are kept at memorials and museums that commemorate the lost souls slaughtered at the Choeung Ek killing fields outside of Phnom Penh, the S-21 prison inside of Phnom Penh, and the killing caves at Battambang. When you visit these sites while doing research for your book *Nothing Ever Dies: Vietnam and the Memory of War*, you sweat profusely in the humidity and afterward return to your hotel room as swiftly as possible on the motorbike or tuk-tuk of your guides, whereupon you spend the rest of the evening without any appetite or desire for wine, unable to forget the fates of the tortured and murdered.

At Coppola's winery, the skulls—real or fake—watch the patrons as they order glasses of Sofia Brut Rosé or Eleanor Red, named after the director's daughter and wife.

> Get over it, snowflake, a reader mutters.
> It's just entertainment. Just a movie.

You try to tell yourself it's just a movie when, as an adult, you go to the rooftop bar of a snazzy downtown hotel and, looking out over the Los Angeles landscape, martini in hand, see a movie projected onto the wall of a neighboring building. Captain Willard is emerging from muddy waters, face in camouflage, machete in hand. You sip the martini, surrounded by LA's beautiful people, as he hacks Kurtz to death.

You whiner, a reader mutters.
If you don't like it, make
your own damn movie.

You're a writer, not a filmmaker. You write your own damn book, *The Sympathizer*, which includes a depiction of a famous Auteur whose talent is matched only by his ego and who looks suspiciously like Coppola but is not actually him. Whoever the Auteur is, many people in Hollywood have read your book, and no one has disputed your characterization of the Auteur, who could just as easily be another very famous director of a very famous American war movie set in Việt Nam, a man to whom you reluctantly sign a limited Pulitzer edition of *The Sympathizer* at the request of a mutual friend. Eventually you see the book, with your signature and dedication to the director, hawked on eBay for $499.

While your Auteur makes a movie that sounds suspiciously like *Apocalypse Now*, it is actually a compendium of AMERICA™'s Vietnam War movies, almost all of which you have watched, an exercise you recommend to no one, especially if the viewer is Vietnamese.

You cackle to yourself for two years as you write the novel, which is your minor revenge on Hollywood and which you think is pretty funny, besides being rather tragic, because you have to laugh at the absurdity of this fantasy in the American imagination called the Vietnam War if you don't want to cry. Joke's on you, after all. Even a kick-ass novel will be lucky if it's read by tens of thousands, whereas millions will watch even a bad Hollywood movie or TV show. The only asses really being kicked belong to the Vietnamese and every Other who haunts the American imagination.

The hypnotic power of Hollywood, AMERICA™'s unofficial ministry of propaganda, is trained on you and millions more in AMERICA™ and all over the world from an early age, every time you switch on the TV or go to the movies. By definition, you are not even aware of being hypnotized. Looking back now, you can see the hypnosis in operation when, a few years after watching *Apocalypse Now*, you enroll at an all-boys Jesuit college preparatory at your parents' demand. The almost all-white, almost all-male faculty features one Black teacher and one Asian teacher. You are lucky your homeroom teacher is one of the few women and a feminist who assigns you Alice Walker's *The Color Purple* and Sylvia Plath's *The Bell Jar*. The majority of the three hundred boys in your class are white, with a few Black and some Latino students. The largest minority is Asian. Three dozen of you. You sense your difference from the white students. Every day at lunch, many of you instinctively gather in a corner of the campus and call yourselves

THE
ASIAN
INVASION

You laugh at yourselves because you have been laughed at so many times already. At Saint Patrick, one classmate asks, Did you carry an AK-47 during the war? Another classmate says, Ah-so, asshole! while bowing and clasping his hands.

You remember their names and faces to this day.

By high school, you sense that the Japs in World War II movies differ little from the gooks in Vietnam War movies. Not that the Asian

Invasion says this out loud. You are each left alone to ponder Mickey Rooney using buckteeth, slanted eyes, and broken English to portray a Japanese landlord in *Breakfast at Tiffany's*, tainting your crush on Audrey Hepburn, who must condone this buffoonery. You silently consider the semiotics of foreign student Long Duk Dong's name in the teen classic *Sixteen Candles*. You wince at the ching-chong jokes poisoning the radio airwaves.

And not just the airwaves. You scrape together a few dollars and coins from what Ba Má sometimes give you and visit the comic book racks at the 7-Eleven across the street from home. You buy your first copies of *Spider-Man, Captain America, G.I. Joe,* and *Sgt. Rock*. You also discover Fu Manchu and Ming the Merciless. Chop Chop the bucktoothed Chinese cook of the heroic Blackhawks fighter squadron. Pulpy war comics with Jap soldiers screaming Banzai! Chinese communist human wave attacks in Korea. Gooks blasted by M16s, strafed by rockets, incinerated in napalm, obliterated by bombs bursting in air.

You begin to understand that you are the Yellow Peril, though when you look at your skin and those of all the other Asians you know, it is never yellow.

A few years later you are a freshman in college. 1989. You open the newspaper or turn on the TV—you forget how you learn the news. A lone white male gunman has opened fire with an AK-47 on Cleveland Elementary School in Stockton, California, not far from San José, killing five schoolchildren and wounding thirty others with a fusillade of 105 bullets (this school shooting should not be confused with the other Cleveland Elementary School shooting in San Diego in 1979, when a sixteen-year-old girl killed the principal and a custodian). At the time, mass school shootings are rare in AMERICA™. The national outcry

after the shooting focuses on the gunman's AK-47 rather than on how
the dead children are Cambodian and Vietnamese and why they are
here because AMERICA™ was there.

> Rathanan Or, 9
> Oeun Lim, 8
> Ram Chun, 8
> Sokhim An, 6
> Thuy Tran, 6

Acquaintances say the twenty-four-year-old shooter, who had attended
the same school

> hated Vietnamese immigrants.

His former school had become 70 percent Southeast Asian, and he
believed the Vietnamese were taking jobs from what he called

> native-born Americans.

His last known words were:

> The damn Hindus and boat people own everything.

Only one of his victims is Vietnamese.

You all look alike.

Those children would be in their forties now. Some of them, maybe all
of them, would be parents with children the same age they were when
they were murdered.

If very few people remember the names of these children or even the shooting itself, some still recall Vincent Chin, bludgeoned to death in 1982 by two white autoworkers in Detroit who mistook him, a Chinese American, for Japanese.

They never go to jail.

Even if you had not heard of Vincent Chin in 1982, you are aware of the Japanese auto industry, whose economical, dependable fleets compete against big, unreliable American gas-guzzlers. You wish Ba Má would actually buy a nimble Honda or Toyota versus the heavy-set American cars they seem to prefer, from a Ford Granada to an Oldsmobile Cutlass.

The television news amplifies this Japanese threat to American jobs, a major feeling relayed by those homicidal autoworkers through the length of their baseball bat.

But the Asian Invasion says nothing. War movies are just stories. Jokes are just jokes. Can't you take a joke? Americans have a right to be angry. Didn't they just lose their jobs?

And what have you to complain about?
Didn't we fight a war on your behalf?
Didn't we welcome all you refugees?
Didn't we save you from communism
and give you the chance to pursue

the AMERICAN DREAM™?

You . . . should be grateful.

colonizer and colonized

Be quiet.

Be polite.

Speak only when spoken to.

You learn this as a Vietnamese child and as a refugee.

But you have a character flaw.

You are an ingrate.

You discover this about yourself with your high school girlfriend, J, whom you meet during your summer at the Great America theme park. She and her twin sister, also J, smile at you when you lock them into the cab of the ride you work on, the Lobster. Your part of Great America is called Yankee Harbor, and while it is hard to look cool working on something called the Lobster while wearing a tricorn hat, a white long-sleeved polyester shirt with a ruffle at the neck, and black bellbottom pants, you try. You must be reasonably successful, for you accomplish the most important goal of your life at sixteen and find a girlfriend.

J, born in the Philippines, immigrated to AMERICA™ at ten. Also sixteen years old, she is as Americanized as you are, since the Philippines spent four hundred years in a Spanish convent and fifty years in Hollywood, as Jessica Hagedorn put it in her play *Dogeaters*. Of the American war that brought Hollywood to the Philippines, one in which American soldiers killed hundreds of thousands of Filipinos in the name of democratizing and Christianizing them, Mark Twain wrote this verse, set to the tune of "Battle Hymn of the Republic," which could easily describe AMERICA™'s Forever War of the twenty-first century:

Mine eyes have seen the orgy of the launching of the Sword;
He is searching out the hoardings where the stranger's wealth is stored;
He hath loosed his fateful lightnings, and with woe and death has scored;
His lust is marching on.

When you meet J, the United States no longer officially colonizes the Philippines but still maintains the Subic Bay naval port and Clark Air Base. For J, arriving in California, itself inevitably Spanish, with her Spanish-inflected surname, must have felt like coming to a home she already knew.

You and J, two colonized kids from Southeast Asia, feel an immediate affinity for each other in Yankee Harbor. Wearing the sartorial signs of American revolution and independence, you have never felt so patriotic in your life. Your crew of teenagers oversees the relatively safe Lobster, a set of spinning cabs that barely leave the ground, as well as the Tidal Wave, a massive machine in which a long train of cars is fired into a loop and back, with the passengers riding upside down twice. For this, you are paid the minimum wage of $3.35 an hour.

Your more experienced coworker, a seventeen-year-old redhead, rides the Tidal Wave during his work shift without the safety bar pulled onto his lap, his hands high in the air and nothing holding him to his seat. When he comes back without having fallen out screaming to his death, he shrugs and says, Centrifugal force.

For the first time in your life, you exhibit physical courage, or stupidity, and follow his example. You scream joyfully as you rocket into the loop and back again. Thrilled to survive, you risk your life over and over. And then, one night after the park closes, you and your crew members hop onto the Revolution, a boat that goes in a circle until it is upside down and stays there, leaving its riders suspended for many seconds. You ride the Revolution with the shoulder harness on but without the lap belt, leaving you upside down with your legs dangling around your ears, laughing and laughing.

Someone who is totally uncool must have reported you and the other crew members to management. For what you have done on the Revolution, the suits summarily fire you from Great America.

What a glorious way to end the summer.

And you have J. You write her love letters and excessively romantic poetry. You sneak out at night to attend her prom and yours. Your parents have no idea about her, since they told you that you cannot date in high school. And when you can date, the only appropriate girls are Vietnamese Catholics. This is very unreasonable. J is Catholic, but that is not good enough. Still, you do not want to hurt your parents. And you fear them. So you keep J a secret, your biggest lie so far to Ba Má.

You cannot see a way to reconcile your desires with their desires, but this does not explain why, when J's mother gives you a ride from their home to the BART station, you forget to say thank you. Mrs. C dislikes you from this first meeting and never stops suspecting that your lack of gratitude indicates something worse about your character. She may not be wrong.

J forgives you, sees the best in you, even though you are also overconfident, cocky, quick to judge others. A natural-born ingrate, you are irked when older Vietnamese people sometimes ingratiate themselves with white people, possibly because you are also very nice to white people. Your people rarely ingratiate yourselves with each other unless you need something badly. But when it comes to white people, your people wish to make up for not being American, for not speaking English well, for reminding Americans of a war they would rather forget, for being guests in someone else's country, although fewer of you live here—2.2 million people—than the number of Americans who fought there, in your homeland—2.7 million people.

But your people do not seek to please *all* Americans. How many times do you hear your people say the Mexicans

contemptuously or dismissively. You don't hear them say

the Blacks

as much because far fewer Black people live in San José than Latinos, whom the Vietnamese just call Mexican. Most Vietnamese people can't tell the difference between Latino populations, but then again, many Latinos use "Chino" to describe any Asian who looks like they might be Chinese.

You are not so offended. The Latinos who call
you Chino have never physically or verbally
assaulted you or made racist
movies about you.

The lesson you learn in San José: Vietnamese are not Americans; Americans are, by default, white; Black and Latino people may be Americans, but Vietnamese people call them Black or Mexican; Vietnamese people are frank about white people behind their backs but are deferential to their faces.

In AMERICA™'s obsession over a Black-white
binary, are you Black, white, or neither?

The model minority understands its place in the racial hierarchy of this country and the world, at least from a colonizer's perspective. Whites on top, Asians next, then Latinos, from lighter to darker shades. Whether the bottom is Black or Native is debatable. The model minority is grateful not to be Black, rarely even thinks about not being Native. You are the model minority's newest model. In 1975, Richard Pryor puts you in your place:

White folks tired of our ass, too. They gettin' them some new
niggers. The Vietnamese. [laughter, applause] But bring 'em over.
Bring all of 'em over. Niggers won't mind. They didn't ask
us shit. We the motherfuckers got to give the jobs up for 'em.

AMERICA™ always needs new Others to provide the cheapest labor,
to absorb the racism, to shame older Others for not working hard
enough and not singing loud enough in the American chorus. If Pry-
or's language still shocks, still violates the border of the unspeakable,
then perhaps that is because he refuses the piety of polite language
or censored words to describe the inherent, fundamental, obscene
violence and murderousness of American life, one that has always
required both the death of Others and the disremembering of those
deaths.

But Pryor, like many Americans, does not know about or forgets Laos,
where tens of thousands of Hmong—perhaps even one quarter of
all Hmong men and boys allied with the Americans—were killed in
combat. The United States repaid Hmong sacrifice by abandoning
most of the Hmong.

Are the ones who make it to AMERICA™ grateful?
What is more obscene, the deaths of the Hmong or the
American expectation that the survivors be grateful?

The model minority expresses its gratitude partly by being successful,
validating the AMERICAN DREAM™ by becoming doctors, lawyers,
engineers. What about police officers?

Police officer Tou Thao is the son of Hmong refugees. He stands with
his back to fellow Minneapolis police officer Derek Chauvin as Chauvin
murders George Floyd by kneeling on his neck for nine minutes and
twenty-nine seconds.

I can't breathe, Floyd says.

Even before the murder of George Floyd,
Ta-Nehisi Coates had written:

The officer carries with him the power of the American state
and the weight of an American legacy, and they necessitate
that of the bodies destroyed every year, some wild and
disproportionate number of them will be black.

and

In America, it is traditional to
destroy the black body—
it is heritage.

Tou Thao has claimed that heritage. His face haunts you, like yours and
not like yours, as George Floyd's face is like yours and not like yours.
AMERICA™ says you and Tou Thao look alike as Orientals, gooks, or
Asian Americans, but does that mean you are alike?

Asian Americans number more than twenty-two million, 6 percent of
the country, but are as diverse as Asia. You join academia. Tou Thao
enlists in the police. You come from a country of colonizers, while Tou
Thao comes from a stateless people. In the United States, where the
poverty rate in 2015 is 15.1 percent for all Americans and 24.1 percent
for Black people, it is 28.3 percent for the Hmong. If anyone from
Southeast Asia might take the place of Black people, it would be the
Hmong, subjected by American warfare and American welfare.

And consider what Frantz Fanon wrote in
Black Skin, White Masks about French colonization:

It is not because the Indo-Chinese has discovered a
culture of his own that he is in revolt. It is because
"quite simply" it became, in more ways than one,
impossible for him to breathe.

When George Floyd is murdered, some on social media quote
Fanon on the impossibility of breathing, but forget to
include the Indochinese. Fanon's point is that under
colonization, none of us can breathe. When we recognize that,
we can all struggle for breath together.

In Minneapolis, does Tou Thao learn the epithet that Richard Pryor
utters with such abandon? Does he hear the same kinds of racist jokes
you hear in California? What does he think of Fong Lee, fellow Hmong
American, nineteen years old, shot eight times, four in the back, in
2006? An all-white jury acquits Minneapolis police officer Jason Andersen of murder.

Your family resettles among working-class and middle-class white
Americans. Many of the Hmong resettle in poor Black communities,
where neither is prepared for the Other. When poor people are forced
together, they sometimes clash. But after Andersen kills Fong Lee, Black
activists rally. Lee's sister Shoua says

They were the loudest voices for us.
They didn't ask to show up.
They just showed up.

Tou Thao shows up and turns his back.

The poet Mai Der Vang writes:

Go live with yourself after what you didn't do
Go and be left behind.

and

To be complicit in adding to the
perpetration of power on a neck. . . .

and

Never truly to be accepted,
always a pawn.

Does Tou Thao understand what the poet, also Hmong, also American, says elsewhere in regard to him?

The American Dream will not save us.

This is blasphemy in an AMERICA™ where the immigrant and refugee must always invoke the AMERICAN DREAM™ and must always give thanks

to be here
(say this part out loud)
and not to be Black, not to be Native
(say this to yourself, or do not say it at all).

As a child, you know of Indians only from the Pilgrims and Indians story you learn in school every Thanksgiving season. As an adult, you write about Thanksgiving for the *New York Times* and describe it as both heartwarming family ritual AND celebration of genocide.

Uh-oh.
Do. Not. Fuck.
with white people's
Thanksgiving, even if all
you tried to do was what the
Great White American Male Novelist
F. Scott Fitzgerald called for.

You will stop calling Fitzgerald the
Great White American Male Novelist when
people stop calling you a Vietnamese
American writer. Adjectives for all,
or adjectives for none.

Fitzgerald says that the test of a first-rate intelligence is the ability to hold two opposed ideas in mind at the same time and still retain the ability to function. So: Thanksgiving can be both lovely reunion and implicit acceptance of genocide. A polite silence.

Some of your readers are not convinced.
How dare you politicize Thanksgiving!
We are only giving thanks for how
the Indians helped the Pilgrims!

But if we really want to be thankful:
Why not give back the land?
Pay reparations and land taxes?
Engage in truth and reconciliation?
Or simply remember history?

As Tommy Orange does in his novel *There There*:

In 1621, colonists invited Massasoit, the chief of the Wampanoags, to a feast after a recent land deal. Massasoit came with ninety of his men. That meal is why we still eat a meal together in November. Celebrate it as a nation. But that one wasn't a thanksgiving meal. It was a land-deal meal. Two years later there was another, similar meal meant to symbolize eternal friendship. Two hundred Indians dropped dead that night from an unknown poison.

Many of those Americans who deny that Thanksgiving is about genocide will never, curiously, discuss genocide the next day or demand it to be taught to their children.

Remembering is the least that can be done. But it hurts to remember genocide. And sometimes remembering what shouldn't be remembered is ungracious.

Americans, like most other peoples, including the Vietnamese, prefer singular myths rather than two conflicting ideas. They expect the people who come to their country to embrace the myths, to learn what to remember and what to forget, as a way of being grateful for being welcomed. But if the giving of a gift might be munificent, the expectation of thankfulness is not. Dina Nayeri—refugee, writer—says

Gratitude is a fact of a refugee's inner life; it doesn't need to be compelled. . . . My gratitude is personal and vast . . . But it is mine. I no longer need to offer it as appeasement to citizens who had nothing to do with my rescue.

Some portion of those citizens who expect gratitude for their nation's greatness and magnanimity will also expect a certain kind of ignorance or amnesia about the nation's misdeeds. As an ungrateful child, you know nothing about genocide, except for the hint that John Wayne provides by killing hordes of Indians in the westerns so beloved by Americans and famous the world over. Albert Memmi, writing in French from Tunisia in his 1957 classic, *The Colonizer and the Colonized*, says that

> the famous national epic of the Far West
> greatly resembles systematic massacre.

Genocide turned into cinematic entertainment and innocent folklore. This is one of the greatest triumphs of the colonizer's propaganda, that children all over the world play cowboys and Indians. As a boy, you identify with John Wayne and the white settlers, since genocide cannot be committed against those merciless Indian savages, as the Declaration of Independence calls Native peoples.

> But in AMERICA™'s binary
> of colonizer and colonized,
> are you, a refugee, the
> colonized or the
> colonizer?

Perhaps you are both. Sometimes binaries are inadequate. In Việt Nam, you were colonized but also colonizer. In 1954, when the country is divided, eight hundred thousand Vietnamese Catholics, including Ba Má, move from north to south, led by Vietnamese Catholic priests, encouraged by the CIA, transported by American and French ships. In the south, you form the power base of the Vietnamese Catholic president Ngô Đình Diệm. The United States supports Diệm and helps pay for the migration.

Does Americanization start here for Ba Má? Does your Americanization begin when you are born in Ban Mê Thuột of the Central Highlands? Montagnards already live there. Does being a colonizer in their homeland prepare you to be rescued by another colonizing country?

                                                                Should you be grateful?

Once, Má mentions the Montagnards who lived in and around Ban Mê Thuột. I felt so sorry for them, she says. They were so poor.

Every now and then you asked your parents about their life in Ban Mê Thuột, but you never asked how they came to settle there among the Montagnards. By the time you ask Ba, he is eighty-eight. He says, We were given a small piece of land in Đa Lạt, which we tried to farm. We sold it and moved outside of Ban Mê Thuột. We sold that land and moved into town to start our business.

Colonization is always about the land.

The Diệm regime sees the Central Highlands of your birth as underpopulated, or populated only by the Montagnards. Settling Vietnamese Catholics in the highlands will help civilize the Indigenous peoples, as the French tried to civilize the Indochinese.

Some Montagnards do not wish to be civilized. In 1957, they form BAJARAKA, spelled from the names of the Bahnar, Jarai, Rade, and Kaho, four major tribes of Montagnard people, also known as the Degar. BAJARAKA seeks independence for a separate nation of Degar peoples. What the Diệm regime calls assimilation for the Degar—a policy the communist government continues after 1975—BAJARAKA calls a

                                                        program of genocide.

You are not accustomed to the charge of
genocide being leveled against your own people.
Your people see themselves as victims of the
Chinese, the French, the Japanese, the Americans,
or else victims of each other. Never as victimizers.
But BAJARAKA claims that

> Diem crushed the BAJARAKA movement with army and tank,
> murdered its peoples and imprisoned all of its leaders. . . . [T]he
> US government knew about what was going on between our
> peoples and the Vietnamese but they did not have any intention
> to stop [the] Diem government from destroying our peoples, our
> villages, our culture, and our traditional way of life.

AMERICA™, built on colonization, assists both the
French and the Vietnamese in their colonizing efforts.
To be a part of this colonization that you did not choose
surprises you.

> He [Diem] forcefully took our good farmlands and . . .
> pushed our peoples to the rocky lands. The Vietnamese
> refugees that Diem settled in our lands began stealing our
> household properties, our livestock, took our farmlands. . . .
> [T]hey said that we were the French influenced peoples.
> Then, they tortured us, imprisoned us, and murdered us

and called the murders an

                                        accident.

In March 1975, as Ban Mê Thuột is being captured
by northern forces, the *New York Times* affirms the
Montagnard point of view, describing your people as

outsiders to the place—who had prospered by their wiles
and their connections, often dishonestly, or at the expense
of the simple montagnards among whom they lived.

You are part of these collective Vietnamese for whom Diệm was a hero.
Your cousin's husband, a man old enough to be your father, hangs a
portrait of Diệm in the dining room of his house in San José in the
1980s. For your cousin's husband, Diệm—assassinated by his own men
in 1963 in a coup approved by John F. Kennedy—was also a martyr.

If you go back to Buôn Ma Thuột, would you return as a prodigal son?
Or as a colonizer? If you call yourself the latter, will your fellow colonizers call you ungrateful?

Perhaps Tou Thao's face haunts you because
you are more alike than you care to admit.

Perhaps you turned your back
on this history in the Central Highlands because
being a colonizer means not demanding to know
what the colonized has never forgotten and
cannot afford to forget.

As for colonizers like you, when colonialism is
truly successful, you do not even realize
you are colonizers.

You just know
you should be grateful.

white and other saviors

The Montagnards who fight with the Americans are trained by the U.S. Army Special Forces, and soon after *Apocalypse Now*, you watch John Wayne's 1968 movie *The Green Berets* on television. It's possible that some Montagards saw *The Green Berets*, since American military advisers showed Hollywood movies to them. Unfortunately, when it came to the cowboys and Indians stories, the Montagnards cheered for the Indians.

The Green Berets is an American western transplanted to Việt Nam. Wayne plays a colonel of the Green Berets, whom JFK dispatched to Việt Nam to save the good, freedom-loving Vietnamese (this means you) from the bad, communist-loving Vietnamese (this also means you). Kennedy, as a senator, once said this about Indochina:

> This is our offspring. . . . And if it falls
> victim to any of the perils that threaten its existence—
> communism, political anarchy, poverty and the rest—
> then the United States, with some justification,
> will be held responsible, and our prestige in
> Asia will sink to a new low.

Could the Prince of Camelot have forecast that one day an Indochinese refugee such as yourself would give a speech in the John F. Kennedy Presidential Library and Museum? Standing in its impressive lecture hall, ready to do the Great Man proud as one of his many offspring, you whisper:

> Hi, Dad. I'm home.

Eventually you realize that *The Green Berets* is a work of propaganda so spectacular and atrocious only the Third Reich or Hollywood could have produced it. In the classic genres of American propaganda—the western and the World War II movie—heroic white men use violent

force to overcome faceless evil or danger embodied by the Indians,
Japanese, and Germans. Good Indians, Japanese, or Germans help the
white American men, and if they do not aid them, or even if they do,
possess the good grace to die nobly.

In the final scene, John Wayne returns from a mission where one of his
men has been killed in a grisly Việt Cộng booby trap, devised by savages
who won't fight face-to-face. The dead man had adopted a Vietnamese
boy, and when Wayne informs him of his foster father's death, the boy
cries, alone once again. Wayne fixes a green beret on his head. You're
what this is all about, Wayne says, walking with him into the sunset.
The sun is setting into the South China Sea. Too bad that sea lies to the
east of Việt Nam, but Americans have always been bad at geography,
cursed by Columbus's mistaking the Bahamas for India. The scene
would work better with the sun rising out of the eastern sea and a new
dawn coming, but Hollywood does not ask Vietnamese people their
opinion about their own country.

You never see the little boy again. His character's name is . . . Ham
Chunk.

> Ham Chunk is played by Craig Jue, not Vietnamese,
> although he is born in the Year of the Pig, like you.
> Jue dies at forty-six from cancer, having acted
> in a handful of television roles.

John Wayne is Colonel Mike Kirby, a good American name for a white
savior fending off savages while saving fellow whites and good little
natives. American soldiers in Việt Nam called the land outside their
firebases "Indian Country." In the American colonizer's imagination,
all natives are Indians. You play the role of good and bad Indians surrounding beleaguered white men like General Philip Sheridan, who

in 1869 said, The only good Indian is a dead Indian. A century later, American soldiers say, The only good gook is a dead gook.

Theodore Roosevelt, future president, was more compassionate in 1886: I don't go so far as to think that the only good Indians are the dead Indians, but I believe nine out of every ten are.

> No wonder some Vietnamese people
> are so eager to prove to white people
> that they are the good 10 percent.

> Should "gook" be capitalized?
> Genuinely curious.

Some Koreans claim to be the first ones so christened, because they called AMERICA™ Miguk, or "beautiful country." American GIs heard Koreans calling themselves "gook." The United States later hired three hundred thousand South Korean gooks to kill unknown numbers of Vietnamese gooks. The novelist Han Kang writes about this in *Human Acts*, as well as about the massacre of Korean civilians at Gwangju by their own army:

> I heard a story about one of the Korean army platoons that
> fought in Vietnam. How they forced the women, children,
> and elderly of one particular village into the main hall, and
> then burned it to the ground. Some of those who came
> to slaughter us did so with the memory of those previous
> times, when committing such actions in wartime had won
> them a handsome reward. It happened in Gwangju just as
> it did on Jeju Island, in Kwantung and Nanjing, in Bosnia,
> and all across the American continent when it was still
> known as the New World, with such a uniform brutality
> it's as though it is imprinted in our genetic code.

Koreans repeat what was done to them by the Japanese, who imitate what white colonizers did to non-white countries. This inhumanity is a very human trait. After the British Empire armed Sikhs and Gurkhas and the French deployed Moroccans and Senegalese in Indochina, these Sikhs, Gurkhas, Moroccans, and Senegalese fought with their colonizers against their fellow colonized peoples.

Some of these Korean soldiers rent rooms in Ba Má's house in Ban Mê Thuột. You do not remember them, or they lived there before your birth. But your brother says

> I was very afraid of them, much more afraid than
> I was of white soldiers. Their reputation
> for terror was that bad.

The brutality of Korean soldiers had already been demonstrated in the Korean War, when Koreans massacred their Korean enemies, real or suspected, an effort led by Syngman Rhee, described by the poet Don Mee Choi as the American-backed angel of genocide. As for the Korean military dictator who orders the massacre of Korean civilians at Gwangju? A veteran of the war in Việt Nam.

> Self-hatred makes the mastered
> meaner and crueler than their masters.

> The self-hating will take out their hatred
> on those who remind them of themselves.

Another theory: "gook" is a variation of "goo-goo," used by American soldiers to describe Filipinos. Many of the American soldiers fighting rebels in the Philippines were veterans of wars against Indigenous peoples in the American West. The West just moved farther west, into the Pacific, until one day the West became the East in Korea and Việt Nam. Who said East is East and West is West and never the twain shall meet?

The Filipinos who embraced the Americans became the little brown brothers to Uncle Sam during four decades of American rule. The "model minority" is just another name for little brown brothers, good natives, sidekicks. The role of the model minority is to be saved by the white man, to be educated by him, to help him carry the white man's burden, and—

if push comes to shove,
not that we hope that it does,
but just in the highly unlikely
worst-case scenario, there it
is in the fine print

—to die for the white man (or white woman).

Good little model sidekick brown brothers or sisters, like your fellow Vietnamese refugees

and maybe you yourself

know their place. You cannot afford to be angry at Americans except in Vietnamese, when some will say out of American earshot that the Americans abandoned you. Remarkable, then, that some Vietnamese veterans finally speak out, in English, or perhaps are just finally heard, on the occasion of the end of the American war in Afghanistan. The parallels between the fall of Sài Gòn and the fall of Kabul may be inexact, but they are evident to these veterans. A former lieutenant colonel, Uc Van Nguyen, says

in the end we felt betrayed.

He refers to the American refusal to help the South Vietnamese defend themselves in 1975. Another veteran, former marine corps gunnery sergeant Ly Kai Binh, says

> I am an American citizen now. . . . But still, we need to keep our promises. That was not done in Vietnam.

These criticisms of American betrayal are still muted, unlike the rage you feel for each other. You take your anger out on each other. In your homeland half of your people fought the other half. But at least there, at home, some of you fought white people, too. Home, where hearth and hurt dwell. Home, where Vietnamese people will always invite you, not expecting you to accept, but if you indeed come, they will, at the very least, serve tea and Danish butter cookies in a blue tin.

Home, where people know how to say your name.
Home, where people can cut you while smiling.
Home, where people put you in your place.
Home, where you fight a civil war.
Home, where revolutions happen.

In 1980s San José, the crime you most fear is the home invasion, when Vietnamese gangsters storm Vietnamese homes, knowing this is where the money and gold are stashed.

> What do you call the north invading the south? Whose homeland is it?

Your parents warn you never to open the door to Vietnamese people you do not know. But when they tell you of Vietnamese gangsters burning babies with cigarettes, you are not afraid. They have already saved you once.

You are certain they can save you again.

part two

The memory stain attaches itself and darkens
on the pale formless sheet, a hole increasing
its size larger and larger until it assimilates
the boundaries and becomes itself formless.
All memory. Occupies the entire.

—Theresa Hak Kyung Cha,
Dictee

mixed feelings

You dislike it when epic books need family trees at the beginning to orient the reader. You also do not like seeing maps in books that serve the same purpose. The exception is for books like *The Lord of the Rings* and William Faulkner's fictions, because Middle Earth and Yoknapatawpha are made-up worlds for which you indeed need maps.

But the immigrant or refugee from some teeming, sweltering corner of the murky Second and Third Worlds, including

Asia

Africa
Latin America

or, basically,

MOST OF THE WORLD

(and their many diasporas)

—this immigrant or refugee needs a family tree and a map to orient the Western (that is to say, minority) reader, with the assumption that you of the global majority are foreign?

Foreign to whom?

At the same time, you can trace your lineage back to only your grandparents, whom you have never met. You would like the privilege and luxury other Americans have of being ignorant of their origins so that you can begin anew, a tabula rasa. You run the risk of being called rootless by the Vietnamese, but what does it mean to be rooted to a country you left at four? White people are never accused of being rootless in an implicitly white AMERICA™. Family trees are optional for those who assume themselves rooted in AMERICA™, even as they expect you to be rooted elsewhere.

But your relationship to your roots, your Vietnamese people, and your homeland is complicated. Once, as a full-grown adult with a PhD, you meet a Vietnamese scholar, about your age, in the UK at an academic reception. Just to make conversation, you tell her you are Vietnamese, too.

No, you're not, she says.

You are so speechless that you do not follow up on what she might mean. You are lying about being Vietnamese? You are of Vietnamese descent but with American nationality? You may be Vietnamese in name but not in spirit?

Mất gốc, they say in Vietnamese.
Whitewashed, in English.
Banana.

You pull on your roots, even if these roots may be the relatively shallow ones of a banana tree. From family lore, you assume your maternal and paternal grandparents come from the province of Hà Tĩnh, where your parents were born in the village of Nghĩa Yên in the district of Đức Thọ. You assume this because your heritage seems eternal, pure, authentic, given how often Ba says to you during your childhood that

YOU ARE 100 PERCENT VIETNAMESE

which is strange, since you look kind of Chinese, or so some Chinese say. Hà Tĩnh is toward the north, 850 kilometers from China, which occupied the country for a thousand years. The chances of Chinese and Vietnamese mutually procreating are therefore 100 percent.

> Once, in college, a friend
> who knows your family says,
> There's a rumor you're adopted.
> She looks at your nose.
> I mean, look at your nose.
> Did you have cosmetic surgery?

You laugh, but when she leaves you go look at your nose, which, so far as you can tell, looks like other Vietnamese noses you have seen, if not all Vietnamese noses. When you tell the story to your parents, your father is incensed. I'll take a DNA test, Ba says. You are my son!

You never take him up on his offer.

> Later your brother says,
> You know how you're not adopted?
> . . .
> Mom didn't leave you behind.

This, too, leaves you speechless.

Because it is probably true.

Your (adopted) sister, chị Tuyết, has been left behind in a country that possesses the fifth-largest army in the world even though it is the fifth-poorest country, or so you learn from an encyclopedia in the early 1980s. The relatives must be starving. Over dinner, the food always plentiful, Ba Má say, If you were still there, you would be drafted into the army. A bộ đội in Cambodia! You could step on a land mine and be killed! Thank God for our good fortune.

You have no idea what is happening in Cambodia. You say
nothing. You rarely have anything to say to Ba Má
and absolutely nothing to say to God. Children
must obey, not speak back.

Nineteen years after leaving Việt Nam, Ba Má return to visit. You are not
invited, but you do not mind. You are focused on being an American and a
Vietnamese American. When you do return eight years later, twenty-seven
years after you left, you go as a tourist and avoid meeting your relatives,
which will be emotionally difficult. You do not deal well with emotional
difficulty, except in your writing. With actual people, you prefer your
emotions like your roads, smooth, straight, and uncrowded. A scouting
expedition to check out the scenery, weather, people, and customs seems
advisable before actually encountering your vast number of relatives.

You do not expect your return to the country of your birth to be a return
to wholeness, to an origin as authentic as your mother's womb, where
you will be overwhelmed by a desire to fall to your knees at Tân Sơn
Nhất Airport and kiss the ground.

You do not believe in wholeness or
authenticity, which require the
opposites of lack and
inauthenticity.

Supposedly rootless and whitewashed, you suspect that everyone is
lacking in some way deep within, especially those most likely to accuse
others of inauthenticity.

Poor you! Torn between East and West!
If only you could overcome the clash of
cultures and fuse your confused selves,
to make a whole out of the hole within you!

So goes the cliché of the identity crisis, in which so-called minorities are alienated from themselves. If your divided selves are the problem, then the solutions must be personal. They require cultural reconciliation. Choose from:

A) marrying a white person
B) trying to be white
C) developing fusion cuisine
D) finding healing in the land of ancestry

These solutions might work for those who seek to be bridges between worlds. But identity crises collectively return from generation to generation not because it is innate to be divided between East and West, but because the colonization and conquest that brought the West into the East still continue in some places. If the colonization does not continue, its effects still do, lingering through the seduction of privilege and power and the ways they divide people into those who have more and those who have less, a division some reject and too many accept.

You do not suffer from an identity crisis because American individualism and Vietnamese collectivism war within you.

You struggle with a political crisis, because the French brutally colonized Việt Nam, with AMERICA™, China, and the Soviet Union taking sides in the resulting civil war between Vietnamese people with different visions of independence, sending you and millions of others into the diaspora, where you are left to re member yourselves.

Although the personal is political, the solution to your political crisis cannot only be a new hybrid of food or a cross-cultural celebration or trying to become more authentically Vietnamese or deeply American.

The solution to colonization is decolonization.

You arrive in your officially decolonized country of origin on a fully booked China Airlines overnight flight that offers the cheapest ticket. It is 2002, only eight years after the United States reestablished relations with Việt Nam, after having waged war for nineteen years by other means through blockade and sanctions. Concrete revetments once used to protect fighter jets still stand on the Tân Sơn Nhất Airport runway, but the American warbirds have long since departed or been repossessed by the victorious Vietnamese. The airport is passably modern, with tile floors, plastic seats, many windows, and air-conditioning. Disembarking passengers rush for the border gates, manned by officers in lime-green shirts and large round hats, some of whom, it is said, will wave you by more quickly if you tuck American dollars in your passport. You do not do so, and the officer asks you a perfunctory question about your being born in this country. By now, he has probably seen hundreds like you, returning Việt Kiều.

Exiting the airport this first time and on the occasions you return over the next twelve years, you are shocked by the heat and humidity after a lifetime of being softened by air-conditioning. None of the hundreds of locals waiting outside the airport to welcome their loved ones seem bothered by the temperature, and you wonder how the French colonized this country wearing suits, long-sleeved shirts, and layered clothing. You wear T-shirts, shorts, and open-toed sandals and must still shower two or three times a day, since a few hours outside leaves you soaked in sweat. Twenty-seven years ago, your body must have been used to this climate, but your body has changed as much as your mind. No matter how many times you return, your body never becomes acclimated, although you are probably to blame, never weaning yourself off air-conditioning.

You negotiate a fee with a taxi driver to take you to downtown Sài Gòn. The price is reasonable, but you can't be sure. Over the next couple of weeks and on return trips, you discover that foreigners are often charged a higher price. People sometimes consider you to be that foreigner, unable to pass for a local. Too tall, too pale, wrong clothes, possessor of a decent accent but a faltering vocabulary. You try to avoid situations where negotiation is expected, like haggling over mangos or lychees with a street vendor, almost always a woman, covered from head to toe and collar to wrist despite the heat, head shaded by a conical hat. When you do haggle, you do so half-heartedly and only because you would appear naive if you didn't.

Má is a master haggler who bargained with customers every day, rapidly calculating in her head. How come you did not inherit this survival skill? Like these women vendors who walk all day with a yoke on their shoulders, she, too, had a hard life. When we first came south, Má tells you as a child at the dinner table during one of her rare moments of sharing her past, I had to pick up buffalo dung to try to make some money.

Why tell him stories like that?
Ba mutters.

Why not? Perhaps Má is proud of how far she has come, a consummate, self-trained, natural businesswoman who rose from a poor, rural childhood where her education stopped in grade school.

Don't talk about that,
Ba says, to you as much as to Má.
Her lack of education is shameful, but

you believe the shame belongs neither to
her nor to your family but to the
society in which she grew up.

In the south, Má is a teenager, a newlywed, a refugee for the first time, having fled from her northern village with her family and your father, who left his entire family behind. At the same age, you are a college student memorizing Byron, Shelley, and Shakespeare because their verses are beautiful. You dream of being a writer, your tuition paid for by your parents. Perhaps that's why you never learned to haggle.

You must bargain to show some self-respect with the xe ôm drivers, deeply suntanned men in threadbare shirts and trousers and open-toed sandals who wait at every street corner, perched on the narrow seats of their motorbikes. Even paying a little extra, the price of a motorbike ride is only a couple of dollars. Việt Nam is the cheapest country you have ever visited, a few dollars for a restaurant meal and thirty dollars for a comfortable hotel room with hot water and your beloved air-conditioning. The only drawback of these family-run mini-hotels is that they lock their doors late at night, compelling you to disturb the night clerks who sleep on the lobby floor.

You cannot bring yourself to stay at the high-end hotels or eat at the high-end restaurants. You take pride in finding restaurants that serve the most pungent flavors, the most native foods, equal to or better than what is served in the Little Sài Gòns of the United States, even if it requires sitting on tiny blue or red plastic stools in humid restaurants. Why the Vietnamese favor these tiny stools and knee-level tables, you never find out.

After dinner, you visit nightclubs with names like Apocalypse Now and Heart of Darkness, throbbing with the beats of American dance hits. You frequent these clubs so often, participating in or at least observing what the government calls social evils, that you witness the lime-green policemen raiding each one. In Apocalypse Now, the music pauses and the lights come on while a squad of cops steps into the office, which you can see from the dance floor. After a decent interval, they emerge, one carrying a briefcase. The lights dim and the music of the Black Eyed Peas resumes. In Heart of Darkness, the police seize all the local women not carrying ID and spirit them away in a police van. The police assume they are all sex workers, which is not true. One of the unfortunate women is your housemate, staying in another room in a local home that rents them out. It is well past midnight when your landlady rescues her from the police station.

If you were to one day retire to Sài Gòn, perhaps you would open a bar with a sign that would flip. During the day: THE QUIET AMERICAN. At night: THE UGLY AMERICAN. Either of these literary allusions would be better than Craters, the bar in Phonsavan near the Plain of Jars in Laos, named after the destruction left by American bombs. The night you walk by the bar, the only customers are young American men in civilian clothes, air force volunteers on a medical mission to aid the local Lao. The one airman you talk to in the airport had not heard of the American bombing campaign that obliterated much of lowland Laos.

Hence the name Secret War,
not to be confused with Marvel Comics'
Secret Wars series in the mid-1980s that you
read and enjoyed long before you
knew of the real Secret War.

The Vietnamese countryside with its bright green rice paddies is bucolic, with no trace of bomb craters that you can see, although unexploded American ordnance is a hazard that kills and maims thousands in the countryside, here as well as in Laos and Cambodia. Bullet holes still mark the walls of the war-shattered Imperial Palace in Huế, with majestic imperial tombs lining the Perfume River. After sweating through a daylong tour of the tombs, you shower and venture out for a cooler evening on a boat where musicians and singers serenade you and your fellow tourists as you watch paper lanterns float on the dark waters. In Hội An's version of Savile Row, you spend too much money on tailors who turn around cheap custom-made suits in less than twenty-four hours. The thread of your bespoke pants unravels within a year.

Leaving Hội An, you take the overnight bus, filled only with foreign tourists, to Hà Nội with its romantic ocher-yellow villas. The dense Old Quarter, with its tight network of alleys and shops, charms you, while the Temple of Literature recalls a quaint time when the mandarins who governed the country were men who had to know literature.

On an overnight trip to Hạ Long Bay you have your own cabin on a romantic junk. Hạ Long Bay is the backdrop of the French romantic epic *Indochine* from 1992, in which a statuesque Catherine Deneuve towers over her squatting Vietnamese slaves—pardon, *workers*—and never sweats even as anti-French revolution breaks out. 1992 is the year you begin thinking about returning to Việt Nam, which you will do a decade later. Not only does *Indochine* appear in cinemas this year, but so, too, does *The Lover*, based on the novel by Marguerite Duras and set in the even more exotic period of the 1920s, helping to popularize the French image of Việt Nam as a steamy setting of colonial romance and regret, of melancholy and mistiness.

The lover, an older, wealthy Chinese man with perfectly slicked-back hair, seduces a willing French white girl, played by Jane March, a British actress who appears white to you but who you later discover has some Vietnamese ancestry. Tony Leung Ka-fai is credited as

The chinaman

and while Duras did write, Il dit qu'il est chinois, that is still not a chinaman. She also describes him as l'homme élégant, which sounds so much better than chinaman.

But cinematic license does mean that while Duras describes the Chinese lover as being rather slight and not even very attractive, the makers of the movie transform the chinaman by casting the very hot and physically imposing Leung (not to be confused with the very hot Tony Leung Chiu-wai, star of a few Wong Kar-wai movies and someone who could also play your father). Cinema transforms how we look at people, things, and places, and while Việt Nam has a cinema, few watch it outside of the country. At the end of the twentieth century, it is the Americans and the French who use cinema to shape Việt Nam's global image, wavering between two different filmic fantasies: a tragic and brutal American war and a sensual and elegant French colony, both of which lure tourists, including you.

These fantasies do not overly concern the Vietnamese unless they work in the tourist business or the memory business of historical museums, which drill a repetitive narrative: the heroic Communist Party saved the country from the French and the Americans and brought the nation to economic prosperity through industry.

While there is considerable truth to
this narrative, the government
allows no further nuance
or other narratives.

What troubles you about Vietnamese communism is that it is not actually communism. If the people do not own the means of production, they should. The troubling irony is that what passes for communism in Việt Nam is capitalism with one-party rule, where proletariat and peasantry are no more in charge than in AMERICA™.

What also disturbs you about purported Vietnamese communism is its fundamentalism, the way it permits only one interpretation of the politically conflicted past and present. Your real home is in language and writing, and it is impossible for you to think of this country as a home when its government does not allow writers to be free.

For a brief moment in the 1980s, the government does allow writers to publish books that tell the truth, or at least one truth, of what happened during the war and its aftermath.

Nguyễn Huy Thiệp, widely considered the best short story writer of his generation, publishes *The General Retires and Other Stories*, which includes scathing portraits of postwar desperation and people scrambling for their own self-interest.

Dương Thu Hương, war veteran and former party member, writes *Paradise of the Blind*, about the disastrous land reform of the 1950s and the Vietnamese sent as guest workers to eastern Europe, as well as *Novel without a Name*, the second-best novel about the war.

The best novel about the war—or so you think—is *The Sorrow of War* by Bảo Ninh, also a northern veteran who barely survived the conflict. Bảo Ninh's classic of war literature concerns ideals and disillusionment, horror and regret, with time and narrative folding back on themselves around a traumatic memory, a trick you eventually borrow for your novel *The Sympathizer*.

Nguyễn Huy Thiệp, the most idiosyncratic, continues publishing sporadically until his death. Dương Thu Hương, who explicitly condemned

Communist Party corruption, is placed under house arrest, her works banned. Eventually she is exiled to Paris. Bảo Ninh, who destroyed the myth of the heroic, noble war veteran, would not publish his second book until thirty-two years later—in English translation, but not in Vietnamese.

In the contemporary era, writers who expose police and government abuses, or who call for more freedoms, are imprisoned by the government.

If you lived and wrote in Việt Nam, you would have to write what you believe and risk jail, or you would silence yourself.

You have no illusions about
your degree of courage.

On the last day of your first trip back to Việt Nam, you sit in a downtown café in Sài Gòn, writing notes on your journey for a book that cannot yet be published in Việt Nam. You are waiting for the monsoon deluge to stop so you can take a taxi to the airport. Motorbike drivers in luminescent ponchos of blue, yellow, and green plow through the spray. A perfect cinematic moment, written by Graham Greene and adapted by Wong Kar-wai, except for you, the sloppy American wearing shorts and a T-shirt.

In photos memorializing your
visit, you are not dapper.
Just damp.

At the airport, you leave the country in reverse, going from heat and humidity and clamor and dense traffic to the air-conditioned orderliness of the terminal where you began. You are leaving with more weight than you entered from the books of Vietnamese photography and art that you have bought, available only in Việt Nam, and you have to heave your luggage from the ticket counter to a separate desk to pay the excess baggage fee. You barely make it to your gate on time for departure, and you are relieved to finally be able to cool down and relax when you take your seat on the air-conditioned airplane. Svelte, soft-spoken flight attendants in scarlet áo dài embody what the country wants for itself, a soothing blend of modernity and tradition. The Boeing ascends, and you look out the window, the patchwork pattern of the land fading away to a vibrant, borderless green

and

just

like

that

you want nothing more than to return.

so . . . where are you really from?

This desire to return home is innocent enough, but the onset of the global plague in 2020 complicates notions of origin and belonging. The plague infects not just the individual body but the body politic of each nation it touches. The body politic convulses, twitches—and remembers.

The Western body politic recalls
the fear of an Asian invasion.

In AMERICA™, the demonization of Asians begins with President ██████, who calls the plague the "Chinese Virus."

██████ relishes his role as the super-spreader of a noxious, ignorant white nationalism that has lurked in AMERICA™ since its origin. A white nationalism that continues to kill: Through guns in the hands of angry, frightened white men. Through the fact that racism, writes the abolitionist scholar Ruth Wilson Gilmore, is

the state-sanctioned or extralegal production
and exploitation of group-differentiated
vulnerability to premature death

found in being victims of warfare and sanctions, police violence and incarceration, exploitation and discrimination, macro- and microaggression, and illness like the plague.

White nationalism is the dominant American identity and has been for centuries, but when white people are in total control, (white) nationalism passes as ( ) nationalism. When this ( ) nationalism is challenged—

by
people of color,

feminists,

and

queer people

because (   ) nationalism,

besides demonizing racial Others,

also

subordinates women

and

regulates sex

and

condemns queerness

—this (   ) nationalism asserts itself,
inflames the body politic,
becomes visibly,
markedly
white.

The fact that ████'s followers include women, Latinos, Asians, even some Black people, means that women and non-white people can align themselves with whiteness and heterosexual masculinity, protecting themselves from white nationalism by pointing at someone darker, more feminized, more easily stigmatized, while hoping to be paid a share of the wages of (masculine) whiteness.

Siding with the powerful and targeting the weaker as viral threats is human, all too human. ████ began his presidential campaign by painting Mexicans as drug dealers and rapists, continued with banning Muslims as importers of terrorism and a foreign religion, and now, with the plague, attacking the Chinese.

The West has long feared the Chinese as a source of contagion. In the nineteenth century, Americans burned down Chinatowns, perceiving them as enclaves for disease. The burning of San José's Chinatown occurred in 1887. Standing in its place now is the luxurious Fairmont Hotel, where you have slept. When the hotel is built in the 1980s, a new landmark of the gentrifying downtown a few blocks from the Sàigòn Mới, you write an article for your high school newspaper describing the architecture.

> You do not mention Chinatown because
> you, the Asian Invasion, do not
> know of its ghost.

██████, a builder of hotels, a man ignorant of history, says that the Chinese virus is also the Kung Flu.

> Some of your Saint Patrick classmates
> thought it was hilarious to ask,
> Is your last name Nam?
> ██████ sniggers in the same register.

The Chinese virus or the Kung Flu takes aim at the Chinese, but to some, all Asians look the same. Anti-Asian violence rises throughout AMERICA™, Canada, Australia, Germany, France, and elsewhere.

> The French of Asian descent declare
> #JeNeSuisPasUnVirus.

In AMERICA™ a woman is splashed with acid on her doorstep; a man and his son are slashed by a knife-wielding assailant; numerous people are called the "Chinese virus" or the "Chink virus" or told to go back to China; people are spat on for being Asian; people are afraid to leave their homes.

> We don't have coronavirus,
> Cathy Park Hong writes.
> We *are* coronavirus.

Being the coronavirus shocks some Asian Americans. Some of you thought you had made progress beyond the viral level. When your high school invites you back, nearly thirty years after the Asian Invasion, to talk to the sixteen hundred young men of the assembled student body, you notice how many more of you there are. You, the model minority: desirable classmate and favored neighbor, the nonthreatening kind of person of color.

> Or are you?

A white classmate from your high school tells you that in the 1980s in his suburban neighborhood of Saratoga, southwest of San José, white people started moving out when the Asians started moving in.

After your talk, a couple of Asian American students tell you how they feel foreign, especially if they are, or are perceived to be, Muslim or brown. This is the same vibe from your youth, when you learned to feel ashamed, or at least embarrassed, of what supposedly made you foreign: your food, your language, your fashion, your smell.

> Your parents.

But these were minor feelings. What is the weight of minor feelings when anti-Asian sentiment remains a reservoir of major feeling?

Anti-Asian racism dictates that Asians belong in Asia, no matter how many generations you have been living in non-Asian countries. Even though you are supposedly invading all these countries, there are not enough of you to make people hesitate in saying Chinese virus and Kung Flu or from asking the classic

Where are you from?

To ask this of
someone of Asian descent
in a non-Asian country
is not an innocent question,
only an ignorant one at best,
a malicious one at worst.

But where are you *really* from?

Are white people
ever asked this question
in a white-dominated country?

Perhaps if they have an accent. But even those of Asian descent who speak fluently in English, French, German, and so on can be asked this question. Assuming foreignness is the first step to assigning blame. Scapegoating Asians in non-Asian countries for a society's ills dates to the nineteenth century, at least in the Americas.

When the usefulness of Chinese workers is finished with the building of the Transcontinental Railroad, politicians, journalists, and business leaders demonize them to appease white workers who feel threatened by Chinese competition.

In Torreón, Mexico, in 1911, a local mob
murders more than three hundred people of
mostly Chinese and some Japanese descent.

White mobs in AMERICA™ also lynch Chinese migrants and drive
them out of many towns. In downtown Los Angeles in 1871, not far
from where you live now, a mob of several hundred murder eighteen
Chinese men and boys. In 1875, Congress passes the Page Act, aimed
at keeping Chinese women out. Anti-Chinese feeling climaxes with the
1882 Chinese Exclusion Act, the country's first racially discriminatory
immigration law. The Chinese become the nation's first illegal and
undocumented immigrants.

What does it mean to be illegal
when the law is unjust?

The cycle repeats throughout American history: big businesses rely on
cheap Asian labor, which threatens the white working class, whose fears
are stoked by race-baiting politicians and media, leading to catastrophe
for Asians:

the Gentlemen's Agreement of 1907
ends Japanese immigration after
the Japanese, who replace the
Chinese, become too visible

the beatings, throughout the early
twentieth century, of Filipino
workers, who replace the Japanese
only to encounter signs saying
NO DOGS AND NO FILIPINOS ALLOWED

the incarceration of Japanese
Americans from 1942 to 1945, which
allows white neighbors to buy (steal)
Japanese American property at
insultingly low prices

the Ku Klux Klan attacks on
Vietnamese fishermen in
Texas in the 1980s

the social downgrading of educated
Korean immigrants, who open
liquor stores and other businesses in
Black and brown communities of
Los Angeles, where, during the LA
rebellion of 1992, the Los Angeles
Police Department cordons off
Koreatown and lets it be burned—

Riot, says Martin Luther King Jr., is the language of the unheard.

Americans blame the Chinese and anyone who looks like them for
the loss of American jobs, even as Americans rely on China and other
Asian countries for cheap commodities that help Americans live the
AMERICAN DREAM™.

ANOTHER AMERICAN
DRIVEN OUT OF BUSINESS
BY THE _____

is a story always available for fearful Americans and those who want to frighten them. The people who tell that story misunderstand a basic fact:

AMERICA™ is built on
the business of driving other
businesses out of business.

Ba Má excel at this capitalist life cycle. No one wants to open new businesses in San José's run-down downtown in the 1970s and 1980s except for people like Ba Má. Easier to blame them or a foreign country or politicians than to identify the corporations and economic elites who shift jobs to other countries, maximize profit at the expense of workers, and care nothing for working people, for some of whom

being racist
is easier than
blaming capitalism.

For too many Asian Americans, the solution is to prove yourselves. Prove your Americanness. Prove your humanity. Wrap yourselves in the American flag, donate to white neighbors and fellow citizens in emergencies, and die in this country's wars, like the Japanese American soldiers who fought in World War II while their families were imprisoned in concentration camps.

Bravery and medals, blood and death, all to prove what should not need proving to people who giggle, chortle, snort, laugh, and sneer when they say to you, or to the cameras, in front of millions, or even just in front of their children, who repeat what they hear—

Jap
Nip
Chink
Dogeater
Slant-Eye
Kung Flu
Chinese virus
Do you know kung fu?
Unidentified Fucking Oriental
Go back to where you came from
University of Caucasians Lost among Asians
Your English is so good
Me love you long time
Love it or leave it
Ching Chong
Chinaman
Gook

disremembered

You learn some of these slurs from the casual racism of television, radio, and classmates. But you also learn some from the books of the public library, the immense white cube on West San Carlos Street named after Martin Luther King Jr. Every Saturday morning, Ba drops you off in front of the library, where you wait with a small crowd of other fanatical readers for the doors to open. Perhaps he and Má think the library is a safe place for you, although it is a place that they may not understand. You grow up in a household without books, except for the schoolbooks and library books your brother and you bring home. No Bible in any language, despite the devoutness of your parents, just Vietnamese newspapers, magazines, and church newsletters. Sometimes you wander into the living room to discover your mother reading with the aid of a magnifying glass. She reads only Vietnamese. Slowly and out loud.

> What do Ba Má think when
> they see you with your books?

You borrow a backpack full of books every week and read them all, totally absorbed. The more fluent you become, the further away from Ba Má that language carries you. Decades later it occurs to you that this might have been what you wanted. As much as you yearn to be closer to Ba Má, they work too much, have so little to say to you. They turn you over to the care of the library but do not realize how the library will steal you from them. By the time they do, you have been kidnapped by literature. By books. By English.

You cannot and will not read anything in Vietnamese, a tongue too thick in your mouth.

> Vietnamese is your mother tongue,
> but you barely talk to your mother.
> Vietnamese is your native tongue,
> but you left before memory.

English is your second language,
but you speak it like a native.

If your real world is limited to house, school, church, and the SàiGòn Mới, the library is its own limitless world. Displaced by crossing from one side of the world to another, you find your place in English, in the endless travel offered by stories. A freedom from a home with iron bars on its windows. No borders between books, no guards to prevent a curious young boy from scarring himself with words hot to the touch.

You have never forgotten the Executioner series, featuring Mack Bolan, an American sniper serving in Việt Nam when the Mafia forces his teenage sister into prostitution, leading their father to kill his family and himself. You can hear the rapid clicking of the typewriter keys in the staccato prose as Bolan returns to enact revenge and, while surveilling the Mafia, consorts with one of the women who work for them.

You take a break to visit your
high school–aged brother in his room,
waving the paperback, its cover featuring a
half-naked redhead with a mafioso holding a knife to
her throat as Bolan points a rifle at both.
What's a prostitute? you ask.
Is that like a Protestant?

Your brother keeps his
gaze on his book for a
very long time.

Finally he says,
Look it up in the dictionary.

In the library, English is your adopted language,
even though it feels biological, and in the
library you are searching for a home,
though you already have one.

Alex Portnoy also feels uncomfortable at home. He is the star of Philip
Roth's 1969 novel, *Portnoy's Complaint*. Perhaps you knew about Roth's
reputation, since you read the *San José Mercury* book review for fun
as you commence your teenage years. You also have inherited your
brother's copy of William Rose Benét's *The Reader's Encyclopedia*, which
you also read for fun. You need to have more fun. What you have instead
is a growing sense of literary history and what is considered important.
Roth is important, the Great American Novelist who actually wrote a
book titled *The Great American Novel*.

Is any other country on this earth so self-conscious about
using its name in the titles of its books? Roth would also
write *American Pastoral*, and there are also *American
Gods, American Psycho, American War, American
Tabloid, American Spy, American Rust, American Son*,
and many more, as well as variations like *Purple America,
Americana, Americanah, Vietnamerica*, and *Amerika*.
Perhaps one day you will write a Not So
Great American Novel titled
American America.

You read a few pages of Roth's first book, *Goodbye, Columbus*, see a
glimpse of the movie adaptation on television with Richard Benjamin
and Ali MacGraw. The Jewish world described by Roth twenty-five years
earlier resonates with your Vietnamese world, especially as seen through
the eyes of a younger, Americanized child who feels his ethnic difference from the norm of white people, sees the oddities of his parents

and community, and understands intuitively that the shadows in the family home are cast by a nearly unspeakable history.

The Jewish people in Roth's books are (in your memory) a little loud, somewhat uncouth by White Anglo-Saxon Protestant standards.

> The white people you know are Catholics, but news, television, and the movies impress WASP ideals on you.

Roth's Jews are determined to climb the social ladder and move to the suburbs, while feeling anxious about losing their roots and becoming too assimilated, especially as evidenced in their children. Not so different from Vietnamese refugees.

> But honestly, all you remember for decades is that the adolescent Alex Portnoy masturbates with a slab of liver from the family fridge, after which he puts the grossly violated meat back in its place for the family's dinner later that night.

Gross!
Who eats *liver* for dinner?

Your family does! But you have not masturbated yet, which is why this scene is hilarious, disturbing, and confusing. The same bewilderment grips you on reading a book about an adolescent boy by Judy Blume, kept in your sixth grade classroom's library, about which all you remember is that his hard-ons embarrass him. You have no idea what a hard-on is. When a girl in your fifth grade class says penis to you, you have never heard of it, having been raised in a monolingual Vietnamese Catholic household where sex, and the biology associated with it, is unspeakable.

At some point in this preadolescent era, you walk home from Saint Patrick with two classmates, one of whom wants to show you his father's collection of *Playboy* and *Penthouse* magazines, which you have never seen before. The three of you study the pictures and centerfolds, which confuse you. In one picture and its caption, naked twins compare their anatomy. Is "anatomy" a dirty word? Soon after, you see the word "anatomy" in a children's book about a seal and become even more confused. You never go to the dictionary to look up the word.

You cannot find *Playboy* or *Penthouse* at the library, but they exist somewhere in a broad rainbow of storytelling and imagination, one end of which reaches into the heavens while the other end embeds in the muck of the earth. *Portnoy's Complaint* may be rarefied art, but its energy derives from Roth's willingness to delve into smut, that lovely word and lovely world. That smut burns in your memory and in your loins, to use another wonderful word you learn from books.

You acquire another word from *Mourning Glory*, an American marine's war memoir you have never forgotten. You stumble across it in the library because you like to browse the war section, for which you must ride the escalator to the second floor, where there are no other children. The marine has sex with a Vietnamese prostitute, then shoots his sperm onto her belly button. What is sperm? Is this where a man is supposed to shoot it? Can a woman get pregnant through her belly button? Decades later you find the book, reread the passage, and realize you have blocked out what preceded the marine's climax:

> I reached down to the floor and picked up the
> loaded .45. I cocked the hammer back and put
> the yawning barrel to the girl's temple.

Would Ba Má have been more shocked at you reading these books or by you risking your life at Great America? Reading these books is risking your Catholic life. Your purity is violated. Your mind, contaminated. Sex confuses. War confuses. Việt Nam confuses. Their tangle is what Americans mean when they say Vietnam, signifying the war, not the country. American shorthand, and a common reference point for the whole world.

> Some years later—1998—future president ███████,
> vascular channel for AMERICA™'s seminal id,
> human Viagra for a limp white or white-
> identifying body politic, describes his
> overactive sex life by saying, It's
> Vietnam. It is very dangerous.
> So I'm very, very careful.

When you are fourteen, you board a bus and travel across town to meet a couple of your friends (actually, your only friends) and watch the global blockbuster *Rambo: First Blood Part II* in the movie theater, circa 1985. American war veteran Rambo, played by perpetually half-naked Sylvester Stallone, returns to Việt Nam to rescue American soldiers kept prisoner by the Vietnamese communists, an enduring myth in the American imagination, one with no evidence. A beautiful mixed-race Vietnamese woman named Co aids Rambo.

> Co—properly spelled Cô—means
> "aunt" or "older lady." Co is
> played by Julia Nickson,
> of Chinese descent.

Co loves Rambo and dies for him when the evil communist captain ambushes them and shoots her. Roaring in rage, Rambo wipes out the captain's squad with his AK-47.

> You do not think too much of this.
> Asian sidekicks and lovers die for
> white saviors all the time.

You enjoy the movie, albeit with a twinge of unease as a member of the Asian Invasion watching the white savior wipe out the Vietnamese commie hordes. Seeing the movie again as an adult, you notice how the actress wears an áo dài in the middle of the jungle, her hair and makeup perfect in the steamy humidity, lipstick gleaming moistly as she utters her dying words in a vaguely accented English:

Ram . . . bo . . . you . . . not . . . forget . . . me?

Rambo embraces Co as her eyes close, her head falls back, and her mouth opens in a shuddering groan, their pose one of orgasmic love-making as much as death.

The movie is also screened for Hmong refugees in Thai refugee camps. Even afterward, one (former) refugee writes you, her parents continue to watch the movie because

its characters closely resemble faces that
looked like ours. As an adult now, I can say that
Rambo was part of the indoctrination of
our love for white saviors.

This is long-distance Americanization. Your Americanization is up close and personal. In 1989, your teenage relatives from Việt Nam, the grandchildren of Má's oldest sister, immigrate to AMERICA™. You are in Southern California at your last-choice college, driving your brother's hand-me-down Buick Skylark coupe. Why don't you take them out? Má asks.

Their English is about as bad as your Vietnamese. You will not have to talk too much at a movie. You choose Brian De Palma's *Casualties of War* as their first American movie theater experience.

Michael J. Fox plays an idealistic soldier who cannot stop Sean Penn and
his squad from gang-raping and then murdering a young Vietnamese
woman. In her death scene, she has been raped, stabbed, and left for
dead on train tracks overlooking a river. But she is not dead. Rising, she
stumbles along the train tracks toward the soldiers who have abandoned
her, dazed, her clothing soaked in her own blood. Shoot her! yells Penn.
Shoot her! The squad hesitates but then obeys. The camera focuses on
her face and body as she is caught in the cross fire of an M60 machine
gun, two M16 automatic rifles, and a pistol. Her body jerks from the
impact of multiple bullets as she screams and screams before she falls
off the train tracks in slow motion. Fox looks over the edge of the tracks
and sees her broken body lying on the rocky banks of the river below,
limbs in impossible angles, face smeared by blood.

Raped and murdered,
desired and objectified,
servile and suppliant,
silenced or screaming,
these are the fates of
Asian women in the
Western imagination,
which is yours as well.

This particular rape and murder is based on the
death of twenty-one-year-old Phan Thi Mao in 1966.
Phan Thi Mao is played by Thuy Thu Le, who graduated
from the University of California at Berkeley, just like you.
Her nickname is Tweety Bird. Her height: an impressive
five feet six. Thuy Thu Le has no more movie roles.
Phan Thi Mao's name with diacritics might be
Phan Thị Mạo or Phan Thị Mão, but you cannot
find anything about her online in Vietnamese.

The white and Latino soldiers who rape and murder Phan Thi Mao range in age from twenty to twenty-two, the same as many of your university students, some of whom come in military uniform to your class on memory and the war in Việt Nam. They have returned from combat in Iraq or Afghanistan or are preparing to be officers in the army, navy, air force, or marine corps. You wonder what, if anything, they will remember from your course.

The longest prison sentence for the rape and murder of Phan Thi Mao is eight years, with eligibility for parole in half that time.

You and your cousins do not say a word
about the movie when it concludes.
Welcome to AMERICA™.

Phan Thi Mao's death scene has lingered with you for decades. As has the scene of the family being massacred in *Apocalypse Now*, and the mother being shot in the head by an American sergeant in *Platoon*, and the circle of vicious cursing, cackling Việt Cộng torturers who threaten Robert De Niro and Christopher Walken in *The Deer Hunter* and force them to play Russian roulette. As much as you have tried to forget your refugee history and as much as AMERICA™ has tried to forget your shared war, neither of you has succeeded. But if you have not forgotten, you have not totally remembered either. And for you, and for the Vietnamese, and in particular for the Vietnamese woman, who stands in for Việt Nam itself, if you are all

invisible and hypervisible

as a condition of your existence in the scene and on the screen of the Western imagination

you are not just forgotten or remembered,
you are both at the same time,
you are seen *and* misunderstood,
seen *and* distorted, seen *and* instantly
forgotten, seen *and* unseen,
you are remembered *and* dismembered

you are disremembered

but—
even as you are the Other who is
disremembered, you also
disremember Others.

When you are twelve or thirteen, your best friend, Chuy, takes you
to his friend's house. The friend, a kid your age or a little older, possesses what you and Chuy, Catholic schoolboys, have been searching for
without success: pornographic magazines. The *Penthouse* and *Playboy*
magazines you pored over and the nude bodies of women with their
vast expanses of flesh gave you a strange, hot, overpowering feeling that
you could not resist. These naked women are very visible, as bodies or
body parts, even if women in general are often invisible, at least to men.

You are an aspiring man.

The friend sleeps in the garage and, under his creaky bed, hides copies
of *Oui, Cheri, Genesis,* and *Hustler.* But before you can get your hands
on those magazines, you must pass a test.

Hey, Chuy says, grinning. Or maybe it's the friend.
Have you popped your cherry yet?

You have no idea what a cherry is or what it means to pop one.

The right answer is: Have *you?*
Or: I know I popped your mama's cherry.

But under peer pressure, your mind is blank. Whether you say yes or no, the answer is wrong. You don't remember whether you hesitantly say yes or no, but both burst out laughing.

> In Việt Nam, American soldiers
> called replacements freshly
> arrived from the States
> Fucking New Guys.
> Or
>
> Cherries.

This is your self-education into something like manhood.

the american question

The immigrant is the Fucking New Guy, or Gal, or Gender Nonbinary Person, in the United States. Fresh Off the Boat or Fresh Off the Boeing, the FNG will learn the harsh lessons of American life like everyone else before them, in an extended hazing ritual from which they might emerge, one day, as Americans. This immigrant is a part of American mythology. Immigrants make America great!

Except when the country shuts its doors to immigrants who are not white, even if whiteness itself is an ever-shifting category. When the Chinese were first immigrating to the country in the nineteenth century, they became the troublesome Chinese question in the American imagination.

How does it feel to be a question? And what, exactly, is the Chinese question?

Whatever it is, the answer is the Irish. Not white in the nineteenth century but white now, even if once caricatured as being almost Black. The Irish take the first step to whiteness by not being Chinese, by not being those who build the Transcontinental Railroad from the west while the Irish build it from the east. After Chinese exclusion, the Irish whiten themselves even further by not being Black. John F. Kennedy eventually makes the Irish permanently white (a feat Barack Obama cannot accomplish for Black people). Saint Patrick's Day helps other Americans identify with the Irish, even if only through a stereotype of Irish drinking.

> The Lunar New Year?
> Mostly celebrated by Asians,
> an exotic spectacle of lion dances,
> firecrackers, and mooncakes.
> Not so popular.

The American fondness for white immigrants goes back at least as far as Founding Father Benjamin Franklin, who in 1751 said:

> The Number of purely white People in the World is proportionably very small. All *Africa* is black or tawny. *Asia* chiefly tawny. *America* (exclusive of the new Comers) wholly so. And in *Europe*, the *Spaniards, Italians, French, Russians* and *Swedes*, are generally of what we call a swarthy Complexion; as are the *Germans* also, the *Saxons* only excepted, who with the *English*, make the principal Body of White People on the Face of the Earth. I could wish their Numbers were increased. And while we are, as I may call it, *Scouring* our Planet, by clearing *America* of Woods, and so making this Side of our Globe reflect a brighter Light to the Eyes of Inhabitants in *Mars* or *Venus*, why should we in the Sight of Superior Beings, darken its People? why increase the Sons of *Africa*, by Planting them in *America*, where we have so fair an Opportunity, by excluding all Blacks and Tawneys, of increasing the lovely White and Red? But perhaps I am partial to the Complexion of my Country, for such Kind of Partiality is natural to Mankind.

The lovely Red recalls the Noble Savage, honored for fighting back and feared as worthy enemies, rather than just scorned as slaves. As for the lovely White, whiteness has expanded to the Spanish, Italians, French, Russians, and Swedes, not to mention the Greeks and the Polish and sometimes, but not always, the Jews, given the endurance of anti-Semitism.

Even these people are now included in whiteness:

> Why should *Pennsylvania*, founded by the *English*, become a Colony of *Aliens*, who . . . will never adopt our

Language or Customs, any more than they can acquire
our Complexion.

The aliens he was talking about? The Germans. Oh, those terrible
dark-skinned Germans!

What would Old Ben have thought of tawny aliens like Ba Má and
you coming to his beloved white Pennsylvania? And could he have
imagined that 265 years after his speech a descendant of swarthy
German immigrants would become the forty-fifth president of these
United States?

But, having become white, ██████ and those like him continue in the
Founding Father's tradition of needing those not white, especially those
who are Black, to help them define their whiteness.

Their borders.

Their nation.

Their selves.

The status of so-called darker people—dark being relative, like being
Eastern—means that whether these people are members of the body
politic is an ongoing question. For example, by 1924, everybody not
white—whatever that means—is locked out of the country, except
Filipinos. Filipinos can migrate freely to the USA as colonial wards of
AMERICA™. Some Americans oppose the American colonization of
the Philippines, not because they believe in freedom for Filipinos, but
because they fear the immigration of brown people. Granted independence in 1946, Filipinos are then cast out of the body politic, becoming
foreigners who can no longer come at will.

The nation's doors finally reopen in 1965, but beginning in 2017, ████ attempts to shut them once more. When he says Make America Great Again, he means make AMERICA™ white again. Going back to slavery days is too shocking even for ████ to utter out loud, but the late nineteenth century, circa 1882, is good enough. Black people are lynched under the rule of Jim Crow. Mexican lands are occupied, Mexicans subjugated. Native nations are being defeated, their peoples sent to reservations. The Chinese are excluded and cannot testify in court, so can be murdered with impunity. Not so hard to do given the prevalence of guns in AMERICA™ and the near-religious belief in the right to own and use them.

The same spirit of armed self-defense extends to the border and how some Americans say they have nothing against immigrants. They just want the *legal* ones.

> To ensure fewer legal ones,
> change the laws. Render more and more
> potential and current immigrants illegal.
> Attack the undocumented first, those
> brown masses surging north
> from the Other America.

No need to panic over the tens of thousands of undocumented Irish and Canadians. Has a (white) Canadian in the USA ever been asked where they're really from?

████ demands a Great Wall across the southern border but not the northern one, as if sealing off the border will seal off the lustful Other within the American soul. Detention camps. Children lost. Children dead. Dystopia in real life, not just in the movies where white people are the central victims of disaster.

After closing the border, go after Asian adoptees whose American parents forgot to file for citizenship. Pursue the refugees who came as children, never became citizens, and committed crimes. Deport them to Việt Nam and Cambodia. Ignore American crimes against their parents from the wars AMERICA™ helped to start in their countries. Pretend there are no obligations to children turned into refugees by these wars.

Destroying families is a part of American immigration law since the exclusion of Chinese women in the late nineteenth century. Chinese immigrant men could not find wives, form families, father children.

> One aspect of genocide: imposing
> measures intended to prevent
> births within the group.

All legal. █████ also wants to cut family reunification, which has allowed immigrants to bring too many people who look like them, invading Great America.

No more refugees either. American guilt after the end of the war in 1975 leads the country to welcome hundreds of thousands of refugees from Việt Nam, Laos, and Cambodia. Cuba, too, because Cuba is communist. But not Haiti, because Haiti is Black. █████ slashes refugee quotas to a few thousand a year.

Calling oneself an immigrant or a refugee, or opening the door to immigrants or refugees, is to oppose Great America by celebrating an Immigrant America that welcomes all and in turn is rejuvenated.

But whether one believes in Great America or Immigrant America, one is invested in American Exceptionalism: the conviction that this country is better than all other countries. Great America is the Ugly American's version of American Exceptionalism. Immigrant America is the Quiet American's version of American Exceptionalism.

Hence the American Question:
Is the real face of AMERICA™
the Ugly American or
the Quiet American?

The Quiet American, more graceful, polite, sensitive, and appreciative of cultural diversity and multiculturalism than the Ugly American, still endorses deploying the CIA and Special Ops and drone missiles to enforce American interests, even if blowing up a few innocents is the unfortunate collateral damage of surgical strikes

even if those few innocents are actually hundreds or thousands or tens of thousands, but how will we know for sure since it is in our interest as Americans not to know the numbers of the dead except for the numbers of our own dead, which we know in exact detail.

The Quiet American does not endorse the surgical malpractice of killing innocents, but neither does the Quiet American do much to oppose it. The Quiet American is not necessarily white. The Quiet American might even be an immigrant. A person of color. A woman. Queer. Trans. Or a mixed-race Black president of the United States who professes, even if ironically, to be

really good at killing people.

Or the Quiet American could be you.

A major American foundation features you in the pages of a major American newspaper as a Great Immigrant. This pushes your rather large button of vanity.

Then an uneasy feeling. You
search quickly and confirm:
Henry Kissinger is also
a Great Immigrant.

Goddamn it.

Immigrant America is better than Great America, but Great Immigrants are also alibis enabling AMERICA™ to execute what Kissinger endorses. Overthrowing the democratically elected Allende in Chile. Carpet-bombing Cambodia and Laos. Supporting the Suharto regime of Indonesia in its campaign to exterminate communists or Chinese. Who can tell the difference? Hundreds of thousands are murdered.

A war criminal
is still a war criminal
even if never convicted,
even if he's a Great Immigrant,
even if he will never be deported,
even if he wins the Nobel Peace Prize,
because Bombing Makes AMERICA™ Great,
but Drone Strikes Make AMERICA™ Even Greater.

good, bad, and ugly

Even if others call you an immigrant, don't call yourself an immigrant.

Call yourself . . . a refugee.

That is what you are, or have been. Immigrants choose when to leave and where to go. Refugees run anywhere they can. The question is: When do they stop running? If you can ever be called a (former) refugee, the adjective will always be parenthetical.

Even now you move and hustle, always working, never satisfied, fearful of what Ba Má experienced. The only insurance is to ensure you have enough to survive the next disaster. You have all you need in your basement, except guns.

So don't call yourself an American yet.

Call yourself a refugee, not an immigrant, because your first solid memories—when you know exactly where you are and with whom—are of a refugee camp. Of separation from Ba Má.

Call yourself a refugee because too many refugees call themselves immigrants.

If Hollywood made an epic
about the refugee experience,
you would be cast as:
A) Dirty Refugee
B) Desperate Refugee
C) Screaming Refugee
D) Grateful Refugee

Perhaps in Europe it's more beneficial to call oneself a refugee, as reporters inform you when they interview you in France in 2017. They tell you Europeans are more accepting of refugees because they are fewer in number and come for political reasons, unlike immigrants or migrants, who come in masses for economic reasons. But only three years later, in the fall of 2020, the Paris police violently break up an encampment of refugees on the Place de la République, where you had stayed in a hostel during your first visit to Paris as a backpacker with bleached blond hair. Everyone mistakes you for Japanese. You have never heard Konnichiwa! so many times in your life. Everyone seems friendly because the Japanese, even if there might be too many of them, visit as tourists with money.

Refugees arrive with nothing and threaten to stay. If there are enough of them, meaning too many, they induce unease or worse.

In this anti-refugee climate, you think you should advocate for refugees, so you give a talk in Boise, Idaho, to a program for refugee high school students. They have written stories, essays, or poems about fleeing from Egypt, Myanmar, Rwanda, Cambodia, and many more countries. What they survived reminds you of this lesson:

The best way to kill a cocktail party conversation is to say you're a refugee.

Refugee experiences unsettle and discomfort people who never had to flee. You don't blame them. You also do not know what to say when faced with emotionally complicated situations.

Start with an easy question for the students. How many of you are refugees? Two, three hands go up. How many of you are immigrants?

Everybody raises their hands.

These students have already absorbed the message: AMERICA™ is a nation of immigrants. Not a country of refugees.

As for your fellow Vietnamese, they may call themselves refugees in Vietnamese, but in English, they often call themselves immigrants. In 1975, some move to Louisiana, where they encounter Hurricane Katrina thirty years later. Tens of thousands of New Orleans residents are rendered homeless, some stranded on rooftops trying to escape rising floodwaters, others trapped in a football stadium trying to survive. When some reporters describe the displaced as refugees, President George W. Bush is outraged.

The people we're talking about are not
refugees, he says. They are Americans.

Many of the displaced are Black, and for
perhaps the only time in history, the civil rights
leader Jesse Jackson agrees with George Bush:

It is racist to call American citizens
refugees. . . . To see them as refugees is to
see them as other than Americans.

You are bemused. It seems that refugees have
succeeded in bringing a racially divided
AMERICA™ together.

This is because refugees are anathema to the AMERICAN DREAM™. Forget for the moment that Black people have a long history of being fugitives and refugees from slavery and Jim Crow. Forget that the Pilgrims were not only religious and political refugees—they were also the Original Boat People! But in the American imagination, AMERICA™

was never founded by refugees and can never become the kind of failed
or repressive country that produces refugees.

Other countries—primarily non-white of the so-called Third World,
large swaths of Asia, Africa, and Latin America—gush refugees because they are broken or breaking apart, or because they break their
own people.

AMERICA™ cannot be broken or breaking.

AMERICA™ can welcome refugees because it is great. So to call Americans refugees is a shock that reveals a truth: the USA can engender
refugees. Because these refugees move only within the United States,
the United Nations would officially classify them as displaced people.
But if they look like refugees and smell like refugees, perhaps they actually are refugees. And no country is so great that it will not produce
climate refugees.

Using words to force us to see anew is critical, if discomfiting (for some).
Once, when you visit a college and say that Japanese Americans were
imprisoned in concentration camps, an outraged (white male) marine
veteran in the audience berates you. But "concentration camp" is the
term President Franklin Delano Roosevelt used until the Nazis spoiled
it. When it comes to concentration camps, Hitler, claims the poet Aimé
Césaire, applied

> to Europe colonialist procedures which
> until then had been reserved exclusively
> for the Arabs of Algeria, the coolies of
> India, and the blacks of Africa.

If "internment camp" is a euphemism for "concentration camp,"
then perhaps "AMERICA™" is itself a euphemism.

An American president embracing the euphemism is unsurprising. But Jesse Jackson—companion to Martin Luther King Jr., presidential candidate, leader of the National Rainbow Coalition who inspired you when you saw him speak at Berkeley—he undoubtedly knows AMER-ICA™ is a myth. A sales pitch that whitewashes enslavement and its consequences. And yet Black people have fought hard to be fully equal Americans. For some, that means claiming AMERICA™ and rejecting any association with refugees.

Refugees are no different. People do not fight their way into AMERICA™ only to reject it or criticize it (except for ingrates like you). Refugees claim to be immigrants because Americans understand the immigrant typology. Here are the steps for anyone wanting to write their own immigrant saga for the American and Western marketplace:

STEP ONE

Hard life in the old world—poverty, war, patriarchy, homophobia, religious persecution, dictatorial regime, etc. If AMERICA™ had a hand in stoking any of the turmoil, do not mention, or downplay, or point out that other countries are worse.

STEP TWO

Daunting challenges in the new world—language barriers, cultural misunderstandings, racism, and condescension, as well as starting at or near the economic bottom, above many Black people (sometimes visible) and Native people (usually unmentioned). Gentle criticism of American racism and capitalism is permitted, even embraced, so long as it is not explicitly decolonial or Marxist and so long as Step Four (see below) is achieved.

STEP THREE

Generational conflict—parents don't understand their American-ized children; American-born or American-raised children don't get their old-world parents. Describe generational conflict as the result of personal differences, familial tensions, and cultural conflict, but not as the direct intimate consequence of colonization with the resulting upheavals of millions, events that AMERICA™ has often instigated.

STEP FOUR

Reconciliation—your grandparents have achieved the AMERICAN DREAM™, and if they didn't, your parents did, and if they didn't, you did. For self-published books, self-help books, and the memoirs of people who are not writers: state reconciliation baldly. Flag-waving is acceptable. For writers hoping to win literary prizes, express reconciliation with great subtlety, mixed with regret and melancholy. Flag-waving: less acceptable.

STEP FIVE

Remember that your people are only the backdrop for your personal struggle to become an individual, someone who has shed your ethnic, cultural, or group heritage as a political identity (although keeping that heritage as a cultural identity is acceptable). Your only political identity is as an American, which is, paradoxically, synonymous with being an individual. Not with being part of a collective.

BONUS POINTS

As an individual, serve as your people's ambassador. Be apologetic for their excesses and their irreconcilable differences with AMER-ICA™ specifically or the West in general. Assume, explicitly or implicitly, that your audience is white. Incorporate food into your title, and/or use excessively spiritual or natural imagery. Use food liberally as a metaphor for cultural differences and assimilation. For example, you could write:

> I introduced my corn-fed, Iowa-raised fiancé/e to a bowl of my mother's delicious pho—a beef broth noodle soup that every Vietnamese person loves . . .

Ignore the fact that no Vietnamese person would need to have phở explained to them. Do not wonder if the Great White American Male Novelist F. Scott Fitzgerald ever wrote, in an early draft of *The Great Gatsby*:

> I offered Daisy a delicious sandwich—two slices of bread between which there is something delicious . . .

Never forget: you are not writing first and foremost for your own people or even the world, as Fitzgerald assumed.

Variations are permitted: perhaps the old world isn't too bad, or perhaps there isn't too much generational conflict. But major variations deeply confuse Americans, particularly with Steps Four and Five. Together they compose the Hollywood ending, where all that has gone wrong is set right, where the individual is affirmed. The American variation of this happy ending accentuates how AMERICA™, for all its flaws and challenges, is

THE GREATEST COUNTRY ON EARTH

The curtain drops. The immigrants or
their children have become American.
THE END.

Or is it?

When you write *The Sympathizer*, you write against this immigrant saga. You write for two years in an oasis of privilege whose roots are planted by Ba Má. They paid for your education through college; fed, clothed, and insured you; gave you a moral grounding in a Catholicism you find problematic but from which you extract a sense of justice and a potent symbology; provided you with their own example of relentless work and sacrifice for others (meaning you); protected and nurtured your ego and self-esteem; and donated, free of charge, a good portion of the down payment on your house overlooking the eastern end of Sunset Boulevard, which, one day, the great-granddaughter of F. Scott Fitzgerald will purchase from you.

The very material conditions for the writing of your anti-immigrant saga are themselves part of the immigrant saga. Even if the spare bedroom in which you write is sparsely decorated, even if you write facing a blank wall, you have a spare bedroom. You possess the celebrated room of one's own that a writer needs, that Virginia Woolf called for. But remember:

> the English writer in her example gets that room of
> her own through five hundred pounds a year
> willed to her by an aunt in Bombay,
> India—an English colony.

And you possess more than a room—you own a house. What a contradiction! And contradictions are great places from which to write

novels. You decline the bonus points and the subtle happy ending of
the immigrant saga, even as you live in subtle happiness. Your protagonist, disenchanted with communism (acceptable) and deeply critical of
AMERICA™ (confusing), does not run to AMERICA™ at book's end
to gorge himself on Happy Meals at McDonald's and transmogrify into
a freedom-loving, alienated, moderately obese individual suffering a
midlife crisis, which might have made the confusing aspects of the
book more acceptable to New York literary editors. Instead, as one of
them puts it, he

just had too much trouble
crawling all the way
inside the voice.

Is this why thirteen out of fourteen editors reject your novel? Is your
voice too foreign? Too weird? Is it that you even have a voice, uttering
words in English, that is strange? Even after *The Sympathizer* is published, another white American editor asks you if your work has been
translated into English.

All you know for certain is that the fourteenth editor who
bought the book, Peter Blackstock, is not American but
English, of mixed race with a Malaysian mother, and someone
who had studied Russian and German, and who edits books
for Grove Press, which publishes the American editions of
Frantz Fanon's *The Wretched of the Earth* and *Black Skin,
White Masks*, works of revolution and decolonization you
have turned to and returned to for thirty years. Perhaps for all
these reasons he sees something in your novel that
the white American editors could not.

While you reject the immigrant story insofar as it can obscure AMER-
ICA™'s settler colonialism and its frequent betrayal of its revolutionary

ideals, some of your fellow immigrants, or refugees, also reject the immigrant story, but for a different reason, one magnified in the age of ███ :

these immigrants and refugees
want to shut the door behind them.

One elderly Vietnamese refugee says of ███ 's refugee policies:

I tell you, this idea he has of keeping out
Muslims is the right thing to do. . . . We are the
good refugees. They're not political refugees
like we were. There are two types of people who
want to come to America—those who seek
freedom and those who go out to destroy it.

Oh, noble sentiment! Oh, freedom-loving, heroic Vietnamese people who genuflect before AMERICA™ and who also toot their own horn and are quick to snitch on those darker, browner, less trustworthy people with the wrong god sniffing at the Golden Door! Oh—

It suddenly occurs to you that you grew up in the second-largest Vietnamese refugee community in the world after Little Sài Gòn, Orange County, California, and you remember that

there were
a lot of bad
Vietnamese refugees!

Taking welfare benefits while working for cash in the ethnic economy? Receiving government housing subsidies while renting out rooms to even poorer refugees? Faking marriage to get immigration status? Faking divorce so supposedly single parents and their children could get additional benefits? Faking car accidents and injuries for insurance money, and treating nonexistent patients to fraudulently claim government reimbursements? Abusing children and wives? Racially discriminating against the Amerasian children of American soldiers, including those children used as passports to the United States by their families, who then sometimes abandon them? Assaulting and robbing fellow refugees, as well as stealing microchips, extorting businesses, running brothels, and dealing drugs? Assassinating journalists with unpopular opinions about the homeland? Going to the homeland and pretending to be rich even if one is a busboy? Finding a girlfriend, mistress, or second wife and living a doubled existence, or, fuck it, just abandoning one's diasporic family altogether for the sweet life back home?

You did all these things, but let's be clear: this is all very colorful! Without this kind of behavior, what kind of stories could you tell? Italian Americans have also been rather colorful. Imagine AMERICA™ without *The Godfather* or *Goodfellas*—impossible!

The Mafia story is the B side of the AMERICAN DREAM™, because crime is as American as apple pie, as American as stealing land and calling it Manifest Destiny, as American as enslaving people and . . . well, let's not talk about that.

All this colorful behavior is now forgotten, or if not forgotten, not spoken of. Instead, Americans extol your people as proof of the greatness

of AMERICA™ in accepting the unwanted, while your people extol
themselves as evidence of the immigrant saga of success.

And yet the majority of Americans
in 1975 did not want to accept
Southeast Asian refugees.

Forgetting this allows anti-immigrant Americans to say they want only
the good immigrants, even though today's good immigrants were yes-
terday's bad immigrants.

As one immigrant put it:
First thing I did after my citizenship?
Climbed to the top of the Statue of Liberty,
gazed upon this great land,
and shouted:

FUCK YOU,

IMMIGRANTS!!!

•

the ronald reagan room

Ba Má always warn you about the bad refugees. Ba Má fear their own countrymen, having come from a country in which their home and business was invaded by a thief with a grenade. Don't call the police, Ba Má also add in the early years of the SàiGòn Mới. In Việt Nam, the police could be dangerous, too.

You learn not to look at a certain kind of Vietnamese boy or man in the eye. The ones with cigarettes in their mouths and hair sculpted into flaring wings with the aid of a hair dryer, styling mousse, and Aqua Net hair spray. The ones who might be gangsters.

Where do they learn that violence? From brothers, uncles, fathers who were soldiers? What blowback from war blew through these homes and families? At least American veterans get a diagnosis: post-traumatic stress disorder. The refugee community stays silent. Unnamable trauma remains a secret shame.

As for the refugees committing fraud, some are simply criminal. But perhaps some learned to cheat and exploit from the war. Americans flooded your homeland with American goods, jacked up inflation so much that honest soldiers could not support families. With war corrupting the entire economy, corruption became a mode of survival.

As for all the doctors, lawyers, engineers, nurses, pharmacists, dentists, and so on—how good are they if they are some of those who want to keep other refugees and immigrants out?

When some people say they want to accept just the good refugees and immigrants, what they really want are the very few exceptional refugees and immigrants.

You, for one, believe in an AMERICA™
that is free and equal for all,
an AMERICA™ where refugees
and immigrants have the right to be
mediocre,
just like every other American.

You look askance at your now nine-year-old, cheerful, playful, American-born, American-raised son, softened by suburbia. He will not grow up motivated by the angst of watching his parents sacrifice their lives for him, which says as much about him as about you. He will not be infused with Catholic guilt and the masochistic desire to suffer, or the belief that if one is not suffering one should be suffering or deserves to be suffering, because you have taken him to church only for Christmas Mass with his grandparents. He will not grow up with the war and refugee experience shaping every contour of his life. He's an American, blessedly free of the past.

This must be corrected.

You tell him that everything he has is because of the sacrifices of his grandparents. You tell him both of his parents and all four grandparents are refugees. You also tell him being a refugee isn't all bad.

Being a refugee gives you the
requisite emotional damage
necessary to be a writer.

That's literally priceless. And you have done
your best to pass on that damage
to your unsuspecting son.

Like many little boys, he loves Legos. Always asks for more. But you cannot give children everything they want. You learned this from your childhood, and you didn't turn out so bad, did you?

Did you?

You tell your son he cannot have these Legos and ask him, Do you know why?

He thinks about it for a moment and says,
Because you're a refugee?

Exactly!

It is never too early to learn empathy for others, including the refugees who make some citizens so uncomfortable. When your son is just a little older, you plan to tell him more about what his grandparents survived. After all, when he was three and came home from preschool talking about Thanksgiving, you taught him another word: "genocide."

Are you a bad father?
Don't answer that question.

What you will tell him:

Good and bad are a binary. One always implies the Other. The pair forces a choice between them and rules out a third. You will tell him how his grandparents pursued the AMERICAN DREAM™ and opened the SàiGòn Mới, only to be targeted by that sign.

ANOTHER AMERICAN
DRIVEN OUT OF BUSINESS
BY THE VIETNAMESE

Ba Má are the Model Minority.   Ba Má are also the Yellow Peril.

Stereotypes: coins with two faces, equally flat, ready
to be spun or flipped, fifty-fifty, either-or.
The stereotyped cannot choose only
one face or the other.
They are both.

You are the Model Minority.   You are also the Yellow Peril.

The Asian version of Dr. Jekyll and Mr. Hyde.
Your own form of alienation
from yourself.

As the model minority, you may have worked hard to get what you have,
but so do all the people suddenly deemed essential workers in the age
of the global plague: farmworkers, meat plant workers, delivery drivers.
Hard work is no guarantee for success. Even if one works hard, one
could still be called lazy. Slave masters called enslaved people lazy even
as they worked them to death. And the stereotype of the lazy Mexican
mocks the same people who pick the nation's vegetables and fruit, doing
work that other people believe themselves too good to do.

Hard work may not even be required if one has the right connections.
Ba Má are your connections, ensuring you have nothing to worry about
except obeying them in every way. Má even lavishes you with compli-
ments, her way of saying she loves you, insulating you with the gift of
unwarranted self-confidence.

And although you are Asian, you possess the
negative and unearned privilege of
not being Black.

Although racism and colonization have singed you because of the war, many of your people do not connect these experiences with those of others. They oppose racism and colonization only when it affects them, which means they do not truly stand against racism and colonization.

Will things differ for your children? Your son attended a progressive preschool in California. One of his best friends was Black. At five years of age, another child called this best friend the epithet that Richard Pryor used freely. How did this child learn this word? Parents, siblings, relatives, the airwaves?

The infection of racism can sometimes be contact traced to a source, but more often racism increases by community spread, as the epidemiologists put it. No single source can be identified because an aerosol of racism saturates AMERICA™.

You cannot prevent your children from inhaling these words. You can only vaccinate them by educating them. Failing to speak out, even with one's family, is complicity with how AMERICA™ perpetuates itself.

You speak out often because apparently you are good at

giving voice to the previously voiceless

as the *New York Times* describes *The Sympathizer*.

Dear reader, have you ever been to a Vietnamese restaurant, wedding banquet, or family gathering? If not, your loss. If so, you know that

Vietnamese people are not voiceless!
They are really, really loud!

As Arundhati Roy says:
There's really no such thing as the "voiceless."
There are only the deliberately silenced,
or the preferably unheard.

To the powerful, voicelessness signals being less than, or other than, human. But it is those who refuse to hear who dehumanize others by silencing them, by not hearing them, or by hearing only what they want to hear. The powerful—that smallest of minorities—anoint the singular voice because they do not want to hear the chorus or the cacophony of the less powerful, that largest of majorities. The powerful want to deal with you one at a time. You immigrant. You refugee. You minority. You native. You token. You. You tell yourself:

Don't be a voice for the voiceless.
Abolish the conditions of voicelessness.

Abolition is the future beyond the horizon. On the long road there, you think it is still necessary to give speeches and write essays and amplify your voice. If you do not speak, perhaps someone else will, someone happy to be a voice for the voiceless who will repeat the euphemisms of the immigrant story and AMERICA™. You must speak out, or you think you must, even if this makes you a professional. A Professional Vietnamese. A Professional Refugee. Hardly a new dilemma to be caught in, as Hanif Kureishi pointed out in 1985 with the Professional Pakistani in his screenplay for *My Beautiful Laundrette.*

The East is a career, wrote Benjamin Disraeli in 1847. And to be from the (very nebulously defined) East can be a career, too. A brand. An identity. A problem. And yet

identity is one of those things that the theorist
Gayatri Spivak says is what we cannot *not* want.
Under colonialism and capitalism, identity is

source of oppression
commodity for exploitation
route to liberation

all at the same time. Understanding identity as
only one of these things is to misunderstand
identity and its complications.

Branded as a Professional Vietnamese and a Professional Refugee, a
former problem and crisis turned into a spokesperson, you are invited
to places you would never have been invited to before becoming a Professional, including a Harvard fundraiser at an exclusive downtown
Los Angeles club. You attend because you owe Harvard, which once
gave you a sweet fellowship. The chairman of the Harvard Corporation
is Jewish, and as he stands with you and a Black woman, a Harvard
staff member, he says to her, A few decades ago, we wouldn't even be
allowed in this club.

You all laugh. Progress!
You silently wonder if Asians
would have been allowed.

You are here on business, you must be on your best behavior, so you
restrain yourself from drinking any more than a few sips of the free
wine, even though you need it. Badly. At dinner, you are seated next to a
man who flew thirty-five missions in the Pacific in World War II. Nearly
a century old, he lives in Cary Grant's house on the Santa Monica beach.
For no reason except perhaps for the fact that you are the Only Asian

in the Room—a not unfamiliar position—and the youngest person there besides the staff, he offers the table a long explanation about why AMERICA™ needed to drop the A-bomb on Hiroshima.

> The former airman, whose bombs probably killed a lot of people, does not look at you. He does not see that you keep smiling. You, the model minority, repaying your debt to Harvard, where scientists invented napalm, a jellied gasoline that sticks to flesh and that the United States used often in Asia, including the firebombing of Japan, which killed more civilians than the atomic bombs. Even Winston Churchill called napalm *very cruel* and was appalled at the USA *splashing it all over the civilian population* and *torturing great masses of people* in Korea— Churchill, whose policies in Bengal helped create a famine that killed up to three million a few years earlier.

The veteran airman's wife, twenty or thirty years younger, asks you why the Vietnamese are so smart. It must be genetics, she says, not joking. I think it's the food, you say with a straight face. The explanation does not seem to bother her.

At a tour of the other major downtown club for members only, which you also have never heard of before, your host explains that the guest rooms have sometimes been used by members for mistresses, although this is (probably) all in the past. You say, Hmm, and nod your head at the shenanigans. Then you deliver a talk in the Ronald Reagan room. You wear a dark blue velvet jacket and a pale pink shirt and remember some lines that Viet Thanh Nguyen wrote in *The Sympathizer*:

> I calmed the tremor in my gut. I was in close quarters with some representative specimens of the most dangerous creature in the history of the world, the white man in a suit.

You decide not to read these lines but different ones about the Los Angeles Police Department that always get a laugh.

No one laughs.
You blame Viet Thanh Nguyen.

In the dining hall, portraits of Great White Men like Clint Eastwood adorn the walls. The guest, or the witness, you have brought along is a woman, a friend. When Zoë visits the powder room, the other women ask her if she is your mistress.

Over filet mignon, you are invited to apply for membership. The club, your host tells you, needs more diversity. They mention a skyscraper-high fee for the downtown club and an astronomical fee for the beach-side club. You are kind of flattered they think you have this kind of money (you don't). And you recall the immortal words of Groucho Marx:

I don't care to belong to any club that will have me as a member.

Or was it Karl Marx who said that? He certainly did say:

The ideas of the ruling class are in every epoch the ruling ideas,
i.e. the class which is the ruling *material* force of society,
is at the same time its ruling *intellectual* force.

You like both kinds of Marxisms. Karl Marxists would benefit from being Groucho Marxists, too, and vice versa, since History is both Tragedy and Farce, not one or the other. You are a dialectical Marxist, but only if the dialectic wavers between Groucho and Karl. Groucho Marxism is funnier if it also has a dose of Karl Marxism, which offers a better analysis of the perils of capitalism—exploitation, alienation, unhappiness, the total destruction of the world, etc.—than what is offered by, say, capitalists. Meanwhile, the lack of Groucho Marxism in actually existing Karl Marxism leads to too many dour, well-meaning novels and dour, ill-intentioned regimes whose consequences are often deadly for anyone with a sense of humor or the absurd, or the willingness to say that even the Karl Marxists, intent on protesting against the abuses of the powerful, can become just as abusive when powerful.

At Berkeley, you temporarily forget the Groucho Marxism from the television of your childhood and learn pure Karl Marxism. You read *Capital*, volume one, by yourself the summer after you storm the faculty club with dozens of other students, demanding greater faculty diversity. You swore then that you would never join any such stinkin' clubs!

                    Not long ago, you joined the faculty
                            club at your university.

                    Not long ago, on revisiting Berkeley,
                            you dined at the faculty club.

                            Both Marxes would be
                            sorely disappointed.

The arc of the moral universe is long, but it bends toward justice, the Reverend Martin Luther King Jr. is often quoted as saying, especially by proponents of AMERICA™ and anyone who wants to demonstrate that they cannot possibly be a racist because they have read one or two of his speeches, or maybe just one or two of his phrases, or most likely just seen a snippet of "I Have a Dream," which is like receiving anti-racist Communion. Does justice include access to clubs like this? If more professionals like you visit or join clubs like this, playing the role of the voice for the voiceless, will the world be better?

After your talk at the downtown club, a member of the audience spots you in the bar. She works in global finance. She's Chinese, maybe even

Chinese American, maybe even an immigrant. You are bad at math and finances, a luxury of having parents who worked hard to make money so you do not have to worry about that stuff. When you ask how many billions she deals with, her smile fades.

Trillions, she says frostily. Perhaps disdainfully. Perhaps both. She departs soon after.

You finish your drink and leave. You never join the club or come back. Why? You've already seen the Ronald Reagan room.

war stories, or your 1980s,
episode I

You trace the roots of your vanity and weakness, your amusement at visiting the halls of power and your curiosity about them, your contradictory Groucho and Karl Marxisms, your existence as a man of two faces who might be a spy, a sleeper, a spook, to your refugee origins and coming-of-age in the era of Ronald Reagan, himself a man of two faces, perhaps the ultimate late twentieth-century embodiment of both the Quiet American and the Ugly American. B-list actor and president of AMERICA™ from 1980 to 1988, the Republican Saint and the costar of *Bedtime for Bonzo*, along with a chimpanzee, defines your childhood and adolescence, the years when you suffer the requisite emotional damage necessary to becoming a writer. Or at least your kind of writer.

Your 1980s overlap with your San José, where you live from 1978 to 1988, arriving three years after the end of Saint Ronald's governorship of California, the largest state of the fifty United States if one does not count the invisible fifty-first: the state of Denial. You spend your adult life in greater Los Angeles, but San José remains your emotionally radioactive core, inseparable from Ba Má. This decade is the second-longest period of her American years when your mother is completely herself. In your 1980s, Ba Má loom over you, always immense, emerged from nowhere, natural outcroppings of towering strength. The idea that Ba Má might once have been children or weak or ill hardly ever occurs to you, except when your mother tells you about the famine.

It might be the morning or the afternoon or the early evening. Daylight shines through the living room window and its red velour curtains. Ba Má work constantly, but there is time for moments like this, the two of you sitting together on the red velour sofa that looks like it belongs in the brothel of one of the westerns always being shown on TV, where the cancan girls wear lace chokers around their necks and hike up their skirts and pinafores to reveal hose held up by garters. Perhaps there were not too many moments like this, which is why you can remember this time when you are perhaps ten or eleven, plucking gray hairs from her head. Má has invited you to do this, offering a nickel a strand. She has been using a mirror to try to see the top of her head, and perhaps she really does need your help. But perhaps she just wants to spend some time with you. Perhaps she knows you will soon enter the Age of Awkwardness, when you are neither a little boy nor a young man. For now, still a little boy, you are attached to Má, relishing the occasions she scratches your back with her long nails in long, luxurious strokes. She is not yet, for you, a completely separate person but someone with whom you are still unselfconscious.

The house is even quieter than usual since your brother left for college. Má gives you a pair of tweezers from the toolbox of her makeup kit, an off-white case a little larger than a shoebox and as sturdy as a suitcase. Its lid has metal latches and, when snapped open, reveals an array of mysterious powders, jars, and devices that hold no interest for you. You examine the part in your mother's long wavy hair. A few silver threads weave through the black layers. It does not occur to you that one day you, too, will have gray hairs. The tweezers are awkward in your right hand, and you use your left to press down around a silver strand, pursing your lips as you attempt to pinch the guilty hair with the tips of the tweezers. The root clings to the scalp, and you are afraid of hurting Má, but with one quick tug the hair comes out cleanly and your imagination provides a satisfying pop of sound. Má stays silent as you contemplate the strand in the light with its tiny bulge of a root at the bottom.

I saw a child dead on a doorstep, Má says.

Perhaps she says this not after the first hair but after the third or fourth. But she says it. The remark comes from nowhere, as you would never initiate a conversation about dead children, and you are not empathetic enough to ask your mother about her childhood. Your range of conversational topics with Má, as with Ba, focuses on your education, diet, religious beliefs, and behavior. Your few hundred words of Vietnamese are not enough for you to attempt to understand Ba Má.

So many people died, she says,
or you think you remember
her saying. Of hunger.

If you have plucked a hair out of her, she has sown a seed in you. Not understanding what she is talking about, you categorize it under the list of Horrifying Things That Could Have Happened to You If You Had Never Left Việt Nam, Including Persecution, Discrimination, Death by Land Mine in Cambodia, General Despair, and, Now, Starvation.

When Má saw this starved child, Má could not have been more than seven or eight years old. Younger than you as you pluck her hairs, although this will not occur to you until many years later. As you extract those hairs, you are unable to imagine that Má was once a child like you.

Many years later, as you seek to understand who you are and where you come from, you read about the great famine that killed one to two million people in the north in the waning years of World War II, induced by Japanese occupiers and facilitated by French colonizers. The total population of the north was a little over seven million.

One out of seven dead is equal to two children in your son's class, dead. Eight of your department colleagues, dead. Three thousand undergraduates at your university, dead.

You don't know what brought this memory on, whether she searched for it or whether it sought her. Put the tweezers down. Embrace her, the way your nine-year-old son does, spontaneously, when he asks you about Má and sees you affected by her death. But you do not. Your family does not embrace.

> As is so often the case, you
> say nothing and keep pursuing
> the gray hairs. A few more and you
> can buy the next issue of *Spider-Man*.

Does your house feel eerie because of these occasional stories that leak out of Má—you do not recall Ba ever telling such stories—or because you fear the dark? So many things must frighten your parents, perhaps even haunt them, but Ba Má never seem intimidated. Only now do you understand that this is how they love you, by protecting you, by never letting you see them afraid.

Decades later Ba tells you that when he saw the location for the future SàiGòn Mới, occupied by a jeans store, he wanted it. With less than fluent English, he asked the proprietor who owned the building, called the owner, persuaded him to sell it, then applied for a loan.

Saint Ronald and the Republican Party would have
loved Ba Má, although not enough to invite
them to their clubs. That privilege is
saved for you.

Ba Má never take welfare, never need food stamps, even if they needed
the entire U.S. government to rescue them from communism, not only
in 1975 but in 1954, when the U.S. Navy boat-lifts them to the south
in Operation Passage to Freedom. Perhaps the refugees believe these
boats will carry them into the future, but perhaps some can also foretell
that they, like these vessels, will be borne back ceaselessly into the past.

You first read about the boat lift in *Deliver Us from Evil*, the bestselling
memoir of one Tom Dooley, so popular that it finds its way to your sixth
grade classroom's bookshelves. Dooley is now mostly forgotten, but in
the 1950s he was an American hero, a navy captain, youthful doctor,
and patriotic Catholic who went to Indochina and helped the suffering
Indochinese, including the

wretched, sick, and horribly maimed

Vietnamese refugees fleeing south from the northern

Communist hellhole.

You imagine Dooley standing on a high peak, gazing
over the coastline and a flotilla of navy ships, as he says

All in Viet Nam dream and strive for freedom . . . the
people who toil in the rice fields with backs bent double and
faces turned to the brackish mud, the naked children playing
in the monsoon, the little fruit sellers in the arroyos of the

> markets and the poor with amputated arm or hand
> outstretched. They have one dream:
> Freedom.

Freedom! Does any other word short-circuit the American brain more than this one, besides, perhaps, "Supersized"? Americans love everything Supersized, including their God, their Dollar, their vistas, their freeways, their houses, their cars, their dreams, their guns, their sexual organs, their amnesia, their innocence, and their mythology of themselves. Whatever their political disagreements, both Ugly and Quiet Americans agree that what the world needs is Supersized Freedom (with a side of military weaponry, since AMERICA™ is the planet's biggest arms seller).

And what kind of American is Tom Dooley? An anti-communist, freedom-loving icon to much of the American general public, and a publicity-hungry, closeted gay man whom the U.S. Navy blackmails into encouraging American involvement in Indochina. His stories of desperate Indochinese and atrocity-committing communists fit the Cold War narrative of AMERICA™, with Ba Má cast as extras in the Greatest Story Ever Told: How the USA Can Deliver the Entire World to the Promised Land.

The rescue of Ba Má, twice, is reparations of a kind for AMERICA™ instigating a war that did not need to happen, given that an ostensibly communist Việt Nam today is on very good terms with the United States. But anti-communism is an American religion, and most Vietnamese refugees, including Ba Má, are devout followers. Anti-communists see the world as anti- and pro-communist, good and evil. This worldview, with no middle ground, no demilitarized zone, fits perfectly with devout Catholicism and its vision of Heaven and Hellholes.

Somehow, in your 1980s, you develop a resistance to this worldview, which later grows into an inherent skepticism of all orthodoxies. When, in the sixth grade, Saint Patrick tells all its students of non-American origins to create a flag to honor their country, you open the *World Book Encyclopedia* and see that the flag of Việt Nam is a red field with a yellow star. At home, you meticulously draw the star on the white poster board you have been given and then color the poster board red and the star yellow. Ba Má are too preoccupied to ask you about this or any other homework, and you hardly talk to them, thankfully so in this case, for the next day you discover that you are none too smart. A Vietnamese student in another grade understood the assignment. Her flag is chosen to represent your homeland: a yellow field with three red stripes, the banner of the Republic of Việt Nam, the anti-communist country where she and you were born and that no longer exists. Your red flag is the flag of your enemies. You, it seems, are already a communist sympathizer without even knowing it. Neither an Ugly American nor a Quiet American, but an Un-American?

The anti-communism of the 1980s and the internal and external war against Un-American activities culminate in the destruction of the Berlin Wall in November 1989, when you are a sophomore in college at UCLA, having transferred from your last-choice university. Mr. Gorbachev, tear down this wall! says Saint Ronald. Tearing down walls and building walls emerge from the same mindset:

Fear of the Other, the Non-
American, the Un-American, the Anti-American.
Fear that the deeply Un-American or very American crimes,
depending on one's point of view, that you have done
to Others or want to do to Others shall be
inflicted on you Americans.

Tear down the wall so your side
can conquer the other side; build that
wall so your side can keep out the other side,
even if the otherness is already inside of you,
was always inside of you, long before
you met your Other.

You do not have political conversations with your parents in your 1980s.
You are aware of what they do not know: that you are, if not yet an atheist or an agnostic, an apathetic when it comes to the religions of God
and anti-communism. But you also do not like confrontation, either
because you are a filial son or because you are a coward. Or both. You
vaguely sense that your future will be as a Godless Commie scribbler
(or so some people see you), but for now you pretend to be the obedient
son who does what his parents order him to do.

> Your parents tell your brother,
> gone away to college, that
> you don't do anything
> they want you to do.

Who are you going to believe?

> Don't answer that question.

In 1982, when your brother tells you he is on his way to Harvard,
you are not happy for him, although you appear so at his high school
graduation party. You are eleven and feel abandoned, again. When anh
Tùng tells you the news about Harvard, instead of singing *Hallelujah!*
you retreat to the bathroom crying. You don't love me anymore! you
sob when your brother follows, even though you have never said I love
you to anyone. Your parents have never said I love you to you. Fellow

Vietnamese refugee Lac Su even titles his memoir *I Love Yous Are for White People*, although many white people tell you they come from hardy European stock where parents also did not say I love you.

But even if no one in your family says so, you know Ba Má and your brother love you through deeds if not words, through sacrificing and being sacrificed, through the offering of their bodies and psyches and time and well-being, through giving up so many pleasures and things they could have otherwise had, through following the example of Jesus, who sacrificed himself, and not God, who sacrificed His only son, which is why you can say, You don't love me anymore!

You make your brother cry, which you have not seen him do since the Christmas Eve Ba Má were shot. You do not come from people who cry or express emotion. Perhaps you make anh Tùng feel guilty. The way he shows his love in the future is to buy you the things that Ba Má won't, or won't even think of: your first banana split, your first computer, your first set of weights, your first stereo and speakers. When you start dating your first girlfriend, J, your brother tells Ba Má you're sleeping at his place when you are actually with J. That is love.

Ba Má married as teenagers, but the American style of dating as teenagers is not something of which they approve. Too frivolous and too dangerous at the same time, a distraction from your education and your future. They fear any threat to your future prosperity, because their origins are in a poor quê known for nurturing hard-core Catholics and hard-core communists. Even though Catholics and communists often oppose each other—viciously—they both believe in one trinity of justice, suffering, and equality, as well as another trinity of redemption, sacrifice, and utopia.

Your parents are hard-core Catholics.
You, you hope, are a hard-core writer.

Ba Má follow a different Word and find comfort in the eternal afterlife, logical given how their entire lives in Việt Nam were stamped indelibly by colonization, famine, war, poverty, and becoming refugees. So they pray to God and the Virgin Mary and in memory of all their dead, including those who passed away when Ba Má had already left. You are too young to remember Má crying when her mother died in the homeland 8,760 miles away, too young to remember Má being sent to the hospital in Harrisburg.

> Your mother comes back, but
> you do not remember her return.
> Má is simply present again.

Maybe you remember the grief, your own incomprehension or terror at something so powerful it disappears your mother. You do not want to feel any emotion so strong it could dismember you, even if that emotion cannot be separated from love, the love your mother felt for her mother, a feeling so strong it dismembered her.

Perhaps you cry because you never forgot being abandoned by your parents, even if you never mention it, even to yourself. Even if Ba Má had not actually abandoned you. And because you never want to feel abandoned again—because you never want to feel what you felt when you sobbed before your brother in 1982—because you do not want to feel any pain at all—you will not cry again for twenty-three years.

> Actually, you will cry again in 1990,
> but you will forget for decades that you did so.

After your brother leaves for college, the house is very lonely and quiet. Unlike most Vietnamese families, which often have four, five, six, and more children, yours is very small, with only two (birth) children.

We tried a lot, Ba Má tell you many times.

Normally reticent about their past, this is one story they enjoy telling, although they do not dwell on the actual effort they must have expended. Your usually vivid imagination is blank. Was it fun for them? Or not? All you know is that they tried for years.

We went every weekend to
pray to the Virgin Mary, they say.

When prayers and effort fail, they adopt their first child, your sister, chị Tuyết, from an orphanage run by nuns. And if there is a God, perhaps He rewards them for adopting a girl by giving Ba Má your brother not long after.

Seven years later, the most important event of your life occurs: you are born.

You hope Ba Má had a lot of fun trying to conceive you.

You do not remember if you remembered having a sister. You last saw her when you were four, and how long did your memories of her persist after that? You do not remember if Ba Má or your brother talked about your sister in front of you. You do remember when you first started thinking of her again, in 1980, when you are nine and she sends a photo of herself. So many Vietnamese refugee families have photos of those left behind. The absent presences. The living ghosts.

What you feel is sadness. Melancholy.
Guilt. You are here. She is not.

Did Má feel guilty for fleeing, for not
being with her mother when she died, for
leaving her adopted daughter behind?

Perhaps all refugees who make it to
safety feel survivor's guilt.

Perhaps all survivors feel haunted, by
the absent presence, by the alternate
universe where they did not make it out.
What if you were the one left behind?
What if you were the negative space in
someone else's life and memory?

And if you feel this way, with no
memories of this sister or the country
back there, what must she feel? And
what must Ba Má feel?

This is a war story.

Another war story: Ba leaving behind his entire family in 1954 to move
south, following Má's family. When your father is eighty-eight, you
finally ask what it was like to leave his family.

It is just the two of you at the dinner table. In old age, Ba, your formerly
stern, driven father, is gentle, quavering, and affectionate. According
to his documents, he is eighty-six. But he was really born at the end of
1933, not October 1935.

Vietnamese people usually do not celebrate birthdays except for the
first and the eightieth, so it's not surprising that your father, confronted
with an official asking for your birthday during that stressful time when
you became refugees, recorded your birth month as March instead of
February. Having two birthdays is perfect for a man of two faces.

Vietnamese refugees who come to AMERICA™ sometimes rebirth themselves, becoming younger or older depending on what they need from bureaucracy or vanity.

> Being a refugee always involves time traveling.
> From one country in one time to another country
> in another time. And most of all living in the
> present while feeling the past, always
> lurking, always haunting.

Over a dinner of red wine and medium-rare filet mignon, which you always cook for your father because he loves it, you ask Ba, Why didn't your family come with you? His family then were mother, father, three younger brothers, and one younger sister.

Ba smiles, looks at his plate, doesn't hear you. Or pretends not to. He refuses to wear his hearing aids.

You don't ask again.
What else could he have felt?
Why must he say it to you?

You remember a black-and-white photograph from your youth, on that bookshelf with no books. Your father with his younger brothers. For years you walked by that photograph without understanding its impossibility. Ba last saw his brothers when they were boys and he was a young man. In the photo stand four middle-aged men.

Then one day the photo punctures your eye and your memory, and you see, at last, the jagged line. On one side the younger brothers, shoulder to shoulder. On the other side, Ba. He has taken two photographs, spliced them together, and framed them. He can at last be with his brothers.

You stare at the jagged line for a long time.

The frame and its photos have disappeared. When did your father decide he no longer needed that picture? You ask if he recalls that missing picture of himself and his brothers, re membered.

Ba smiles, shakes his head, says, No, I don't remember.

You let it go because he has let it go. You,
who have forgotten so much,
understand that forgetting
can also be a blessing.

say my name, or your 1980s,
episode II

You are forgetful of some things (the emotionally complicated) and not of others (the historically complicated), or so you tell yourself. You tell yourself history stays with you because of your name. You are so Vietnamese your name is

VIỆT

How are you supposed to forget the past, where you come from, your mother tongue, when you see and hear the name of your people every day? To ensure you do not ever forget, your last name is that of a dynasty, one so popular about 40 percent of your people bear it, forty million people in Việt Nam and abroad, a Nguyễn homeland and diaspora, a nation in and of itself, seventh most common surname in Australia, second only to Smith in the Melbourne phone book.

You might have been called George Washington if you had been born in the United States. The TV reality show *House of Ho* features a family of rich Vietnamese Americans in Houston with sons named Washington and Reagan. Your generation had Tom Vu, who created infomercials about getting rich in real estate with bikini-clad white women cavorting around him on a yacht.

As a child in the era of Tom Vu, the most famous Vietnamese in AMERI-CA™, you go on a school field trip to Monterey in the California Bay Area, including a propagandistic visit to the Defense Language Institute, which teaches military personnel the foreign languages needed to be more culturally sensitive soldiers, interrogators, and invaders.

A nice young white man with red hair and glasses, a Quiet American wearing a Vietnamese áo dài who speaks more Vietnamese than you do, translates your Vietnamese name into English:

BRUCE SMITH

You prefer George Washington.

In Vietnamese, your name is more distinctive, Nguyễn Thanh Việt, with Thanh, your father's first name, grafted onto yours, distinguishing you from all the many others, including quite a few criminals, named Nguyễn [fill in the blank] Việt. Reborn on paper in AMERICA™, you become Viet Thanh Nguyen. The diacritical marks, part of a Romance language alphabet created by Portuguese missionaries and promoted by French rulers, are somehow too foreign for Westerners when attached to Vietnamese names and words.

But accent marks on French words?
Bien sûr.

Other Americans still find it hard to pronounce or write your name. How many times have you seen "Nugyen" or "Nyugen"? But it never occurs to you to change your name, since you are

100 PERCENT VIETNAMESE

... until your parents decide to become American citizens.

Má fails her exam the first time. You sit beside her as she takes the oral examination on which your own citizenship depends. You believe you would pass, your English flawless and your indoctrination into Americana perfect: George Washington and the cherry tree and Betsy Ross and the flag and Paul Revere's ride and Johnny Appleseed and Paul Bunyan and Babe. You are all-American! But what are your parents?

When they become citizens, they surprise you by changing their names. Nguyễn Ngọc Thanh becomes Joseph Thanh Nguyen. Nguyễn Thị Bảy becomes Linda Kim Nguyen. Joseph and Linda meet AMERICA™ halfway by erasing their diacritical marks and changing their first names. They know who they are and feel no disjuncture using one name among Vietnamese people and another among Americans.

But you, evacuated from your country of origin before you knew what it was to be Vietnamese and replanted in AMERICA™, are hybrid. Vietnamese American. An American of Vietnamese ancestry. Whitewashed, according to some. A banana, according to others, yellow outside, white inside, displayed in the American supermarket of assimilation among the coconuts, apples, and Oreos. The sellouts who are never actually sold out, always being replenished.

So when Ba Má ask if you want to change your name, you hesitate. But you try on different ones. How about . . .

Troy

Maybe you are thinking of the actor and heartthrob Troy Donahue from the 1950s. Maybe Troy resonates with Jane Fonda's son, Troy, named after the Vietnamese revolutionary Nguyễn Văn Trỗi, executed in 1964 for his attempt on the life of Secretary of Defense Robert McNamara. Maybe you remember the city of Troy from reading *D'Aulaires' Book of Greek Myths*. Handsome, revolutionary, classical Troy.

But if you could rename yourself Troy, you would never be the person who could write these words. In another universe, however, you are a news anchor or corporate lawyer or realtor named

Troy Wynn

You don't know who first thought *Win* was the best approximate Anglicized pronunciation for Nguyễn, but it has caught on among Vietnamese Americans, beating out *Neh-goo-yen* or *Noo-win* or *Noo-yen*. Some go so far as to change the spelling of your surname to approximate its sound in Vietnamese. As a teenager, you see France Nuyen in *Star Trek* and are excited and confused—is she Vietnamese? She is! The first Vietnamese person you see on-screen, cast as a green-skinned alien whose tears, if they touch a man, compel him to fall in love with her.

These name changes attempt to reduce alienness, yet each embodies awkwardness. Or do they?

Does anyone blame
    Kirk Douglas, born Issur Danielovitch?
        Rita Hayworth, born Margarita Carmen Cansino?
            Tony Curtis, born Bernard Herschel Schwartz?
                Marilyn Monroe, born Norma Jeane Mortenson?
                    Or John Wayne, born Marion Robert Morrison?

AMERICA™, mythological land of remaking, self-creation, fabulous fiction, where anyone—*anyone*—can be a celebrity, a movie star, president. Vietnamese people should not be held to a different standard, but the reason you cannot easily become Troy Wynn is because you are not white. These movie stars are white or can pass for white—the line between whiteness and passing for it sometimes thin—but an Asian person with a surname not Asian inspires confusion.

Changing one's name also differs from others changing one's name, as the French do when they sometimes spell your last name as "N'Guyen." Could you write "Macron" as "Makron," or "de Gaulle" as "Degaw," even if they came to your country? If people can say and spell the name of movie star Timothée Chalamet, people can say and spell Nguyen, or better yet, Nguyễn, in all the full diacritical glory imposed on you by the French colonizers from whom Chalamet also descends.

> If Chalamet, Schwarzenegger, Kissinger,
> Roosevelt, and Obama are American
> names—if ███ is one, too—
> then so is Nguyễn.

Because you believe in the power of language, you cannot further change the name that makes you who you are, a name already compromising with AMERICA™. You cling to your Americanized name as a sign of your hybrid authenticity, your refusal to be completely assimilated into a culture that can be hostile, skeptical, or indifferent to people who look like you. Yes, AMERICA™ has changed you, but you will try to change AMERICA™, if only by making this country say your name. If only by becoming a writer of a Not So Great American Novel.

all about your mother, or your 1980s,
episode III

The 1980s deposit in you a sediment of confusion and emotion that requires decades for you to sift through. In sifting through these feelings, you learn how to be a writer. The confusion and emotion are due at least partly to watching Ba Má struggle through the hardest decade of their lives in the United States, until the thirteen years beginning in 2005, when your mother falls gravely ill. She never recovers.

> Your brother the doctor tells you Má's diagnosis. Twice. You cannot or will not remember, any more than you can recall the names of her many medications, so you ask him to email you, so you can write it down, so you can remember. Major depression, anh Tùng writes you. Don't mention the other part.

You do not witness every day of those thirteen years. Only Ba does. You are, however, present for every day of the 1980s, until leaving for your last-choice university in 1988. You pack your few belongings into anh Tùng's Acura Integra, and he drives you south down the I-5 to Southern California, a long, monotonous stretch of road flanked by farms, orchards, and ranches, whose only blessing for those passing through is that it is the fastest route by car through Central California. Your destination is the unironically named Inland Empire, which, unlike San José, will at least have a movie named after it by David Lynch. Much less popular than the song by Dionne Warwick, but more hipster cred. Once there, anh Tùng buys you sheets, pillowcases, a bike. He gives you his college-era stereo speakers, heavy wooden boxes that you keep for thirty years. Your parents give you, among other things, a rice cooker, which, by the end of your first year, becomes a laboratory for black mold growing on uneaten rice.

You are thrilled to get as far away as you can from San José, even if it is only 330 miles to your Inland Empire. Only many years later do you feel a degree of shame. Ba Má sacrificed so much for you. And you repay them by fleeing.

The truth is your years in San José damage you, but what is the cause of that damage? Your future teacher Maxine Hong Kingston, who grew up in Stockton in the 1950s, only a couple of hours from San José, put it this way:

> Chinese-Americans, when you try to understand what things in you are Chinese, how do you separate what is peculiar to childhood, to poverty, insanities, one family, your mother who marked your growing with stories, from what is Chinese? What is Chinese tradition and what is the movies?

As for you, how do you disentangle the peculiarities of your family and your lives from adolescence and testosterone, high literature and pornography, San José and Hollywood? What is your own personal strangeness and what is the dismemberment?

Leaving San José behind means not writing about it, putting time and space between it and you. The Silicon Valley is L.A. minus twenty years, your high school classmate Peter Malae writes in his novel *What We Are*, and perhaps that is why, after two decades of living in Los Angeles, you finally find it bearable, if not comfortable, to return to San José.

During those twenty years, you return only to visit your parents, the occasions suffocating you with a feeling of being an alien in a consumerist city where people work, shop, and raise children until they die, or so it seems to you. But maybe you resemble Malae's narrator, who says:

I was a native son of the Silicon Valley,
however much I disavowed it in
gesture and attitude.

In the 1980s, Silicon Valley is being born. Apple is beginning its domination of the world. Somewhere and everywhere in San José, Vietnamese refugees work on assembly lines or do piecework at home, soldering
microchips, some of which end up in the Atari video game console that
Ba Má buy for you in middle school, along with the occasional game
cartridge that costs an exorbitant thirty or more dollars, proof that you
were not always neglected. Malae—whose Samoan father and uncle
both fought with AMERICA™ in Việt Nam—describes the feel of your
quadrant of San José, driving

> down Alum Rock, its ruined lanes unreadable, and there are
> paisas at every street corner, on bikes, on scooters, at bus
> stops, taquerias with futbol posters of Mexico vs. Argentina
> over the door, signs diverting traffic around mounds of gravel
> that have been uprooted and left in the sun, pho houses
> stuffed with Vietnamese hunched over their steaming bowls
> of noodles and rice, and straggler whites using forks and
> talking (you can tell even from outside) way too loud, and
> beauty salons proprietored by women named Tiffany Le and
> Michelle Nguyen, their names in English and Vietnamese
> detailed in flowery pink paint on the windows, a Dunkin'
> Donuts with no one in it, a triangular eyesore still called
> Wienerschnitzel, Walgreen's, 76, 7-Eleven, the bright yellow
> foothills in the nearing horizon rising slower than the sun.

Turning right on Capitol Expressway, you drive to the home of the
AMERICAN DREAM™ that your parents buy in South San José.
They move in 1987 to this new upper-middle-class subdivision of
nearly identical houses: two stories, stucco walls, Spanish tile roofs,

a green carpet of lawn, and twenty-three hundred square feet of space, at the base of those bright yellow foothills and on a quiet cul-de-sac, far from any freeway. Ba Má hire a moving company, itself a luxury, to transport your belongings to the new house, which feels like a mansion with its towering cathedral ceiling in the living room. The red velour sofa has disappeared, replaced by brand-new white leather furniture that matches the white walls and evokes the sleek decor of *Miami Vice*.

Your bedroom, on the second floor, was the nursery for the previous owner. Someone's effort to remove the baby's decorations has made it worse, leaving ragged and torn remnants of a strip of wallpaper running beneath the low ceilings, featuring pastel teddy bears banging on drums. More than thirty years later, the teddy bears are still there.

Your parents no longer run the SàiGòn Mới, renting it out instead and opening a jewelry store next door. 759 South Tenth Street would seem far away except you drive past it every Sunday returning from Vietnamese Mass. Seeing that brown house every weekend and then every time you return to San José and go to Mass with Ba Má still does not make it easy to write about it. Eventually you write a short story about that house and that time, featuring a mother very much like Má and a father not like Ba. The story is titled "War Years" because you cannot separate that era of the SàiGòn Mới from the war's shadow.

You have never forgotten about Má telling you how a thief armed with a hand grenade attempted to rob their store on Ama Trang Long street in Ban Mê Thuột. You were two and do not remember the man with a grenade, or Ama Trang Long street. Is this your first brush with violence and perhaps death?

Your second is the invasion of
your hometown and the refugee
flight from Sài Gòn.

> Your third is when you, a child, run across
> South Tenth Street on a red light and get
> bumped by a pickup truck whose driver
> has slammed on the brakes, sending you
> flying ten or fifteen feet. You are not too
> smart. The shaken driver walks you to the
> 7-Eleven a few feet away from your near-
> death experience. He buys you a toy car
> and some Bazooka bubble gum, the one
> with a comic printed on the inside of the
> wrapper.

> Your fourth is with Ba Má, when you finally
> experience and remember what their life
> has sometimes been like.

You are sixteen, the summer after your junior year, and beginning to
feel like a young man. You replace the glasses you have worn since the
second grade with contact lenses. Your father no longer cuts your hair,
and you have begun a lifelong journey to find the perfect stylist. You
are working at Great America, and Ba shows you he loves you by taking
an hour off every day from the SàiGòn Mới to drive you there. You take
the bus home and, without complaint, eat what Ba Má make for dinner.

After the table is cleared, you help with the day's accounting. Spread out
on the dinner table are cash in bills and coins, checks, and occasional
money orders, with half the day's revenue comprising food stamps and
coupons from Women, Infants and Children and Aid to Families with
Dependent Children.

AFDC coupons are big and yellow, while food stamps come in the bright colors of Monopoly money. You apply red ink to the stamp pad and stamp the back of each of the coupons, food stamps, and checks with the name and address of the SàiGòn Mới. You sort the cash, enter the amounts in the ledger, and punch the numbers without looking at the calculator.

You know these numbers by heart.

You do not feel wealthy or even middle class, though you are the latter, perhaps better. Your parents do not believe in allowances, fashionable clothes, or vacations, but you never hunger. For food. You attend private school. You borrow books from the library, but until your job at Great America you own none outside of schoolbooks. Then you use your wages to buy secondhand books and comic books.

To make up for all the things they do not allow you, Ba Má give you the biggest room in the house, the master bedroom with its view of the freeway entrance ramp. This luxury is not like what you see on television, where the master bedroom is always reserved for the parents. From the 1950s, *Leave It to Beaver*, *Father Knows Best*, and *The Adventures of Ozzie and Harriet* feature happy smiling white people, fathers and mothers with handsome children in tasteful middle-class homes. Not a freeway in sight. From the 1960s and 1970s, *The Brady Bunch*, *The Partridge Family*, and *Happy Days* offer more of the same, except the white people are in color instead of black and white. Also no freeways.

Is this exotic display of what white people wear, eat, and say to each other fantasy or reality?

You enjoy comedies about Black people, too: *The Jeffersons, Good Times, Diff'rent Strokes, Sanford and Son*. Even a show with a Chicano protagonist, *Chico and the Man*. But no comedy exists about people who look like you.

And nothing is funny about your family. A movie of your family's life in the brown house might be made by Wayne Wang, whose 1980s movies *Eat a Bowl of Tea* and *Dim Sum* capture the claustrophobia and struggle of Chinese immigrant life. Households without music or laughter, genuine or canned. Plenty of tears, so little joy.

At day's end, your parents are too tired to be joyful. Nothing's funny about refugee life. Right?

Nothing funny about iron bars on the windows.
Nothing funny about Ba checking all the doors and windows before bed.
Nothing funny about telling you not to open the door to strangers, not after being robbed with a grenade and shot on Christmas Eve.

The knock on the door comes on a summer evening. Still daylight outside. Your parents wear the casual clothes they change into after work, white undershirt and shorts for Ba, semitransparent nightgown for Má. You are all barefoot. You don't remember what you are wearing, but it is likely the clothes that you consider cool: a T-shirt with a surfing logo, blue jeans with the cuffs rolled up and twisted to taper at the ankles for the pegged look that is the fashion among your high school classmates.

The knock can be heard by all of you, since there is never any music in your house, no news on the radio or television, no TV turned on while dinner is being prepared or eaten. No one comes to the house unannounced except Jehovah's Witnesses. All three of you head for the front door, a few steps from the kitchen. Má arrives first. She looks through the peephole and says, Allô?

I have a package for you, he calls.

If he were a Vietnamese stranger, Má would never have opened the door. Does she open the door because he is a white man? Speaking English? Even if he is not the postman?

Má unlocks the dead bolt, peers through the slightly open door. It takes him an instant to shove past her. Behind his back is not a package but a black revolver with a long, slim barrel. The gunman's hair is dirty blond. He wears a faded blue denim jacket. To you he is old, but gazing back from the crest of your middle age, you see that he is young, perhaps in his mid-twenties. He points the gun at Má, at Ba, at you, yelling, Get down!

For an eternal second, there is no past, no future, just the present and the muzzle of the gun. You can still see the barrel of the gun, a .22. A very small caliber, not like Dirty Harry's .44 Magnum. Afraid of acting afraid, you do not scream, beg, cry, or say anything. This is not happening to you. This cannot be real. When Ba kneels, so do you.

> Part of you feels immortal. Part of you
> thinks you will die because you do
> not want to be embarrassed.

The gunman's attention focuses on you and your father, the men of the house. Poor guy. He is not a professional, though he is enough of a pro to have followed Ba Má home from the SàiGòn Mới. If he were a real professional, would he have ignored Má, standing by his side? Does he see her as a weak, hysterical woman? Does he overlook her because she is an Asian lady with poor English? The kind of Asian woman he has likely seen so many times just from randomly watching TV? The anonymous older, silent women in street scenes and marketplaces and brothels who serve as the backdrop to the attractive young Asian women in movies like *The World of Suzie Wong* and *Sayonara*?

He underestimates Má.
So many people have misread her,
including you.

Má, by the door, sees that he is not looking at her but at you and Ba, sinking to your knees. Má's scream shocks the gunman, Ba, you. The scream stuns all of you into paralysis for a moment, enough for Má to dash by the gunman and run outside, still screaming.

Astonished, he turns and starts after her, and you are thankful he is not a professional, because if he were, maybe he would have shot Má or tried to. But he doesn't, and the moment he crosses the threshold, his back to you, Ba leaps up, slams the door shut, and locks it, stranding the gunman outside.

With Má.

Through the movie screen of the living room window, its red curtains drawn back, you see her, Má, fleeing down the sidewalk in front of the evening traffic flowing toward the freeway. The drivers and passengers must be amazed to see a woman in her nightgown. Watching the spectacle, they are unaware that she is running for her life, running to save her life.

And yours.

Again.

the care of memory

Policemen in dark blue uniforms appear shortly after you call from the sole telephone, hanging on the wall in the kitchen. Your family is not a telephone kind of family, no one, beginning with Ba Má, enjoying small talk or conversation in general. You have good phone manners but only a few friends, none of whom call you on the phone. You are respectful calling 911 and telling the dispatcher that your mother is somewhere outside with the gunman. You do not remember if your voice shook.

A fleet of squad cars arrives. You do most of the talking because you are, at sixteen, the only translator, however imperfect. The sergeant in charge, a sturdy white man with graying hair, gathers Ba Má and you at the dining table. You describe the gunman and the gun, and the sergeant gently says, Tell your parents not to be afraid. I'm going to take out my weapon. He has two on his belt, a pistol with a magazine in the grip and a silver revolver with a thick barrel, probably a .357. He unholsters that one and shows it to Ba Má and you, pointing the gun in another direction, so you can compare its size and muzzle with the gunman's. Did his gun look like this? You know something about guns and say, It was a revolver, but the caliber was smaller. And the gun was black.

You are not worried that the sergeant might harm Ba Má or you, and Ba Má did not hesitate in having you call the police. Times have changed since they opened the SàiGòn Mới and did not trust cops. They are people of property, as you will one day be, and they understand that the police are there to protect people like them.

The police sweep the neighborhood, and within an hour the sergeant seats Ba Má and you in the back of a police cruiser, which takes you a few blocks away to where a potential suspect is being held. The sergeant shines a spotlight in the eyes of the suspect so he cannot see you. Is that him? No, you say. Ba Má agree. A white man. But not the same white man.

The police eventually leave with their report. You never hear of the case again. Perhaps Ba still has documentation, kept in the filing cabinet in his bedroom, along with his funeral plans. The picture of your mother running down the street exists only in your mind.

You wonder if she thought often, or at all, of her flight down the sidewalk, one of several moments of heroism in her life. Perhaps the confrontation with the gunman did not amount to much compared with everything else she encountered. Perhaps she never saw her escape as heroism but merely as survival. Or perhaps the gun in her face was another blow against her foundation, another crack that would grow over decades.

                              You have cared for this memory
                              for decades, but you never ask.

When Má dies thirty-one years after the gunman points his gun at all of you, it is not unexpected. She does not receive an obituary in any newspaper, but perhaps you have been writing one in your mind during the last thirteen years of her life, all of it marked by severe illness, including the three years at the end when Ba can no longer take care of her and Má is spending her days and nights in a Memory Care Unit staffed almost entirely by Filipinas. When you visit her, the initial smile on her face and the recognition in her eyes soon fade. She turns her gaze away and retreats into her own world.

                              Does she remember
                              nothing or everything?

Your father pays all the very expensive bills. Ba Má prepared for this all their lives, saving so you would not be burdened by their care. What does it matter that you get very few of the toys you want. What does it matter that your parents never say I love you during your childhood. What does it matter that they rarely spend time with you, squeezed as you all are in the classic immigrant and refugee dilemma: the more parents sacrifice for their children, the further apart they grow from them.

Sacrifice is love. In his seventies, Ba takes it on himself to care for Má for a decade, refusing all assistance. As he liked to tell you in the years after the SàiGòn Mới closed, theirs was a love match, not an arranged marriage. They chose each other and did not waver, so far as you know, for sixty-eight years.

I had my pick, he says one night at the dinner table, Má laughing in pleased embarrassment. I visited with a lot of the girls. They were interested in me. I was a tailor, so I had a skill. Your mother wasn't just pretty. She was smart and ambitious, too.

He still remembers this.

The world in which Ba romanced Má was a black-and-white one, a different age, more tumultuous and more glamorous, when taking photos was a special occasion for which one dressed up, when one's entire generation was haunted by famine and war, division and displacement, colonialism and cataclysm.

You were born toward the end of that age, in black and white. You have not asked Ba if he remembers the photo he took of you and Má. You are two or three years old, walking down the road holding your mother's hand, between the towering trees of a rubber plantation, a natural cathedral. Your mother wears sunglasses and a floral áo dài, her hair in a bouffant. This is the most glamorous photo you have with your mother, when Má is almost your entire world. She and you will never be this glamorous again.

You do not remember this.

Childhood photos are imbued with poignancy, parents knowing that what they remember, their child may not. As for Má, what did she remember? A question you ask yourself almost every time you think of her now.

The director Hirokazu Kore-eda captures this question perfectly in his masterful film *After Life*, set in a way station between earth and Heaven. The guests are the recently dead, in transit to the afterlife. They must decide what single memory they will live with eternally. The staff restages this memory and films it, creating a brief movie that will be eternity for the newly dead.

The conceit is genius. Movies are like memories, memories are like movies, and eternity is an infinite loop of memory. The problem: Which memory? The staff members are those who have become stuck in transit, unable to decide. In limbo they stay, condemned, or privileged, or both, to care for the memories of others.

If you died now and had to choose an eternal memory, it might be this moment in a photograph when you speak your mother tongue, your mother the most powerful woman in the world, both of you unaware of all the future holds as you walk toward your father.

A memory you do not remember.

She remains the most powerful woman in the world to you for many years, even in Harrisburg when you and your brother do something to upset her—you forget what—and she whips you both with a switch from a tree, the only time you remember her hitting you. You cannot be more than seven and you smirk at your brother. His laughter outrages your mother even more. But she does not or cannot hit you any harder, her strength undercut by this new American life. Or by her love for you and your brother.

The next time you see her weakness, she is in a ward. Not the Memory Care Unit of her final decline. The Asian Pacific Psychiatric Ward in San José, earlier in her life, when you are still a child. Patients in gowns mumble in corners. Má, not herself. Má, one of these patients. The experience and the memory disturb you. Or so you think.

Fortunately or unfortunately, you kept a journal during this time, because you had read somewhere that writers should keep journals and you fantasize about being a writer. When you were eighteen, you told a college roommate that F. Scott Fitzgerald published his first novel, *This Side of Paradise*, when he was twenty-three. You had read it. You told your roommate that you also plan to publish your first novel when you are twenty-three. He was impressed. It's good to set goals. You miss yours by twenty years.

The journal exhibits your lack of talent and discipline. It is fitful and fragmented, written inconsistently over a few years in high school and college. In later years, when you return to Ba Má's home, after they have gone to sleep and the house is quiet, the journal waits for you in a milk crate of school folders and notebooks, nestled in a closet with a few scraps of your past: a T-shirt from Saint Patrick with the names of all your classmates, your high school graduation cap, the blazer you wore to your senior ball that you thought made you look sleek and sharp and that now seems cheap and synthetic. The bedroom is a time machine, transporting you back to your teen years when all you wanted was to leave San José forever. You lie on the bed with the same bedspread from those years, a tumbler of Laphroaig on the nightstand, and you discover once again that the journal is actually a horror story. You horrify yourself at what you were.

On February 18, 1990, you describe Má's situation this way in your journal:

> Mom's in the hospital for depression. It's a psychiatric ward, basically, but very clean, very nice, much better than the sanitary white hospital rooms I normally see. It's more like a rest home, except where all the doors have to be left open and all the visitors must have their presents and gifts screened for dangerous items. Mom looks OK. She should be home in a few days.

Which is true: the past the way you remember it now, as disturbing and unsettling, or the past as you wrote about it then?

> Truth is, I barely even thought about Mom at all. I wouldn't tell this to anyone, I think.

What is wrong with you?
Why don't you feel anything?
Your lack of feeling frightens you.

On the next page, more than a year and a half later, you write this on October 6, 1991:

> I am reading Erich Fromm's *Art of Loving* for answers. Unfortunately most of it seems to deal with living, not loving.
>
> ----
>
> My father called me last night. We hadn't talked since the first of the month, and his voice, harsh with his accent and my own quick tinge of guilt,

Whatever Ba said, you did not write it down.

The comma indicates you had more to say. But you never write another word. Because you are not yet a writer. Because you do not like this person in these pages, though this person is you.

This person incapable of feeling, of loving.
This person you do not care to remember;
this person you fear you still might be.

your education

Nevertheless, this earlier version of you, this ghost of you with his horror story, will not let you go. His writing has found its reader, you, in words you wrote to yourself and archive in the milk crate as self-evidence. The further you move away from that time when your mother is in the Asian Pacific Psychiatric Ward, the more your memory changes it. For years afterward you think your mother is in the Asian Pacific Psychiatric Ward when you are a child, because the visit to the ward frightens you and makes you feel vulnerable.

> Why, then, do your words from
> that time indicate no fear
> and no vulnerability?

Perhaps because you are a student at UC Berkeley and you feel, for the first time, that you are a part of a cause and a movement. By the spring of 1990, in your first semester, a sophomore transfer from UCLA, you are taking an introduction to Asian American history.

> You are immediately radicalized.

You wonder why you never learned any of this history. It turns out that it is not you who is whitewashed. It's AMERICA™ that is whitewashed, erasing the Asians it has exploited and dehumanized. Also expunged, edited, or sanitized: the wars and conquests that brought so many Asian and Pacific Islander immigrants and refugees to the United States, from the American conquest and colonization of the Philippines, Hawai'i, and Guam to the American role in Korea, Việt Nam, Laos, and Cambodia, countries where considerable numbers of the people did not want Americans there. And you, the Asian Invasion, realize that

> Asians have never invaded AMERICA™.
> It's AMERICA™ that has invaded Asia.

You join the Asian American Political Alliance, a group of equally angry and passionate students who claim descent from the college students of the late 1960s who refused to be called Orientals or Asians and re-invented themselves as something altogether new: Asian Americans. These Asian Americans claimed their place in the Third World Liberation Front, an alliance of radical students who believed liberation comes from cross-racial and international solidarity, from being not only anti-racist but also anti-war and anti-imperialist. You are no longer a faceless part of an Asian Invasion. You are an Asian American. You have a face, a voice, a name, a movement, a history, a consciousness.

A rage.

As part of a coalition of students of color and white allies, you Asian Americans stage protests to demand more diversity in a mostly white faculty and in a curriculum that marginalizes your histories and experiences. Your protests are not revolutionary, and yet there are those who see these efforts, then and now, as dividing the country and destroying Western civilization.

Your heroes are anti-colonial revolutionaries, public intellectuals, committed writers, galvanizing teachers. From the latter, you learn about the astounding concept of tenure: a professorial reward that guarantees academic freedom, because tenured professors cannot be fired.

Academia's hook sinks into your eye.
It is still there, thirty years later.

In the classroom, you study history, politics, theory, and literature, focusing on moments and movements of decolonization, revolution, or resistance. Outside the classroom, you learn how to organize people, build a network, plan protests. You begin with marches and rallies. You end with taking over the campus administrative offices and then the chancellor's office, dozens of you storming in, sitting down, refusing to leave. You raise your fists and chant, The people, united, will never be defeated!

You are having the time of your life!
And it's only your first semester!

The campus police jab at you with batons. You back away, shrink from the front line. When you lock arms with fellow protesters, the police break up your blockade by bending your thumbs until you let go. They process you at a mobile booking station and send you on your way. This happens to you twice, not just once like most of your peers.

You didn't come to Berkeley *not* to be arrested.

But there's no jail. You're nice college kids. At one of the protests, some Asian American friends wear suits and ties to show how respectable they are. A prominent civil rights attorney is good enough to represent you pro bono. Not good enough to get you acquitted, it is true, but that is because you are really, really guilty of two counts each of trespassing and resisting arrest.

You leave UC Berkeley with four misdemeanors,
three diplomas, two arrests, and an abiding
belief in solidarity, liberation, and the
power of the people and the
power of art.

Art can decimate as well as liberate. The popularity of *Miss Saigon* reminds you of this. This musical reheating of the *Madame Butterfly* story has become a huge theatrical hit. In it, an Asian woman falls in love with a white man and gives up her life so her child can live free in the West. The microwaved version moves from Japan to the brothels

of Sài Gòn during the war, with the role of the Eurasian engineer given
to a white man who tapes his eyes to slant them.

>No matter how often you look at yourself in the
>mirror, your eyes do not seem slanted. But perhaps
>those with slanted eyes cannot see their own slant.

You write your first op-ed for the college newspaper, condemning *Miss
Saigon*. A friend tells you that one of the most beloved English professors, whom you also like, does not approve. Perhaps you wrote a terrible piece. Perhaps you are a barbarian or a Philistine. Or perhaps the
professor thinks someone else is you.

That someone else is the other Viet Nguyen, also an English major.
He is short and gay and looks nothing like you, or he looks exactly like
you, depending on who is looking. The other Viet Nguyen's professor
dislikes him and thinks you are him when you apply for graduate school.
For this, you almost do not get a fellowship, which would prevent you
from accepting Berkeley's offer of admission.

Or perhaps the professor didn't appreciate your application. Influenced
by the Marxist literary critic Terry Eagleton's *Literary Theory*, you believe
SOMETHING MUST BE DONE. Literary criticism, you argue, can
change the world.

>Oh, youthful illusion!
>You do not realize that your criticism
>can never hope to change the world
>if you cannot also change yourself.

Thirty years later you write another op-ed about the revival of *Miss Saigon*,
this time for the *New York Times*. Challenging art with politics, and vice
versa, brings out the critics then and now. Your hate mail has a common

theme: How dare you reduce Art and Love to politics! How dare you trample Freedom of Speech and Artistic Freedom and AMERICA™ with your Soviet Russian Chinese Maoist North Korean Totalitarian Writers Union Authoritarian Communist Socialist Marxist Anti-American Drivel!

These freedom-loving critics would likely laud the brave dissident
writers of China, North Korea, Russia, etc., and look down on
the apolitical conformist writers of those regimes. But is
nothing in the West worthy of political wrath when it
comes to art and writing? It must be so wonderful to
be free of anger, to have nothing threatened by the
outrages committed by your society, to have
never been on the receiving end of your
society's wars police actions missiles
guns bombs whips nooses batons
coups death squads black sites
laws statutes policies
epithets jokes gazes
denials and
silence.

In fact, you take Art and Artistic Freedom and Freedom of Speech and the Exchange of Ideas very seriously. So seriously that you ask a beautiful young woman to go to New York City and spend a huge amount of money (for students) on fourth-row seats for *Miss Saigon* so you can See for Yourself Rather Than Just Judge.

All around you and your gorgeous date are audience members weeping at the climactic spectacle, the heartbreaking tragedy of an Asian woman killing herself for a white man and giving him their child. There's even a Huey helicopter! Like the one that landed on the roof in Sài Gòn to rescue desperate Vietnamese! Like the ones from which American soldiers slaughtered innocent Vietnamese!

When your lovely companion is equally unmoved—disgusted, really—you sense that you have made the right choice, and vice versa. Lan, your future wife and first reader, an aspiring scholar and an aspiring writer like yourself, takes a photo of you gagging under the marquee, a document now lost or otherwise you would share it, because you are that kind of person.

Watching *Miss Saigon* continues your education into how a part of AMERICA™ and the West enjoys seeing Asians. You think you know something about this AMERICA™ because you grew up surrounded by white American culture, so much so that your first publication in college is a long essay for *Asian Week* on "Growing Up in White America."

The essay earns you a seat in Maxine Hong Kingston's nonfiction writing seminar along with thirteen others. Kingston is the author of *The Woman Warrior*, a 1976 landmark of feminist memoir and Asian American literature. A classic of American writing. You are lucky to be in this cozy, dim seminar room. Every day you sit on a couch a few feet from this writer whose *The Woman Warrior* is said to be the most widely taught book in college classes, and every day—

you fall asleep.

At the end of the semester—December 1990—Kingston writes each student a note. You bury yours in the milk crate of school folders and notebooks, but the paraphrase glows in your memory:

You seem very alienated. You should make use of
our university's counseling services.

You never make use of the counseling.
You become a writer instead.
You haven't turned out
so bad, have you?
Have you?

Thirty years later, the writerly you digs up Kingston's letter and re-reads it:

> I believe you are trying again and again to
> approach the heart of your story (mother
> lands in the hospital). But you have not gotten
> to the center of things.

> My observation is that you seem alienated
> and depressed. You said that falling asleep in
> class is your normal behavior; I think it is a
> sign of withdrawing and not functioning.

> Taking joy in life and being generous in the
> giving of yourself (such as giving praise or
> criticism to other students) are healthy states
> that I want for you to work on and achieve.

> Did you notice that I asked you to give me
> questions? There are no questions in your
> letter. Questions are creative and dangerous.
> To ask a question is to be open to change. For
> you to be a good writer, Viet, you need to be
> open, engaged, speaking, hearing, awake.

These are the questions you should have asked yourself:
Are you, in fact, alienated and depressed?
Can you be generous to your fellow writers?
Can you be open, engaged, speaking, hearing, awake,
especially if you have never been before?
Can you get to the heart of the story?
Can you go where it hurts?
Can you cut to the bone?

portrait of the writer as a young fathead

It's enormous. Your hat size is extra large because extra extra large isn't easy to find. The size of your head has nothing to do with the rest of you, which is of average height and weight. At two years of age, your head is a touch bigger than your nine-year-old brother's. Your brother is beautiful, but you . . . look kind of bewildered. A foreshadowing of your years as a fuckup.

You do show a flash of early talent when, in the third grade, you write and draw your first book. *Lester the Cat* is a minimalist character study of Lester, an urban cat, stricken with ennui. Bored with city life, Lester flees to the countryside. There, in a hay-strewn barn, he falls in love with a country cat.

You have never even petted a cat in your young life, but you must have captured the authenticity of urban feline alienation, for the San José Public Library awards *Lester the Cat* a prize. Since Ba Má cannot leave the SàiGòn Mới to take you to the ceremony, your school librarian picks you up from home and treats you to a hamburger across the street from the library. The hotel restaurant, the first one you can recall sitting in that does not serve Vietnamese food, strikes you as incredibly luxurious. You don't remember the white-haired librarian's name, but you are eternally grateful to her and to the San José Public Library for setting you on the path to more than thirty years of misery in trying to become a writer.

Eventually you give *Lester the Cat* to J. The book fades from your memory, as does your childhood promise. Kingston gives you a B+. You were, she tells you decades later, the worst student in the class.

At twenty-one, you are a better literary scholar than writer. You stay at Berkeley to pursue your doctorate in English, but promise yourself that once you get tenure, you will do whatever you want, since you cannot be fired.

You will write.

As a literary critic, you want to criticize colonialism, capitalism, and racism and to study literature by people of color, especially Asian Americans. You tell your English department chair, one of the most famous American literary scholars in the country, that you want to write a dissertation on Vietnamese American literature. He gazes at you with mild concern through his glasses and says, You can't do that. You won't get a job.

Perhaps true, perhaps not. But you are outraged. The right response is not to accept the status quo but hope to transcend it. If not today, then in the future. Your department, however, believes in tradition and the canon, requiring you to read *Beowulf* through Chaucer and Shakespeare, the Romantics and the Victorians, the realists and modernists, so you can talk to your entire profession.

Too bad much of the profession cannot talk back to you.

As a professor of Chicano literature in your department tells you with an edge of anger, the door to his office closed, They expect us to read their literature, but they won't read ours.

So-called minorities must always know the minds of the so-called majority. But they assume they need know nothing about you. Their ignorance is a privilege, a luxury you cannot afford.

A quarter century later, in response to students demanding greater diversity in the English curriculum at Barnard College—the same cause you campaigned for as a student at Berkeley—the college's Emerita Helen Goodhart Altschul Professor of English says:

You need to have read some Shakespeare, Milton, Tennyson. This
is good background for an English major. The brutal part of my
mind says, "If you don't like it, don't major in English."

Love it or leave it. The professor has said the
quiet part out loud, the part you suspect is
sometimes or often said in the privacy
of faculty clubs, cocktail parties,
conference receptions, and
tenure reviews when the
audience is all white.
She continues:

> Many professors would feel that if you don't give
> the basics of the British literature supplemented
> by American literature, you simply can't
> understand some of the moderns.

You grew up in San José, California, so mentally colonized
by the English culture you encounter in the library and
on television that you become an Anglophile. As an
adolescent, you read *Vanity Fair* and *Tom Brown's
School Days* for fun. But the brutal part of your
mind says if one does not read the literatures
of people of color and the colonized,
one cannot understand that

> slavery's profits make European modernity possible,
> as does the European exploitation of the Americas and
> its Indigenous peoples. The bloodstains from these
> profits are laundered through the denial by Europeans
> of their inhuman behavior.

Understanding how English literature often
participates in this denial and projects
this inhumanity onto the enslaved
and the colonized is good
background for an
English major.

At Berkeley, you become what academics call an Americanist. You obtain your first passport so you can travel to international conferences. During your oral examination in nineteenth-century American literature, the examining professor spends half the time interrogating you about one scene in *Moby-Dick*. Fortunately, you have read *Moby-Dick* (loved it!) and remember the gold doubloon nailed to the mast of the *Pequod* by Captain Ahab.

You write a dissertation on Asian American literature, a field in which you can find an academic job because of the struggles of an entire Asian American movement that has succeeded in making Asian Americans and their writings more and more visible. This movement lives inside and outside of academia, from organizers and politicians to artists and activists. Your dissertation is partly about how literary and political struggle go hand in hand, how both are needed for changing and transforming self and society, voice and art. You write about Sui Sin Far (*Mrs. Spring Fragrance*, 1912), Carlos Bulosan (*America Is in the Heart*, 1946), John Okada (*No-No Boy*, 1957). Almost no one who does not teach or study Asian Americans has heard of them, even Bulosan, who was famous in his time.

America Is in the Heart dramatizes the migration of Filipino men to the Depression-era United States. Allos, the narrator, becomes Carlos in the United States and then, by the end, Carl. This work of fiction and autobiography foreshadows today's autofiction, so fashionable when written by white people, not so fashionable when written so much earlier by a colonized person. Bulosan understood that the borders between genres do not matter when colonizers routinely violate existing borders and create the borders they want, while the colonized are forced to cross those borders just to survive.

America Is in the Heart was published during World War II, when AMERICA™ knew it had to live up to its rhetoric of freedom and democracy. So, after hundreds of pages depicting American colonization in the Philippines and brutal racism against Filipinos on the American West Coast, a politically conscious Carl (as in Karl Marx) concludes by saying:

> It came to me that no man—no one at all—could destroy my faith in America again. It was something that had grown out of my defeats and successes, something shaped by my struggles for a place in this vast land. . . . [S]omething that grew out of our desire to know America, and to become a part of her great tradition, and to contribute something toward her final fulfillment.

This ending puzzles you for years until you understand that it makes sense if Groucho Marx reads it aloud, waggling his eyebrows and rolling his eyes at every mention of AMERICA™, the most exclusive club of all. Bulosan should have been a Great American Novelist, but by 1957 he was dead on the steps of Seattle City Hall, ill with tuberculosis and alcoholism, tracked by the FBI at the peak of American anti-communist paranoia. Caught between AMERICA™ as a welcoming heart and a colonizing hammer, Bulosan's epic is really a Not So Great American Novel.

So is *Tripmaster Monkey*, Kingston's satirical, loving depiction of hippie Asian American artists in San Francisco and Berkeley during the countercultural revolution of the 1960s. The hero is the idealistic playwright

Wittman Ah Sing, and since the novel is also about AMERICA™ as the land of democratic Whitmanian possibility and AMERICA™ as imperialist warmonger, it should be a Great American Novel but is not mentioned as such by those who keep track of such things.

It's mostly these literary people who have heard of Kingston in a mostly nonliterary world. Only when you mention Amy Tan and her immensely popular *The Joy Luck Club* do other people start nodding. Wayne Wang directs the movie adaptation starring the hunk who could also play your father, Russell Wong. He smashes his fist into the red meat of a watermelon and then eats a handful of it with juice dripping down his chin while he smirks suggestively at a youthful Ying-Ying, played by Feihong Yu (the older Ying-Ying is played by France Nuyen of *Star Trek* fame, who could also portray your mother in the epic movie of her life if Joan Chen or Kiều Chinh are unavailable).

When you encounter *The Joy Luck Club* at eighteen, it is the first book you have ever read by an Asian American (and by someone who attended college at San José State, a few blocks from your brown house). Your literary models have been Jane Austen, Lord Byron, and Percy Shelley, writers completely alien to Ba Má. English exists only for your own pleasure, irrelevant to the world of the SàiGòn Mới. *The Joy Luck Club* reorients you, along with works by many other Asian American writers: Jessica Hagedorn (*Dogeaters*), Theresa Cha (*Dictee*), David Henry Hwang (*M. Butterfly*), Frank Chin (*The Chickencoop Chinaman*). Asian Americans have written in English since the nineteenth century, beginning with Sui Sin Far's sister, Onoto Watanna, the Japanese pen name of Winifred Eaton, born in Canada of a Chinese mother and English father. Through Asian American literature—and Native literature, and Chicano literature, and Black literature, and anti-colonial literature—you construct a literary inheritance for yourself in addition to the genealogy of the Anglo-American-European canon, which is also yours. And you wonder:

Perhaps writing can be an act of justice. Perhaps through writing
you can illuminate the shadows of the SàiGòn Mới, the brown
house on South Tenth Street, the realm of Vietnamese
refugees. Perhaps writing can be beauty and
light and also rage and anger.

And if you cannot write a dissertation on Vietnamese American literature, you will write Vietnamese American literature. In the early
1990s, only a handful of books have been published by Vietnamese or
Vietnamese American writers in English. You are determined, against
the dehumanizing force of Hollywood and its crimes of representation against Vietnamese people, to humanize the Vietnamese and give
them a voice.

This is a mistake. You will not be able
to say why for years or to do
otherwise for decades.

So you attempt to be a writer, although you do not dare call yourself
one. You write poems: a sonnet about your absent sister, another ear-
nest one in free verse titled "Cambodian Boy on a Stairway," about a
black-and-white photograph featuring a survivor of a rocket attack. The
poignancy of that lone boy moves you deeply.

Unfortunately, this does not make you a good poet.

You stop harming yourself and others with your verse. Essays and nonfiction are closer to the academic writing at which you excel. This is
how you end up in Kingston's nonfiction seminar.

You remember falling asleep in her seminar. But you do not remember
writing about Má in the Asian Pacific Psychiatric Ward until you open

your shabby archive decades later and are surprised to learn from the essays you had written in Kingston's class that your mother was in the ward when you were nineteen.

Not when you were a child.

Your big head holds so many big ideas and remembers so many things about important books, down to the doubloon on a mast in a thick novel written in a language your mother barely reads.

But you cannot or will not remember

who you were

when your mother was not

who she was.

your own personal archive

In order to re member your self and your mother, you examine the paper fragments of your past. Your journal indicates that you visited your mother in the Asian Pacific Psychiatric Ward in February 1990. In your writing for Kingston, you describe yourself as feeling

numb.

Your brother the medical student calls your mother's affliction a

neurosis.

The dictionary calls a neurosis

a relatively mild mental illness

but not

a radical loss of touch with reality.

Really? You perceive this ward, its patients, and your mother as

insane.

None of the patients, your mother included, appears to be a member of your reality. When a woman named Trinh rolls on the floor, a ward attendant, a Black woman, gently picks her up. Then

Trinh stands in the middle of the floor before us. Her
language is a mixture of Vietnamese and baby talk and
maybe something of her own thrown in. She gapes out the
window. She begins clapping her hands and singing in a
disjointed, breathless way, like a child singing too eagerly.

You might as well be reading fiction. You have no memory now of this scene or how most of the patients are Asian and Vietnamese. Your description of one of your characters in your short story collection, *The Refugees*, applies to you, or perhaps you applied your self-description to him:

> His habit of forgetting was too deeply ingrained, as if he passed his life perpetually walking backward through a desert, sweeping away his footprints, leaving him with only scattered recollections.

But you possess a vague image of the ward, because Má returns in 2005 when she embarks on her final departure from your reality. What you mostly recall from 1990 is your discomfort among these patients, your shock and terror that your mother is here. She is not herself. Or perhaps she is herself. Herself as another. As your Other.

> A white patient walks by, one of the few white people in this ward. She says, "Tell your mother not to worry about dying. We all felt that way when we first got here. We all get over it." I nod at her to recognize that she exists.

The patients do not exist for much of the world outside the ward. This is perhaps especially true for the Asian patients, coming from people, such as your own, who rarely, if ever, discuss mental illness. Embarrassing. Shameful. You do not feel this way, but you can only write about Má's voyage into surreality now that she has died.

And what right have you to do even that?

But perhaps you tell this story so you
can recognize that your mother

existed, exists, in all her selves, and
that she was not and is not alone.

You do not recall what brought her to the Asian Pacific Psychiatric Ward
until you read the words you wrote as a nineteen-year-old:

> Someone out there—if not everyone—is trying to kill her.
> They crawl through the sewer and emerge through the
> toilet. She was waiting for them, locked in the bathroom,
> when my father decided enough was enough and
> knocked a hole in the door to reach her.
> It was my bathroom.

If you cannot remember this, why do you remember the reverse, the
night Má chases Ba into the other bathroom in the hallway? When Ba
locks himself inside, Má smashes holes into the door with a chair, all
the shouting in Vietnamese you don't understand.

But you do remember the many times you, as a boy, as a teenager, dash
into that same bathroom and lock the door, beating your father by a few
steps before he can beat you. In fact, Ba whipped you only once, with
his belt, and while you no longer remember what you did to provoke
Ba, you remember how you screamed and bled, how Má grabbed Ba's
arm and begged him to stop. You might have been nine or ten. You
did not blame Ba then and you do not blame him now. Who are you to
complain about one beating when they had been shot. But the fear of
another punishment makes you finely attuned to those moments when
the stress of the SàiGòn Mới breaks Ba and makes him turn on you.
You remember the fear and you fear that you are a coward, running and
hiding rather than standing up to Ba. Sometimes you are quick enough
to grab a blanket and pillow, preparing yourself for a long night. But
you never have to sleep in the bathtub. Ba always, eventually, comes to
the locked door and pleads for you to come out.

This is his true self—the tender one.

Ba, so fastidious about everything, so protective about you, never letting you hang your arm through the open car window because, he says, you will lose it in a car accident—this Ba never bothers to fix or replace the door Má has smashed. Although you remember how the gaping holes in the bathroom door reveal its hollowness for the rest of your years in that brown house, you possess no image of sitting with your mother in the ward.

> She recognized me, but I was no more important in her world than the rest of the ugly furniture. She looked ahead at the opposite wall. Her mouth remained slightly open, her eyes slightly glazed, but she didn't move.

Is this the same gaze you will see later in the Memory Care Unit?

> She wouldn't hug us or touch us, but instead shied away like a timid child. She stood on the middle of the floor and smiled vacantly as we said goodbye.

You believe these things happened, even if you cannot re member them, including how Má ignores the grapes and orange juice Ba has brought, and while Ba talks to a social worker

> the tears started to come from me and I got up before anybody saw me crying, because nobody had seen me cry since the sixth grade. I walked into the bathroom without saying anything to her, but I don't think she noticed anyway. I locked myself in the bathroom stall, and my first sob made me gasp.

You do not remember fleeing from Ban Mê Thuột and Sài Gòn because you were only four, but why can you not re member these things from your late teen years? Why can you not re member yourself? You have been dis membered and disremembered, by Hollywood and colonialism and racism, yes, but also by no one other than you.

You have forgotten that Ba Má would sometimes threaten you. They tell you to obey them, because if you do not, you could upset Má. She could relapse. A threat that can only have meaning if Má had, at one point, collapsed and left the real for the surreal, as she did in Harrisburg. Emotional blackmail, you tell yourself. And then you forget the threat. Perhaps because it turns out to be true.

What you finally re member, provoked by these paper fragments, is this:

Throughout your childhood and adolescence, Ba Má want to shape you into a moral, hardworking, upstanding, 100 percent Vietnamese Catholic. You disagree with their intention, but you respect them. They are not hypocrites. They never deviate from their moral beliefs, their grinding work schedules, their nightly ritual of the Rosary, their weekly attendance at Mass, which, on retirement, becomes daily.

But they verge on fanaticism. During your time at Great America, for example, you buy a pair of gray checkered pants with your own money from the teen fashion department at Macy's in Eastridge Mall, rolling up the hems and twisting them tight around the ankle. You can never imagine wearing pants any other way, especially like those poor adults—your teachers—in their baggy chinos.

Má sees these checkered pants as what delinquent Vietnamese refugee youth wear as they smoke, hang out with the opposite sex, do poorly in school, style their hair into outrageous heights, and go to nightclubs and garage parties, all that is good and fun in your mind and wild and destructive in Má's imagination. She berates you, says you are not respectable and proper, that you are dooming your future. She orders you to return the pants. You do.

And seethe.

The lesson you learn is the need to keep a secret life. You are already adept at secrecy and silence. In Ba Má's house, you are an American spying on them. Outside their house, you are a Vietnamese spying on Americans and their strange ways and customs, including the forbidden, fantastic world of dating, seen in John Hughes movies like *Pretty in Pink* and *Weird Science* and *Some Kind of Wonderful*.

Then you meet J at Great America. She lives fifty-six miles away. To see her, you take a bus and then the BART, a trip of three hours each way. You sell your beloved comic book collection to pay your long-distance phone bill. You maintain the secrecy for three years, until you run out of money and start calling J on Ba Má's phone bill. On January 4, 1990, Má says:

> "Your father doesn't even buy himself
> ten-dollar shirts. He wears your and your brother's
> hand-me-downs. Now, every time you call, he has to
> pay ten or twenty or thirty dollars."
> And she cries.

By January 9, your parents find your letters and photos with J under your bed. You never see them again. You are outraged at this violation of your possessions, your memories, your affection for J, your chance to live your life like the white teenagers in the movies. Ba Má are incensed because, all of a sudden, they discover that their quiet, sullen, usually obedient, vulnerable boy, not yet a man in their eyes, has been lying to them. And worse—is becoming someone they don't even know. You write:

Mom threatened to have a heart attack.

Ba Má demand that you end the relationship. You have no car, no money, no guts, and you owe your parents loyalty and love. So you tell Ba Má you will not see J again, although you keep seeing J. You have become used to living a secret life, with two faces and two selves, only one of which you reveal to Ba Má. What harm does it do them if they don't know of your other life? You avoid thinking about what harm it does to J, who tolerates the situation. Your mother and father compromise in their own way. They offer to set you up with nice Vietnamese Catholic girls. The last thing you want is a nice Vietnamese Catholic girl.

Eventually, though, you marry a nice Vietnamese Catholic girl—Lan, who is also so much more. But, like you, she knows how to wear the appropriate face for certain occasions. Not a false face. Just the right face.

Five weeks after discovering your secret affair, Má departs from reality and enters the Asian Pacific Psychiatric Ward, a fate arguably worse than the threatened heart attack. Perhaps you fear that you are the cause of your mother's departure, a fear that you never articulate for yourself, until now. Perhaps this unspoken, unacknowledged fear is why you will forget for the next few decades that your mother warned you.

You: the cause.
Your mother: the effect.

Seven or eight months later, in the fall of 1990, you will try to write about the Asian Pacific Psychiatric Ward in Kingston's seminar, try to get to the center between your two selves, try to get to the crossing between reality and surreality, try to re member what you have already begun to disremember.

As for your journal, you will only write one more entry, nineteen months later. The final word in your belated, fitful attempt to be a writer?

Guilt.

the inventory of yourself

Má recovers. Comes home. Does not return to the Asian Pacific Psychiatric Ward for another fifteen years. You continue keeping secrets from her and Ba, a double life not atypical of immigrant and refugee children, or so you tell yourself.

Ba Má want to protect you from dangers you do not see; you want to protect them from knowledge they do not need. And they must own secrets you do not even know about. Isn't a true secret, by definition, something whose existence is not known? As for you, which secrets are worst? Being an atheist? Reading Marxist theory? Getting arrested? Seeing J for five more years until the relationship ends?

i.e.,
that is,
in other words,
she dumps your sorry ass.

J refuses to be your secret any longer. She keeps *Lester the Cat*. You wonder if she still has it but never ask. She does not need to hear from the person too weak to stand up on her behalf, content to live a double life that she did not ask for. When does duality become duplicitousness? When does having two selves lead not to double vision but to self-deception? The last time you see her is at her wedding to a Vietnamese groom. At least you did not ruin all Vietnamese people for her.

You marry Lan. Although the most important thing about her to Ba Má is that she is a Vietnamese Catholic from a good family, the most important thing about Lan to you is that she is a poet, as well as beautiful. Your delighted parents pay for the very loud wedding, held in a Chinese banquet hall with the same elaborate ten-course Chinese meal served at every Vietnamese wedding, a bottle of Hennessy cognac on every table for the four hundred guests, most of whom you do not know. No one expects you to enjoy your own wedding. What a Western idea!

You meet Lan during a dark night of thunder and rain in an Oakland loft next to the railroad tracks, at a poetry reading you organize, where she reads her poems at the open mic. Her lyricism smites you. In addition: She, too, fled Việt Nam. She, too, ended up at Fort Indiantown Gap. She, too, migrated again from Pennsylvania to San José. She, too, is a book-loving misfit. Perhaps you crossed paths in the camp, even played with each other. Perhaps you wandered down parallel aisles of the library at the same time, ignorant that your fates would one day intersect.

Someone needs to make a movie about this love story. Wes Anderson? A perfect Wes Anderson movie! Except Anderson makes charming movies only about whimsical white people. You are not whimsical.

Lan reads your every word, often more than once, never complaining even through the long early years of false starts and atrocious experiments. More than anyone, she knows your writerly ambitions, which you share with few. You are a professional literary critic, a professional professor, and if your desire to become a novelist is revealed, your writerly colleagues might see you as a dilettante, while your scholarly colleagues might categorize you the way zoologists regard animals: as an object of study, taxonomy, and curiosity, deserving of some love but perhaps also a little disdain.

You are, as always, divided. Are you a critic or a writer? Scientist or beast?

On the way to getting a PhD in English, you learn a new language: Theory. A mix of intoxicating strains of thinking, particularly, for you,

Marxism, deconstruction, and poststructuralism, energized by global anti-colonial struggle and the insurgent writings of American people of color.

> You acquire a voice,
> but you do not know
> it is not your own.

It is the voice of someone imitating the masters of Theory. To outsiders, Theory often appears dense, complicated, opaque. But your twentysomething self is genuinely inspired by the conviction that theorizing is a way of plunging beneath the surfaces of texts, things, the world, to understand how art, power, and politics operate. You set out to master this discourse that criticizes the world through criticizing the text.

> By the end of your doctorate,
> the discourse masters you.

During your job interviews for university positions, professors hostile to or skeptical of Theory ask you to explain your dissertation in what they call "plain language."

> Whose language is plain?
> ████ speaks plainly.
> Is that something to aspire to?

The skeptical professors also ask you to explain an idea you pick up from your theoretical reading: interstitiality. You cannot yet articulate, in two minutes or less, how your entire existence is interstitial. At the interstices. At the intersections, the junctions, the crossings. Of languages, cultures, ways of thinking, and political belief.

You are forever in between that place and this place, dis place and displaced, a site of unease that will always be home. You will never be quite comfortable anywhere, because what if homes are not only places where everything is happy and resolved, but also just as likely places of discomfort and dis ease. Welcome home. Love it or leave it.

> You always stand somewhere inside
> and outside of every language you
> encounter. Orphaned in Vietnamese.
> Clumsy in French. Adopted in English.
> Mastered by Theory. Awed by Fiction.

Once, in a graduate seminar on literature, border crossing, and migrants, your classmate, a daughter of Mexican immigrants, says she wants to write something her mother could understand. You appreciate her sentiment. But you could never write something Má would read.

> And because you cannot, or will not, you
> give up and give yourself wholly over to
> Theory. Not hard to do, because when
> you offered yourself first to English,
> you cut off your mother tongue.

It was not a conscious decision.
Yet it was. As conscious as a child
could be about amputation.

English comes with consciousness and with memory. Memories begin, in your own narration to yourself and of your self, in English. English is present most hours of your life through school, reading, television. Vietnamese slips away, spoken only with Ba Má. Through Vietnamese they teach you tradition, discipline, etiquette, religion. Punishment and shame. Obedience and dread.

> Also love. But you do not know that and
> feel that until after you leave home,
> when hearing Vietnamese being
> spoken, even by strangers,
> will evoke for you the
> sound of love.

Your parents hire a family friend to teach you Vietnamese in your early teen years, but you are a reluctant student. The friend was a doctor in your homeland, but with his degree worthless here, he has to study to become a doctor again. All you remember is the title of the novel the poor man uses in his classes with a bored kid: *Anh Phải Sống*.

Even in college, Ba Má still try, hiring an older cousin, the son of Má's eldest sister, to teach you Vietnamese. Old enough to be your father, the cousin is a former soldier who survived the reeducation camps. His teaching text: the Bible.

You see yourself as Ba Má and these Vietnamese teachers might have seen you: quiet, reticent, sullen, resisting their efforts to reach you, dwelling in a private life of fantasy and escapism. Becoming American. Becoming alien.

Now a father, you want to keep your own son close. You try to create the intimacy you once had with Ba Má but which the SàiGòn Mới destroyed. You read to him often, and he learns to love books. Some of the sweetest words you hear are, Daddy, read me a book, which he says even when he can read on his own.

Reading by himself, he takes one of his first steps away from you. But whatever miscommunications may await, it will not be because you do not share a language. For him, his mother tongue is your adopted tongue.

You do not cut off your mother tongue in one sharp slice. You saw at it gradually, as your English becomes ever sharper, ever finer. You do not encounter bone, but you do not cut your mother tongue off completely. The stub still wags in your mouth, proficient enough so that when you return to Việt Nam, people say,

Your Vietnamese is so good
. . . for a Korean!

As a child, you must have made the decision. You could not speak both languages like a native or like a master. The worst possible outcome: speak both languages poorly. The next worse outcome: speak English like a foreigner but retain your mother tongue. The best outcome: speak English like a native, Vietnamese like a child.

Even a child's Vietnamese
lets you know you are still Vietnamese.
In a Los Angeles pharmacy, as an adult, you
hear a man speak Vietnamese on his cell phone.
He is weathered, his clothes perfunctory,
perhaps a working man in some kind
of manual trade. He says, voice
tender, Con ơi, Ba đây.
Con ăn cơm chưa?

Tears in your eyes then,
tears in your eyes now.
So sentimental, even cliché,
but these tears let you know
you are still Vietnamese.

In your childhood, Ba Má say to you, every day,
Con ăn cơm chưa?

They greet visitors the same way:
Ăn cơm chưa?
An expression of care and concern,
bred from the desire to see loved
ones and friends well fed.

No one takes rice, or eating, for granted.

> As children, during the great famine, when
> there was not enough rice, your parents
> had to eat manioc, the tuberous root
> of the cassava tree. You find its
> white fiber tasteless. A couple
> of times in retirement your
> father boils manioc and
> eats it, smiling, out
> of nostalgia.

However much they economize, Ba Má never stint on food. Con ăn cơm chưa?

Ba Má come home from long days at the SàiGòn Mới and still prepare the usual three-course dinner—meat, vegetable, soup—anchored by a gigantic pot of jasmine rice, lifted directly from the rice cooker and placed on the dining table. Con ăn cơm chưa?

You never want for food, but you must eat everything on your plate. Boiled, unseasoned offal. White slices of rubberized intestine. Chewy slices of yellow tripe. Bite-sized morsels of muscular chicken gizzards and tender chicken hearts. Bristly beef tongue, decades before it becomes a hipster staple. Dark chocolate-colored liver, before it attains a Rothian sexual connotation. Con ăn cơm chưa?

You eat it all, and more than thirty years
later, whenever you finish roasting a
whole chicken, you take it out of
the oven, stand by yourself at
the counter, and eat the
gizzard, liver, and
heart, because
no one else
will.

Rice stands for food; food stands for love. Your father counts the bowls
of rice you eat at every meal, protests if you eat fewer than three.

How do you translate the word "you" into Vietnamese when there is
no exact translation, when every "I" and "you" is always about one's
relationship to the other? On television, Americans of the same family call each other with the word "you." Shocking. Your own son now
addresses his father with "you," because you do not call yourself "Ba"
and do not call him "con." In cutting off your mother tongue, you also
cut off more. Father, Dad, Daddy—they nudge your heart but do not
move you to tears. Yet.

Con ơi, Ba đây.

Your nine-year-old son and three-year-old daughter may never know
what these words mean. Not what they mean literally, which your son
already does, but what they mean emotionally.

You know your place when you say those words, when those words hail
you and place you in the branches of the family tree. The entire history of
what it means to be Vietnamese, the record of war and loss, of struggle
and sacrifice, of the parent's love and the child's filiality, condensed into
these simple words and their sound when spoken out loud.

Ba, Má, con. The holy trinity. Who needs love when you have sacrifice? And if your mother and father never said I love you to you, did you ever say these words to Ba Má?

Perhaps the first time you say the word "love" to another person is when you tell your brother, You don't love me anymore. Anh Tùng tells you he does love you, which he will not say again until decades later, after Má dies. Even then, you find it almost impossible to say I love you to him in return. But you do.

The next person to utter these words to you is J. You are about to leave for different colleges. I love you, she says, over the phone.

> You freeze. You stutter. You cannot make your tongue
> say the same words. The silence grows longer and
> longer until she says goodbye and hangs up.

Weeks later, in your first year at college, a new friend will say I love you out of friendship.

> You freeze again. You do not understand why anyone
> would say this to you, much less actually love you.
> She smiles kindly, or awkwardly, and lets the
> moment pass, never to bring it up again.

You cannot say I love you because you do not know how to love, or if you do, you do not know what love feels like. Many years later, you understand: you are afraid. Of feeling. Of being vulnerable. You lack the courage to love. To be open to others, who might hurt you as much as love you.

You hide behind Theory. A shield of mastery behind which you can be objective, unemotional, invulnerable. You learn to distrust the subjective.

The irrational. The experiential. The ambiguous. The emotional. The vulnerable. All the things that can undermine your mastery.

You think but do not feel.

The result is that you can examine a text closely as a doctor of letters, but you are utterly incapable of examining yourself. You, the zoologist, never the beast. You, the reader, never the text.

What if you are both?

pilgrimage

For seven months from summer to winter in 2003, you and Lan stay in the eleventh arrondissement of Paris, where English is rarely heard and Americans rarely seen, a few steps from métro Voltaire. You are newly married, and you have just been tenured. You cannot be fired, short of committing a crime, and so you are here not to write another scholarly book—

> your best friend from high school tells
> you he keeps your academic book
> by his bedside to help him
> fall asleep

—but to write your book of short stories while living in a one-bedroom apartment on the third floor of an unadorned building on the unfashionable rue Richard Lenoir. No Haussmannian splendor and no elevator, but you and Lan are young and in love, with only one suitcase each.

If going to Paris, a city famous for its writers, is a literary pilgrimage for you, Ba Má visit you in Paris that fall intent on a religious pilgrimage. Their idea of a good time: visiting the major Catholic shrines of western Europe. Over five days, you escort them to Lourdes in southwestern France and Fátima in Portugal, with a stop in London. You pack a bottle of whiskey to relieve the stress, but are proud of yourself for orchestrating this vacation of a lifetime for Ba Má.

This is their fourth international voyage. Their first was fleeing their homeland. If forced migrations make one cosmopolitan, then refugees and migrants would be considered some of the world's best-traveled people. They are far more worldly than those who never leave their countries and yet look down on these cosmonauts, whose odds of surviving their journeys are as bad or worse than those of astronauts.

To see for yourself where Ba Má's epic journey began, you make a pilgrimage to Nghĩa Yên, your father's quê, in 2004, as soon as you leave Paris. A child of the diaspora returning to the quê is a kind of pilgrim. Where your parents were born and spent their childhoods is a shrine. And you, who do not believe in God, believe in Ba Má.

You prepare carefully for this visit, which you do in your thirty-third year. During your first trip in 2002, you were a tourist. For this occasion, you are a student. You study academic Vietnamese for several months at the Việt Nam National University in Sài Gòn, aka Hồ Chí Minh City, if by studying one means going to lots of nightclubs and bars, including after-class sessions with your sole male teacher. It is he who tells you that in Vietnamese culture the father's quê is the son's quê as well. Between the two of you, you can easily drink ten large bottles of Tiger beer, which the waiter brings in a crate. You study very, very hard.

You rehearse the complex terminology of familial honorifics so you know what to call a paternal uncle versus a maternal aunt. But no one warns you, least of all Ba Má, that the people of Nghĩa Yên, Đức Thọ, Hà Tĩnh, speak such a peculiar, regional dialect that even the word for water is different. So this is why I sometimes find it hard to understand your parents, Lan says.

> Only then do you realize you have grown up
> being spoken to in a Vietnamese that
> perplexes other Vietnamese.
> This explains everything!

You are delivered to your quê by the bombastic husband of your cousin, daughter of a paternal uncle. She comes from a family who feels indebted to Ba Má for having sent money to help them survive the rationing years after war's end. You plan to take the train from Hà Nội to Vinh, the nearest large city, but the bombastic husband insists on taking you in his chauffeured Mercedes. The bombastic husband, a businessman with a swimming pool in his urban gated mansion, is the new Việt Nam with its capitalist hopes. Your father's brothers are the old Việt Nam. Rural and poor. The three of them and many of their children and grandchildren are waiting for you when you finally arrive at the ancestral home late in the evening. At least two dozen people, from the elderly to the tiny. Is this what it means to be Vietnamese? Never to be alone?

Unfortunately, you like to be alone.

The ancestral home is a walled compound with three houses, one for each uncle. Your paternal grandfather, whom you never met, built this compound. When you tell one of your language teachers that the compound has running water and electricity, she is impressed. Your quê has a reputation for being a difficult place to live.

Nghĩa Yên is where Ba was born, but you do not visit your own birthplace because Ba says, You can never go back to Ban Mê Thuột. He believes the communists will persecute you for being his son. You have no such fear because you have no memory. But you also cannot disobey him, though you have disobeyed him many times before. Mostly you follow this command out of respect, but Ba also succeeds in planting a tree of fear inside of you. What if he is right?

Your sister, chị Tuyết, who still lives in Ban Mê Thuột, now Buôn Ma Thuột, comes to meet you in Nha Trang, the beachside city where Má fled with your brother and you in 1975. Your rendezvous is the house Ba Má owned during the war years, a few blocks from the beach. You take a taxi from your budget hotel and arrive on a quiet side street drenched in sunlight. The house is modest by suburban California standards and middle class by Vietnamese standards, with a gated courtyard in which motorbikes are parked. Ba Má let her oldest sister live in the house during the war, and somehow during those years your aunt divided the villa—this is what Ba Má call the house—in two to rent out half of it. Ba Má mention this story once or twice, bemused. Your aunt is now the owner. How she managed to keep the house after the communist victory, you never find out. You never ask.

You are glad someone in your family got to keep the house. You just wish it were your sister. But you do not bring this up, given the shakiness of your Vietnamese. Conversations proceed with you catching 50 to 80 percent of what is being said, enough to understand the gist but salted with just enough doubt that you can't be certain you've heard what you've heard. Your usual method of conversation is to keep asking questions and let the other person respond, but even that is limited if you are unwilling to ask certain questions.

> What did she think when she saw your backs, when she closed the door, when she was all alone? What was the next morning like? The day after? What did the cadres say when they came for the house and threw her out? What was her time like on the volunteer youth brigade after the war? Where was she sent? For how long? How did she meet her husband?

All these questions come to you now, but none occur to you at your aunt's house near the beach, or if they did, you couldn't ask. Or would you even dare to ask

> what does it feel like to be the adopted one?

You don't recall then what Kingston wrote to you after her seminar:

Questions are creative and dangerous.
To ask a question is to be open to change.

Sometimes you wonder what your life would have been like if Ba Má had not succeeded in leaving. It is your sister who has lived this other life. She stayed but did not get to keep the family home and business in Buôn Ma Thuột or the house in Nha Trang. Má, on fleeing Ban Mê Thuột, had left behind gold that she could not carry and instructed her sisters to share it with your sister. Your aunts never did so. Another reason not to return to Buôn Ma Thuột is that you have no desire to meet these aunts who you feel cheated your sister.

You last saw her twenty-nine years ago, a moment you do not remember because you were four. You have only ever seen your sister in two photos, taken in her young adulthood. The woman you meet is a mother of two in her forties. Fashionable. With makeup. You marvel at each other's presence, at each other's faces. She cries. You do not. After her tears come smiles and laughter for both of you. You learn that she likes to sing. And have fun. Having fun is something Ba Má, your brother, and you find difficult. You are a serious family.

If you had been left behind, you would probably feel unlucky, resentful, envious, conflicted, abandoned, betrayed. If your sister feels any of those things, or has ever felt any of them, she shows no sign. She appears only happy to see you.

At your aunt's dinner table, your sister, whom you knew by her nickname of Tuyết but who now calls herself by her proper name of Hương, wears a sleeveless leopard print dress. Your aunt and your cousins laugh about the time Ba Má finally returned home in the early 1990s on their

third international trip, as soon as the United States reestablished political relations and lifted the embargo it had imposed in 1975—a soft war
after the hard war. Your relatives are amused because of your father's
paranoia, how he insisted on keeping his and your mother's suitcases
under their bed for fear that someone would disturb their contents. But
given that your aunt's house was once his, perhaps he was justified.

Ba is the eldest son. A dutiful man who loves his family, a faithful
Catholic who believes in helping the poor, he must have felt his obligations to his parents and siblings keenly. But the financial and emotional
costs must have been heavy: three brothers and a sister on Ba's side,
five sisters and a brother on Má's side, as well as all their children. And
your (adopted) sister.

In advance of your own visit to your quê, Ba gave you a list of relatives
and the amount of money each one will get from you. You have, for each
relative, an envelope with American dollars, as Ba Má undoubtedly did
as well. On the Thanksgiving after their return from Việt Nam, Ba—who
had previously insisted on your absolute Vietnameseness—proclaims,
over the turkey, We're Americans now.

They never return after that.

You remember their quê, the compound crowded with relatives, the
vast green farmland stretching beyond the walls. That land sinks into
utter darkness once night falls, and you understand why Ba Má cannot
return to the quê for good. They have traveled too far in both space and
time. As have you.

Your only connection to your quê is a silken thread of memory and
feeling, invisible to the human eye. You wish you could say that after
twenty-nine years of distance from your sister, you pulled on that thread

to bring you closer to her. But you did not. Or could not. Seeing your sister in Nha Trang is, for you, a kind of pilgrimage, a ritual visit to see someone enshrined in your memory. But having conducted the pilgrimage, there may be no need to return.

Your relationship with your sister is a war casualty. Or perhaps your inability to have a relationship with her is a war casualty. Or perhaps in any parallel universe you would still be emotionally numb.

> If the war dismembered your
> relationship with your sister,
> did Ba Má disremember her?

You cannot speak for Ba Má, but you certainly have. Your sister, Tuyết, is an absent presence; your (adopted) sister, Hương, is a present absence. Never having quite forgotten your sister, you have never quite re membered her either. You cannot blame the war or anyone else for this, the way you see her as if she were still rooted to the earth and you were on the moon. Or Facebook, which is where you see her now nearly every day, visible but distant.

Astronauts eventually return to Earth. But cosmonauts like Ba Má permanently escape the gravity of home.

> Is this the root of your own willingness to leave home?
> San José too small for you as, perhaps, the quê
> of Nghĩa Yên became for Ba Má?

> Nostalgia is, literally, homesickness,
> with those afflicted yearning for
> their home. But what to call
> being sick of home?

For devout Catholics, the real home is not earth but Heaven, their long-ing for it perpetual. How else to ascend and fulfill that desire but by becoming a one-way cosmonaut, voyager, risk-taker? Nothing riskier than faith in what cannot be seen, heard, touched.

> Your parents call their object of faith God.
> You call yours justice. All of you, in
> your own ways, are true believers.

Thus, Ba Má's second international trip, around 1988, is a pilgrimage to the Vatican and Jerusalem with their church. That trip's sequel is this European pilgrimage in 2003 for which you are the tour guide. The bright colors of the architecture in Lourdes, where the Virgin Mary appeared to a peasant girl, remind you of Disneyland. Tourist shops sell crucifixes of every size, plates adorned with the Pope, Virgin Mary statues, snow globes, and lockets. You buy a cologne-sized bottle of holy water for your father-in-law. Your parents bathe in this holy water while you wait outside the baths. Devotees light candles as they promenade through narrow streets to evening Mass, while formations of nuns glide by in black and gray habits.

Fátima impresses you with its severity. Nestled in green mountains and supposedly named after a Moorish princess kidnapped by a Christian knight, Fátima commemorates another Virgin Mary sighting. Visitors approach a grand basilica with a towering spire by crossing an expan-sive square. Those desperate for the Virgin Mary's help shuffle across the square on their knees. In grimmer days, the knees of the faithful would be bloody and bruised. Now the pilgrims wear kneepads. Ba Má pray at Fátima but do not crawl. They do not need a miracle. They have already saved themselves, with the aid of the U.S. government and God.

You never tell Ba Má you are an atheist because you do not want to upset them. Protecting Ba Má is how you show you love them, even if they do not know it, even as you do not remember all the unspoken ways they love you. Being their tour guide is another way of showing love. Ba Má put themselves in your care as someone finally an adult. Getting married is the first real sign of your adulthood. Grandchildren is what they want next, but fatherhood terrifies you.

You buy yourself time with this pilgrimage. Surprisingly, you enjoy yourself, happy to see Ba Má delighted as you escort them to the Eiffel Tower and Versailles, Buckingham Palace and Lisbon. Ba Má prefer the cleanliness of London over the dirtiness of Paris. In the Paris Métro, Má laughs recalling how, as a girl, she rode the bus without a fare, hiding underneath a seat.

> Years later you will understand this memory when
> you take an oversold night train through central
> Việt Nam, third class, kids sleeping under your wood
> bench, a stranger dozing on a stool in the aisle,
> forehead against your chest.

Your terror of fatherhood comes partly from seeing what motherhood inflicts on Má. The mother of your childhood wields a beautiful smile. She loves to adorn herself. She is statuesque and elegant, authoritative and powerful. But the SàiGòn Mới exhausts her, ages her, diminishes her. Or maybe she would shrink anyway as you grow and reach her height, then exceed it. In your teen years, you begin to notice the age in her face, the way you see the age in your own face now, compared to the freshness of your children. They absorb your life as you absorbed Ba Má's.

But this pilgrimage signals the end of
sacrifice. The war years, long past.
SàiGòn Mới, no more.

You will take them to all the Catholic shrines in the world. You might even go back with them to Việt Nam, to re member.

It is the fall of 2003. Má is healthy.
Neither of you know that in two years
nothing will be the same, ever again,
for her. Or you. Or me.

part three

We are adult because we carry with us the mute presence of
the dead, from whom we ask counsel in our present actions,
from whom we ask forgiveness for past offenses.

—Natalia Ginzburg,
A Place to Live

forgetting, deliberate and accidental

You. And me. Such an odd couple.

The only way I have been able to write about myself is through writing about you. You are me, but seen from a slight distance, or the greatest distance, which is the space between one and one's self.

You are my excuse to write about me, because I find myself too boring to go on about and also too frightening to think about. What kind of person is capable of the disremembering I have done, to myself and to others, like my (adopted) sister, like my mother?

Only through writing about you can I attempt to re member, not only you, but also myself. And perhaps, in writing and re membering, you and me, engaged in this delicate dialectic, can become something greater than the sum of our disjointed parts.

If re membering has proven so difficult for you and me, can either of us be blamed for forgetting? Americans, who continually struggle to be greater than the sum of their parts, live in a culture of forgetfulness, that fifty-first state of Denial. This is a country where so many would rather not remember what the poet William Carlos Williams calls the

orgy of blood

from which the nation was born and that still soaks the land so many citizens, including those who were once refugees, continue to profit from. At best, many of my fellow Americans disremember these atroci-ties as things to be regretted, accidents drowned in the wake of the nation as it sails inevitably toward the dawn. But is that light the sun or the glow of the atomic bombs AMERICA™ dropped on Hiroshima and Nagasaki, not to mention the sixty-seven bombs that the United States tested on the Marshall Islands?

When it comes to forgetting, AMERICA™ is not exceptional. Nations forget or disremember history all the time. History that contradicts the nation's image is suppressed, erased, rewritten, or expelled along with the people who might bring up that history through their memories, such as the Vietnamese who were defeated in the war. The revolutionary victory of 1975 re membered the country of Việt Nam, north and south, even as it dismembered the southern republic. When we, the defeated or their descendants, return to a re membered Việt Nam, we know our stay is conditional. We must refrain from politics, accept communist legitimacy, not bring up the past, not cross the red lines.

But to speak of our lives as refugees is already to cross a red line.

When my short story collection, *The Refugees*, is published in Việt Nam, the censors remove "War Years," the only autobiographical story I ever wrote, about the SàiGòn Mới and the white gunman. The father in the story is mostly not Ba, but the mother in the story resembles Má, and you resemble the child who narrates. Má once told me of a Vietnamese woman who came to the SàiGòn Mới and demanded money for the anti-communist cause. In my usual fashion, I asked no questions of Má. Writing a story is my way to ask questions and provide answers. In the story, I call this woman Mrs. Hoa and imagine that she lost her husband and son in the war. I know people like Mrs. Hoa, their anti-communism personal as much as political.

The censors must have felt like they knew her, too.

Communism censors the SàiGòn Mới in Việt Nam, but capitalism erases the SàiGòn Mới from San José, an echo of how colonialism sought to efface the still-surviving Muwekma Ohlone people of this land on which the SàiGòn Mới once stood.

This tragical farce or farcical tragedy is why your Karl Marxism needs your Groucho Marxism. Ba Má and other Vietnamese refugees are so

successful in gentrifying the decayed downtown that the city gentri-
fies it even further. By the 1990s, everyone knows the way to San José
because it is a bedroom base for Silicon Valley, and this renewed San
José needs a new city hall . . .

across the street from the SàiGòn Mới.

The Vietnamese who remade the old downtown are too déclassé for
the new downtown. The city forces Ba Má and the other Vietnamese to
sell their businesses at an insultingly low price. Ba Má and the others
learn another sentence of the American story: hire a lawyer to sue for
a fair price. But whatever they are paid, they must concede that having
been hypervisible, they must now be invisible.

A brand-new city hall that looks like a seedpod from the Death Star
rises from a foundation of amnesia, as metallic and glossy as the tech
world whose tax revenues fund it. I will not see it for over a decade.
Every time I return to downtown San José, I avoid Santa Clara Street.
Too painful to see a parking lot where the SàiGòn Mới once stood, no
sign left of their labor or sacrifice.

The city plans to build a symphony hall on the absence of the SàiGòn Mới.
I love that a symphony can spring from the SàiGòn Mới's refugee roots.

I hear America singing

white Walt Whitman writes, and so even in a ghostly way, Ba Má can
participate in the American chorus, the one Langston Hughes writes
about when he says,

I, too, sing America.

But somewhere along the way the plan changes. The city sells the property for many millions of dollars, evidence that Ba's intuition to do
everything he could to buy this property was correct. Where Ba Má once
shed blood and sweat now looms a gigantic luxury apartment complex,
the Miro, the tallest building in San José, evocative of, possibly, the
artist Joan Miró. The symphony, never more than an idea, is silenced,
replaced by a $288 million

high-rise urban retreat

where you can

live beyond your expectations

for approximately $3,000 to $12,000 a month in rent.

This, too, is AMERICA™!

Or at least my off-key version,
terrible singer that I am,
neither Black
nor white.

Against erasure, against silencing, against the obelisk
of lifestyle capitalism with a chic veneer of artistic
sophistication for the technocratic consumer of the
planet, stands not a song but these words, this book—

which retails for approximately sixteen to
twenty-seven dollars and which can eventually be
bought, used, for less than a dollar, or simply borrowed

—this memorial pressing against the inevitability
and necessity of forgetting. The forgetting of the
collective, my own forgetting,
Ba's forgetting.

A memorial, despite its name, is also a testament to how much has
been forgotten, the infinite background of all that cannot be recalled, as
well as all the disputable facts that must be interpreted, against which
the solid fiction of cohesive remembering stands out.

Strange that I, best known as a fiction writer,
cannot remember in this way. I can only re
member.

Ba no longer remembers Fátima and Lourdes, visits I dreaded but now
seize on as cherished memory, when Má inhabited this reality and I
was a good son.

What he does remember: Paris and London. And what he remembers
most:

Those curtains in that hotel room, he says wistfully.

The Marriott hotel where we stayed, near Big Ben, with its conjoining
suites for Ba Má and for me, had floor-to-ceiling bright yellow curtains.

I modeled the curtains in the living room on them.

A tailor in his youth, Ba cut and sewed the curtains himself upon his return from London. Now, every morning and afternoon, he sits and naps on the plush brown leather sofa, hands clasped on his chest, illuminated by the soft golden light filtering through the closed curtains.

Sitting on that sofa, one sees on the opposite white wall the photos of Ba Má's fiftieth wedding anniversary in 2004, coinciding with the fiftieth anniversary of the partition of Việt Nam, of the beginning of their refugee life together.

> Even as a country is divided, a future of blood
> foretold, marriage brings together two families
> and two lovers—a great detail for a novel!

During this anniversary Ba wears an off-white suit; Má, a golden áo dài. The plump, pink-cheeked bishop of San José presides, ornately robed in his chasuble, bedecked with a miter, and wielding a tall staff over his Vietnamese sheep.

A year later, in December 2005, during the Christmas holiday, I sit on this sofa, stunned. Something in Má has suddenly broken.

There is no visible cause for this crack between our reality and her surreality. She was retired, enjoying her life: perfecting a handful of recipes, picking something different each day from her extensive wardrobe for the daily Mass she attended with Ba, taking pictures with her grandchildren. Now she is in a hospital, detained against her will and ours. I learn that doctors can put patients in a seventy-two-hour hold from which their loved ones cannot rescue them. This is one of the few facts I remember.

I do not keep a journal of this time.

And I call myself a writer?

In the absence of words, my memory is blank. A space as white as

bone.

Almost no memories because you choose to forget and I am not willing to remember. Partly to protect you and me. Partly because remembering what I cannot remember would be an act of fiction rather than fact.

Fact: I am unable to recall what happened to Má, whether I was even there for her breakdown, what she looked like, how long she was in the hospital, or its name, or how she eventually returned to the same Asian Pacific Psychiatric Ward from so long ago.

The fact is that I also refuse to re member. I do not call my brother to ask for his help in sharpening my memory and my prose, the better to saw against

bone.

I reject memory. I accept my amnesia. Because—fact—the Asian Pacific Psychiatric Ward is the most terrifying place I have ever been, and the seventy-two hours of my mother's detention in that hospital whose name I cannot even fathom is the most unsettling time of my life. I would trade parts of my body, even shorten my life, rather than be afflicted like the patients of that ward, like the people undergoing that detention.

Like Má.

Forgetting the painful things is necessary for some of us. As long as we eventually simmer that

bone that we cannot cut through. Have I
simmered that bone enough? Can
I taste that marrow of
memory?

After the doctors release my mother from detention, after she leaves the Asian Pacific Psychiatric Ward, after we gather the legal documents Ba needs to control Má's fate, we deliver my mother to a nursing facility.

My memory resumes at this halfway house between the surrealism of the Asian Pacific Psychiatric Ward and the realism of life with Má at home where she belongs. The nursing facility, neither luxurious nor cheap, resembles a hospital but is mostly a refrigerator to keep human beings alive until they are ready to die.

If a quiet library with towering walls of books and hushed patrons and my own leather armchair is my vision of eternal bliss, this refrigerator is, if not Hell, a purgatory with tiled floors, brightly lit hallways, bland meals under plastic covers, incapacitated patients, the constant bustle of nurses, therapists, visitors, the buzz of televisions.

I have never seen anyone
reading a book in
this purgatory.

Most of the staff, clad in nursing scrubs or polo shirts and chinos, are Filipinas. American colonization in the Philippines created this route for nurses to come to AMERICA™, while draining the Philippines of its own medical professionals and depriving the children left behind of their mothers, exported to take care of Americans and many others around the world.

Where is the televised dramatic comedy about these
women? Call it *Filipinas*. Or *Feelings*. All those
Filipina actors and dancers who worked in
Miss Saigon are waiting.

As I numbly watch the patients, they lie numbly in their beds or sit
numbly in wheelchairs in the hallways. Old and ill, or old and dying.
Occasionally someone screams. I do not want to end up here.

My mother stays for days, or weeks, or months. I can't remember.

What I do re member is that this time is different from the other
times.

While driving my brother and father away from our most recent visit with
Má, I realize that Má will not get better. As they discuss Má's condition, I
understand that Má will never descend from her surreality to our reality,
except for occasional, brief visits. I am ambushed by myself, sobs and
tears rupturing the wall that separates you and me, me and myself. It
has been fourteen years since the last time I was so waylaid by myself,
when Má was in the Asian Pacific Psychiatric Ward the first time.

Neither my father nor my brother says a word as I grip the wheel and
struggle to see through tears.

I recover. I get ahold of myself. I put you back where you belong.
My father and brother resume their conversation. I
resume driving.

We never speak of this moment.

After the nursing facility releases Má, Ba brings her body home. But not her
mind. Not fully. Her thoughts travel most of the time through a different,

parallel universe. Still, she sometimes returns to our reality, enough to notice how Ba, beginning at age seventy-two, when he should be circumnavigating the world via Boeing, remains earthbound. Homebound. He cares for Má without complaint for the next ten years, ignoring entreaties from my brother and me to hire the help that he can easily afford.

As a child, I watched Ba cook dinner, shop for groceries, vacuum the house. The typical Vietnamese man is allergic to these chores. This routine of mundane deeds, I understand later, is love.

> In 2012, the Austrian filmmaker Michael Haneke,
> whose work I admire, makes *Amour*, about a
> loving husband and wife in their eighties.
> A stroke disables the wife, leaving her
> helpless in her husband's care. Out of
> deep love, he suffocates her, then
> starves himself to death in
> their Parisian apartment.

> Haneke. Always a crowd-pleaser.

> Not the right director to make
> a movie about Ba Má.

Their amour is about endurance. Both know how to suffer and sacrifice, without the reward of recognition from anyone but their sons, without the drama of a murder-suicide or a crucifixion.

Má's many medications, arrayed in a repurposed cookie tin, prevent such theatrics. The meds calm her. Reduce the chance of self-harm. Keep her from breaking fully free from our reality. So tightly is she leashed in orbit that Má is very quiet, moves slowly, does little. But she recognizes me and her grandchildren, even if the glow of recognition quickly fades.

Unlike Haneke's two-hour, seven-minute movie,
this quiet play, as slow and puzzling as
Happy Days by Samuel Beckett,
goes on for a decade.

Beckett also wrote, in *The Unnamable*,
You must go on. I can't go on. I'll go on.

How appropriate for refugees, of whom
Beckett was one. As for Ba Má,
they have only ever gone on
and on and on.

Má will not count as one of war's casualties, but what do you call someone who loses her country, much of her wealth, her family, her parents,
her (adopted) daughter, and her peace of mind because of the war?

So many of war's casualties are never counted. Never commemorated,
never named on walls, never written about in novels and plays, never
featured in movies. The refugees, the suicides, the disabled, the un-
sheltered, the traumatized, the ones who have departed this reality.
The ones never known.

Vietnamese people, how do you separate what is unique to you and
your own personal trauma

from war, colonization, the division and reunification of the country?
from becoming a refugee or staying behind or being left behind?
from being the child of refugees, soldiers, witnesses, survivors?
from being the child of those who didn't survive?
from being Vietnamese?

How do you separate yourself and
your memories from History?

How do you separate your
presence from so many
absences?

Questions I can only
ask, never answer.

obituary

In 2015, after a decade of taking care of Má by himself, my then eighty-two-year-old father surrenders. Ba moves Má to the kind of benevolent nursing home seen in movies or soap operas, usually reserved for white people, hushed and carpeted, a piano in the common room that my father plays for my mother when he visits. He taught himself to play the piano as an adult and the mandolin in his old age.

> Sometimes I wonder what he could have become if he had the education my son has, with his private piano teacher. But then he would not be the father he became, and I would not be the person I am.

My mother stays in the Memory Care Unit, again staffed almost wholly by Filipinas, where residents eat together in a sunlit dining room with silverware, plates, table service, and bland food with very little salt. Baked chicken, broccoli, mashed potatoes—a disheartening diet for someone who ate Vietnamese food her entire life. Even my little boy rejects the square of Jell-O on his grandmother's plate. The residents coo over him, but the next time we visit, they have forgotten who he is and exclaim over him again.

His presence, and mine, makes Má smile. After that initial warmth, her eyes shift and fixate on something only she can see. She is as still as water in a plugged sink. Her pills don't always work. One day I learn that she has broken her arm by jumping on and then falling off her bed, or so the staff says. A doctor, whom I never see, adjusts her meds. Her arm, permanently injured, huddles against her body or floats by her side, useless.

> I cannot now re member if it is her left or right arm.

In 2018, Má's condition worsens. A stroke, anh Tùng says. She needs X-rays, MRIs. The Memory Care Unit can no longer attend to her. She returns to the nursing facility, the setting for a horror movie more frightening than anything Hollywood can dream up because it is real life, or real death. A Hollywood drama is finished in two hours, but finishing off a human being can take much longer than that. In Má's case, thirteen years of slow erosion, a death inflicted cell by cell on her body and mind.

Ba calls for a priest. A middle-aged one with graying hair soon arrives in his black uniform with its white collar. He stands over Má's bed to bestow last rites, delivers the words in Vietnamese. I don't understand the words. Má doesn't open her eyes.

The rites are done in a few seconds, the priest present for a few minutes. I expect solemnity from the Vietnamese holy man, a pat on the shoulder for Ba, a rote expression of comfort, but the man offers no words of care, not even pretending to share in the sorrow of my father. The priest could have been washing dishes for all the feeling he exhibits as he makes the sign of the cross.

Father. Son. Holy Ghost.

Ba. Me. And this—

memory, history, memorial—

this spectral thing I was already thinking of as
Má lay dying, my art the closest I come to the
spiritual. Or the ghoulish. I looked at Má then,
as I had many times earlier, and thought:
How will I write about this?
About her? And
her ghost?

Ba Má had gone to Mass every day during retirement. Ba Má helped raise the money that built the Vietnamese church where those Masses were held. I expect more from this Vietnamese priest than the brush-off this man gives Má as he waves his hand in the air. But I say nothing. Ba is thankful, shakes the priest's hand, bows a little. If my father is grateful, who am I, the ingrate, to say anything. Perhaps when I am aged and shaky and vulnerable like Ba, I, too, will be grateful.

Má can end her days in this purgatory or at home. So we bring Má back to the suburban house of her AMERICAN DREAM™. The vast, verdant lawn is now an expanse of dirt, Ba too tired and distracted to maintain it. I sleep in an upstairs bedroom, the same one I slept in the last two years of high school. The shower pipe groans and rattles when I turn on the water. The room is hot in the summer, the air-conditioning too weak to rise to the second floor.

But this is December. The house is cool, especially the downstairs bedroom where Má sleeps. We wheel her rented hospital bed into the family room, with its television that has barely been watched since Má fell ill and the stereo system no one listened to even when Má was well. Background music is not a part of family life. The house is usually as silent as an empty church. There is no soundtrack as I watch December 22 turn to December 23 while Má takes her last breaths, thirteen years almost to the day from her final breakdown. Ba, my brother, my sister-in-law, and I are the only witnesses.

Má was born in 1937 as Nguyễn Thị Bãy, a poor girl in a poor northern Vietnamese village. She dies in 2018 as Linda Kim Nguyen, American citizen, traveler of a life both ordinary and epic.

At seventeen, she married and became a refugee for the first time.

At seventeen, I almost did not
graduate from high school
because I nearly failed
precalculus.

At thirty-eight, a mother of two biological sons and one adopted daughter, Má became a refugee for the second time, her sequel starting in an alien country.

At thirty-eight, I, with
no children, struggled
with writing a short
story about Má.

Má's first name is Bãy. Giving children numbers as names was common in rural Việt Nam. Families often had so many children. Some would not survive. Why give a girl a real name?

As a girl, the seventh child, she deserved no more.

Má hated this birth name. In her last decades, she wanted to be called by her American name, Linda. But both her names feel alien on my tongue. I never called her by her name, only Mẹ as a child, Má as an adult. Her refugee path shaped even what I called her. Northerners say Mẹ, southerners say Má, and I, as always, am somewhere in between.

Most Americans who met Má probably only saw her mortal, unextraordinary coil. If they knew anything about her, they might know she had been a shopkeeper, businesswoman, refugee. If they knew nothing about her, she was another Asian woman who did not speak good English. Mẹ, or Má, never wanted to mention how she received only a grade school education. I am telling on her, and yet she should be told

on, even if it is not my secret to tell. Look at what Má accomplished with just a grade school education, overcoming everything—*almost* everything—except her mind.

> Defeated, like so many
> heroes, not by others
> but by herself.

A hero but not a soldier. People like Má who will not be remembered by History are also a part of History, drafted as reluctant players in horrific wars. Unlike soldiers, these civilians, many of them women and children, never get the recognition they deserve. Some endure more terror, see more horror, than some soldiers. And the wars of the twentieth century—including the ones in Việt Nam—killed far more civilians than soldiers.

> Civilian stories can be war stories, too.

Perhaps what happened to my mother was simply her body and mind's fate. But History and war took their turns hammering Má. Unnerving her. Breaking her.

> My mother, child
> of colonization
> and war.

> Me, grandchild
> of colonization
> and war.

Also the child of Ba Má, who chose each other. For all that Má was lost to us for so many years, my father's love was not lost to her. She saw this reality from the orbit of her surreality. I know because the last words Má

says on her hospital bed in the family room before she says the Lord's
Prayer with my father are for my father, to my father:

> Em yêu anh.

> This I will translate, even if the
> translation is not enough:

> I love you.

After the Lord's Prayer, silence.
My brother the doctor gives Má morphine
while my sister-in-law the doctor watches.
Má's breathing slows.

> I lean close to tell Má in Vietnamese that I love her.
> She lived a good life. A life of hard work and
> sacrifice. A heroic life. A life that
> demanded so much strength,
> devotion, and love.

> I don't know where Má
> found those qualities. But I am
> the beneficiary. These words, this faith
> in her, this betrayal of her, are the outcome.

Má's eyes do not open. She gives no sign of hearing.
Her breathing finally stops. It is midnight.
Her journey on this earth, complete.

> My mother is mine and my
> mother is also Other to me.

My brother makes a phone call. In an hour
a courteous stranger who might be Filipino arrives
with a gurney, fills out a form, takes away my mother,
leaves the empty hospital bed in the family room,
and drives my mother into the night.

                                I remember Má loved me.

                                        Everything else

                                            I can forget.

memorial

"War Years," the story about my mother, takes me years to
write, and before that even more years to find the will to write. As for
the words in this memoir, this history, this memorial, this book that
could have been a Not So Great American Novel and perhaps even is
one if re membering is fiction as much as fact—

I waited my entire life to approach these words. Perhaps I also
waited for Má to pass away before I fabricated my stories about her,
or retrieved my stories about her, my tales nothing more than
garments shed by her ghost.

Má dies before the plague begins. If she had been alive,
would she be one of the thousands of elderly and infirm
trapped in their nursing homes? Would my last glimpse of
her have been through a window? During the disaster, not
yet over, more than a million Americans and more than six
million people all over the world die. The body count
continues. Who will memorialize them? And how?

The global plague exacerbates another illness that has always
existed in AMERICA™, our predisposition to murder. The
police murder George Floyd in 2020. In 2021, a white man
with a gun murders eight people in Atlanta, six of them Asian
immigrant women working in massage parlors.

Soon Chung Park, 74
Suncha Kim, 69
Yong Ae Yue, 63
Hyun Jung Grant, 51
Xiaojie Tan, 49
Daoyou Feng, 44

Anger surges against Asians in many countries. In
AMERICA™ and elsewhere, women compose the majority
of victims. Of physical verbal symbolic brutality. Of the
violence of stories that stir, seduce, and shatter (some of) us.

How many Asian women, often Vietnamese, have I seen
killed or murdered on-screen or onstage? Did this shape how
I saw Má, who, to some, looks like these dead women?
Sounds like them, too, with her imperfect English?

Apocalypse Now, 1979. *Rambo: First Blood Part II*, 1985.
Casualties of War, 1989. *Miss Saigon*, 1989. Outdated?
Watchmen, an HBO TV series in 2019, ends with the
spectacular death of a Vietnamese woman, the mysterious
Lady Trieu, a visionary scientist and a trillionaire

ANOTHER AMERICAN

DRIVEN OUT OF BUSINESS

BY THE VIETNAMESE

with utopian ambitions that her enemies see as dystopian.

Lady Trieu is played by (Vietnamese American)
actor Hong Chau, who could also portray my
mother in the story of her life that HBO will never
make, although HBO is producing a TV series of
my novel, which means if you haven't read
The Sympathizer yet—you never have to read
The Sympathizer. Just watch it on TV.

Would the makers of *Watchmen* have dared to
kill Lady Trieu after the Atlanta shootings? Or would that
fantasy be too close to reality? Too disturbing to be
dismissed as just a story?

Lady Trieu met the inevitable fate of the Yellow Peril,
slaughtered by that most American method of mass
termination, aerial bombardment, albeit in a hail
of frozen squid dropped from outer space
(don't ask). At least she got to say some
appropriate last words as she saw
her fate coming for her:

Đụ má.

Her words are subtitled:

Motherfucker.

The violent deaths of Asian women are not just a story. All
those who can walk away from a book, movie, or play do not
realize it is a privilege to dispose of stories. The privilege of
being part of a majority, when almost all the stories center on
them. They live in the luxury of narrative plenitude.

Few stories feature those of us who dwell in narrative
scarcity. When featured, we are, far too often, distorted. Each
appearance then matters. Too much. No story can handle the
weight. This onus of representation is unfair to us and to the
writers, artists, filmmakers, actors, and storytellers who speak
about us and for us whether we want them to, whether they
want to. And when a story attacks us, when a story repeats
over and over and over, it is no longer just a story. When the
story drills us, it inhabits our minds as narrative, as
mythology, as fantasy that can become reality, as
Full Metal Jacket shows.
As reality shows.

The white male shooter who murdered the
Asian women in Georgia is part of a lineage that
took root with the arrival of European settlers and
continues through the gunman who killed five
schoolchildren in Stockton. The killer says he is
not a racist but a sex addict bent on removing
temptation, as if sexual desires can be separated
from racial fantasies. Regardless of his lie or self-
deception, he targeted these women because
they are Asian women.

I watch *Full Metal Jacket* at home, sometime during college.
Me so horny, Papillon Soo as Da Nang Hooker says to a pair of
marines newly arrived in Sài Gòn. Me love you long time.

In 1989, 2 Live Crew scores a tremendous hit with
"Me So Horny" from the album *As Nasty as They Wanna Be*,
one of George Floyd's favorites in high school.
The refrain: Papillon Soo saying, over and over,

Me so horny.
Me love you long time.

This is how much of the country, perhaps the world,
sees and hears Vietnamese women. Perhaps all
Asian women sound like this to some non-Asians.

I cannot laugh at this movie, at Stanley Kubrick the auteur, at
his masterful cinema. I can stop watching. I don't. I have
learned to watch women and keep looking.

In the climax, a character known only as VC Sniper
(Ngoc Le, in her sole film appearance) picks off marines in the

battle for Huế. When the marines capture the castrating sniper,
they are startled to see the sniper is a mortally wounded young
woman. Shoot me, she whispers over and over. Shoot me.
These marines are young men trained in boot camp to march
with phallic rifles on their shoulders while clutching
their crotches, chanting:

> This is my rifle, this is my gun,
> this is for fighting, this is for fun.

Joker—the marine whom Papillon Soo propositions—
cocks his .45 pistol and shoots
VC Sniper.

> How much difference exists, Kubrick implies,
> between a woman saying fuck me and shoot me
> in the war-saturated masculine imagination,
> which is also mine?

The novelist Larry Heinemann understands this
imagination, too. Reading his *Close Quarters* as a boy, I
am scarred forever by a scene in which American soldiers
gang-rape a Vietnamese sex worker whom they call
Claymore Face because of her acne scars. Like the
marine in *Mourning Glory*, they, too, hold a pistol to her
head. This, the real climax. The battle that follows against
Vietnamese enemies, terrible as it is, is the denouement.
Heinemann wants to disturb his readers because war, which
he experienced, disturbs. In his novel, idealistic young men
transform into monsters. Not just killers. Rapists.

If I am infuriated by the violation and depiction of
Claymore Face, if I am horrified because I have never

raped anyone and cannot imagine myself capable of this
human behavior, am I disturbed at all that soon after
reading the novel I begin looking at girls and women,
feeling great pleasure and therefore becoming complicit in
what is done to them or what might be done to them?

And if I have never aimed a gun at a human being, I am
still complicit in the American machinery of death,
whether aimed at fellow Americans or our
Others beyond our borders.

> Even if at times I am also an
> Other to my fellow Americans.

The novelist Laila Lalami, born in Morocco but an
American citizen like me, says that Others like us are only
conditional Americans, our citizenship suspect due to
origins, ancestries, religions. Sometimes this
suspicion results in murder.

Americans might mourn the victims of the lone white male
gunman, but for the most part they do not mourn the
millions of victims of the greatest acts of anti-Asian
violence, the wars and colonization that AMERICA™ and
other colonizing countries have carried out in Asia.

> How many people, including the French, know
> the French navy shelled Hải Phòng in 1946 and
> massacred 6,000 Vietnamese people?

Many Asians flee or migrate to the very countries that
bombed, shelled, invaded, or colonized them. Even with
conditional citizenship, it must be safer inside the

AMERICAN DREAM™ than outside,
behind the guns than in front.
Until it isn't.

> Before being murdered, Xiaojie Tan claimed her
> AMERICAN DREAM™ by opening a
> massage parlor in a shopping center:
> Cherokee Village.

Ba Má, my brother, me. We began our AMERICAN DREAM™
in a refugee camp at an American military base:
Fort Indiantown Gap, Pennsylvania. The

> early settlers in this region

says the fort's official history

> worked hard to make a living
> coexisting with the native people.

The region's boosters say

> a fortification was established in the area
> of Fort Indiantown Gap, during the
> French and Indian Wars, to protect the
> settlers of the area from the
> Susquehannock Indians.

There are probably no Cherokee, or very few, in Cherokee
Village. The American military forcibly expelled the
Cherokee from Georgia in 1838, then compelled them to
migrate west on the Trail of Tears, what the Cherokee call
the Trail Where We Cried.

More than four thousand Cherokee perish.

The Susquehannock, also known as the Conestoga, numbered
as many as seven thousand in the year 1600. Diseases
brought by the colonizers diminish them, as do wars with the
colonizers and other Indian nations. Only a few hundred
survive by century's end. In 1763, twelve years after Ben
Franklin's speech praising the whiteness of his Pennsylvania
and the need to keep it pristine, vigilantes called the Paxton
Boys murder almost all the remaining Conestoga, peaceful
farmers and craftsmen. The killers, white men who

             suffered no legal consequences for their actions

come from Paxton Township. The township is sixteen
miles from Fort Indiantown Gap, where we arrived and
where we were grateful. My parents claim our AMERICA™
by buying their first home in Lower Paxton Township.

             Daoyou Feng, Hyun Jung Grant, Suncha Kim,
             Soon Chung Park, Xiaojie Tan, and Yong Ae Yue
             may or may not have known of the Trail Where
             They Cried. But when Asian immigrants and
             refugees like them, like Ba Má and me, come to
             claim AMERICA™, we also claim this history.

             And sometimes this history claims us.

For most of my life, I do not think about the name of Fort
Indiantown Gap, do not seek out its history or memory.
That, too, is the power and violence of stories. Of
mythology. Of the fantasy that Ba Má and I are not
touched by the history of AMERICA™ and its genocidal

origins, by its ongoing colonization; that we and others like us do not perpetuate that history and present by coming here as refugees, immigrants, or settlers and becoming shareholders in the war machine, the ultimate condition of our citizenship.

The Lancaster County sheriff recorded the names of the Conestoga people murdered by the Paxton Boys. So far as I know, this record is their only surviving obituary.

Murdered at Conestoga Town:
    Sheehays
    Wa-a-shen (George)
    Tee-Kau-ley (Harry)
    Ess-canesh (son of Sheehays)
    Tea-wonsha-i-ong (an old woman)
    Kannenquas (a woman)

Murdered at the Lancaster Workhouse:
    Kyunqueagoah (Captain John)
    Koweenasee (Betty, his wife)
    Tenseedaagua (Bill Sack)
    Kanianguas (Molly, his wife)
    Saquies-hat-tah (John Smith)
    Chee-na-wan (Peggy, his wife)
    Quaachow (Little John, Capt. John's son)
    Shae-e-kah (Jacob, a boy)
    Ex-undas (Young Sheehays, a boy)
    Tong-quas (Chrisly, a boy)
    Hy-ye-naes (Little Peter, a boy)

Ko-qoa-e-un-quas (Molly, a girl)
Karen-do-uah (a little girl)
Canu-kie-sung (Peggy, a girl)

Survivors on the farm of Christian Hershey:
Michael
Mary (his wife)

Their descendants live.

open secrets

I am Má's descendant.

What does it mean to write my mother's obituary, my mother's story, to claim descent from her?

Especially since Má would not want me to write about her this way. Not that she ever forbade me. She trusted me, whose books she never read but was proud of anyway. And since she never consented to this story, written in a language she had difficulty reading, am I betraying her?

If I do betray her, can I be loyal at the same time? Her life is epic and yet quotidian, deserving to be told and known, according to me if not her. Her story matters because she is Má, but it also carries weight because it resembles those of many other (Vietnamese) refugees.

Heroic as she is to me, perhaps Má is not exceptional to anyone but those who love her. But saying my mother may be more typical than exceptional is no loss. When I hear stories of other refugees and what they survived

                                                                    or not

I am immediately captured by their gravity. Not the same as Má's, but similar. Not exceptional, but common. Not stereotype, but history. Each one deserving a story. Each one with potential to be portrayed. And perhaps betrayed.

I write about Má because I believe stories matter, but if stories can dismember as much as save, what does my version inflict on her? If I re membered everything about Má and wrote it down, is it betrayal? For example, in "War Years," my adolescent narrator says that

my mother wore only a nightgown of sheer green fabric
without a bra. She wasn't aware of how her breasts
swayed like anemones under shallow water, embarrassing
me whenever I saw those dark and doleful areolas with
their nipples as thick as my index finger. My mother's
breasts were nothing like those of the girls in my class,
or so I imagined.

Some readers are offended. Is it a defense to say Má wore such a nightgown in my adolescence, her way of relaxing after an exhausting day at
the SàiGòn Mới, discomfiting me enough so that the memory seeks me
out without my consent, even as I cannot seek out other memories, like
what occurred in the Asian Pacific Psychiatric Ward? Or is mentioning
the fact and memory of that nightgown already betraying Má?

Whereof one cannot speak,
thereof one must be silent

wrote Ludwig Wittgenstein. True for nations, corporations, individuals. But I have been silent for so long about so many things that now
and then I find it hard to know when to choose silence or speech.
Sometimes one speaks too much, while sometimes silence speaks
for itself.

If recalling this memory for others to see is, possibly, a betrayal, what
about forgetting? If blankness and whiteness riddle my imprecise
memory of Má, is that also treachery?

Turning memory's dial, we veer between what
Paul Ricoeur, the philosopher, calls
"unhappy memory" versus
"happy forgetting."

Unhappy memory, all too common, is when the past
arises from the grave and arrives armed and
lethal, seeking revenge or justice.

I prefer justice, the condition for happy forgetting,
when the fatal and fateful past, satisfied, returns
to a peaceful slumber from which
it will not rise again.

But if we have happily forgotten,
how will we know the fact of
our own amnesia?

Days go by, weeks even, when I do not think of my mother, unaware
even of my lack of reflection. Is that happy forgetting? If so, and if forgetting is necessary to moving on, why does the remembering of my
forgetting feel like another betrayal?

Writing thus becomes a way of re membering, for the act of writing is
when I most feel Má's presence. But writing is also a way of forgetting,
allowing me not to think of her after I am finished, Má and the past
safely behind me.

Remembering and forgetting Má says something about her but also
about me. The storyteller telling on himself. And what I can tell is that
in writing about my mother as my own, someone who is part of me as
I was part of her, my mother is also my Other.

The Other is someone too close to us.

I cannot *not* remember my mother. And
my Other. But how do I re
member her?

The easiest thing is to recall someone dearly my own (my mother) and someone who is an Other (also my mother) and thus *represent* her, and implicitly through her all Vietnamese refugees and their struggles, to make her, them, us, a part of AMERICA™ and maybe even Việt Nam. To humanize us. To include us. This was my ambition when I began trying to write decades ago.

But to humanize and to include are mistakes.
Proving what does not need to be proven only
concedes our inferiority to people who never
question their own humanity, even as they
dehumanize us, invade us, murder us—
the colonized, the conquered, the Indigenous, the
enslaved, the exploited, the non-white, the non-
male, the non-straight—and then invite us to do the
same inhuman things to Others. In the name of
humanity. Kill the savages. In order to save them.
Then teach the survivors and descendants. The
language of the humanities. So they can speak.
Properly. Politely. Of this fraught history. That is
not history. But still present.

Đụ má!

Strange how an obscenity inspires nostalgia in me. But this is how some of us talk to each other! And yet the language in which I write is the master's. I know very few Vietnamese who curse in the master's language to the master's face.

In this language, we hold our tongues,
for those who claim English as
their own are watching
and judging us.

But why refrain from obscenity when
our existence is due to the obscene?

So many of us who fell in love with stories feel the pain of being silenced,
erased, distorted, raped, killed. So we demand for ourselves the power
of speech, of narrative, of (self-)representation, about people like us.
Like Ba Má.

> But if (self-)representation
> matters, it is also
> not enough.

For those of us who are writers and storytellers, the masters tell us to
show, don't tell. A law of representation to keep us in our place. Since
many of us have so much we want to tell. Even if we want to show the
telling at the same time.

> "You must not tell anyone,"
> my mother said,
> "what I am about to tell you."

Kingston begins *The Woman Warrior* this way, naming the taboo and
breaking it at the same time. In so doing, Kingston creates a parable
of the writer's ultimate task:

find what must not be told
and tell it.

> But is this honesty or betrayal?
> Sometimes telling the secret is both.

I see Má's face as she exhales her last. Did she ever forbid me from telling her story? No. Because she never thought I would. She trusted me, who cannot trust my own memory.

Having been represented by me, does she now matter more than when she wasn't? So many stories have already been created about women somewhat like her by writers somewhat like me, ambivalent about telling on their mothers, revealing their secrets.

If Má's life had secrets and
is itself perhaps a secret, let it be said
that two kinds of confidences exist
to be confessed and told on:
the private secret and
the open secret.

Private secrets are common enough in the storytelling world: illness, divorce, alienation, infidelity, and the like.

Like Má's life.
And death.

These are the kinds of secrets expected of a book like this. Matters of the self, and only the self, not the collective, are the drama for an American storytelling world that honors showing over telling; that sneezes when politics nudges too close into fiction, poetry, movies, and television; that associates telling with the uncouth acts of writers who are barbarians or, even worse, *communists*.

Art, in the free West, in AMERICA™, is above politics. Instead of being sentenced to reeducation camps and forced labor, instead of being disciplined by socialist realism and Writers Unions, free writers in the

West, especially AMERICA™, are dispatched to campuses to work on their *craft* as *creative writers.*

"Creative"—a curious and anxious adjective, as if writers exist who do not want to be creative, as if being creative were more important than anything else, like being critical.

To be creative without being critical risks being apolitical. A lack of politics *is* the politics of the dominant American literary world, leading many American writers to avoid certain open secrets.

The open secret dares us to acknowledge its presence. If we
tell on the open secret, we anger the many
who do not want it called out.

The open secret of AMERICA™ is that white people founded it on
colonization, genocide, slavery, war, and white supremacy,
all of which continue shaping the self
and the Other.

The open secret of AMERICA™ is that we
do not call colonization by its name.
Instead, we give colonization
another name:

the AMERICAN DREAM™

But, some protest, we do talk   Yes, but we contain their
about these horrors, especially   disturbance through
in books!   (self-)representation!

And yet (self-)representation is a euphemism.
Open secrets spawn euphemisms,
the deadly dialect of the powerful.

Open secrets and euphemisms abound. The "special military operation" of Russia's invasion of Ukraine. The "Department of Defense"
for a United States almost always at war. Or the "Cold War," a frigid
euphemism allowing great powers to distance themselves from the
hot wars they fought, instigated, or supported in other countries. The
latest battlefield: Ukraine.

The American Pentagon press secretary becomes emotional talking
about Vladimir Putin's atrocities in Ukraine:

> It's difficult to look at some of the images and
> imagine that any well-thinking, serious, mature
> leader would do that. I can't talk to his psychology,
> but I think we can all speak to his depravity.

When was the last time an American official was teary discussing the
hundreds of thousands of civilians killed by American weaponry and
sanctions, or by the warlords and strongmen we support?

> It was a pity

the idealistic and innocent CIA agent Alden Pyle
says of Vietnamese civilians killed by his bombs
in Graham Greene's *The Quiet American*

> but you can't always hit your target.
> Anyway they died in the right cause. . . .
> In a way you could say they
> died for democracy.

For Americans, the open secret is our own depravity,
which must be passed over in silence.

To learn a little of these open secrets and hot wars, readers can turn to writers like me, born elsewhere and rebirthed in AMERICA™ as literary proxies for the less powerful, ethnic representatives in the so-called culture wars over the nation's past, present, and future. As the novelist Rabih Alameddine, also an American, among other identities, says:

> Those of us who fall outside the dominant culture
> are allowed to speak as the other, and
> more importantly, for the other.
>   . . . I get Lebanon.

My assignment: Việt Nam.

The euphemism of (self-)representation is that we proxies usually do not get assigned AMERICA™ itself. Too big of a subject for our little selves. No, AMERICA™ belongs to the Great White American Male Novelists. They write from and about the bright center of empire, without ever calling it as such, while we write from the shadows and far reaches.

Our power comes from witnessing death and suffering, or witnessing the trauma endured by our parents. We are called on to offer testimony about this pain, but we are not the prosecutors, defenders, and magistrates who make the case, write the definitive opinion, hand down judgment. We are expected to show our grief, not to tell on why this grief exists.

This grief . . .

> When Má dies, I gently close her eyes,
> as Ba asks. Then he tells me
> to close her mouth.

Her skin is already cold when
I lift her jaw, and when
I let it go, her mouth
falls open again.

Her voicelessness invites me to
speak for her. That is also
representation's
temptation.

Can I be her representative?
Make her story mine?
Through Má and others like her, can I,
can we, demand our share of
representation in this country,
in the world?

When we make that demand, those who oppose us no longer say stories are just stories. Instead, they blame us for destroying (Western)
civilization, or at least AMERICA™, by demanding narrative plenitude
for our voices, experiences, memories, and histories in the curriculum,
the canon, the country.

Representation matters, but inasmuch as it is a cure, representation is
also an affliction, condemning us to isolation as proxy and alibi.

have I found my voice

do you hear me

or must I translate for you

As an esteemed, white-haired Ivy League Americanist once said with a genteel smile after I visited his graduate seminar and spoke for an hour of my work on the war in Việt Nam:

It is a cri de coeur!

Yes. It is.

The powerful are not frightened by the less powerful claiming their one small grief, uttering their soulful, heartfelt, irrational howl. A ration of grief keeps the less powerful alive but weak, divided from each other, blaming each other, more easily conquered.

To unscrew ourselves from the colonizer—or his replacement, risen from the ranks of the colonized, someone who looks like us but is more than willing to screw us—we must imagine solidarity with others who do not seem to be like us but whose sorrows we can and must share. As the powerful share their secrets in order to become even more powerful, the less powerful must share their griefs to prevent their one grievance from becoming a poison.

Unscrewing ourselves and undoing representation's curse goes by another name:

decolonization.

Decolonization tells us representation matters, but that we fool ourselves, curse ourselves, if we believe that representation is enough. We must also own the means of representation. And production. And that if colonization is always about the land and its violent appropriation, decolonization is about returning the land and dispelling the greatest euphemisms of all: "civilization" and "humanity." In whose names the massacres have been committed. In whose names the corpses have been disremembered.

Writers who see themselves only as individuals practicing art in isolation, who can only show but never tell, are less able to protest being cast as a representative and a voice for the voiceless, a cursed condition writers may bemoan to no end—

> no end unless writers see themselves as engaging
> with open secrets, refusing euphemisms, and being
> but one voice among many, including the dead
> with all their private secrets.

Now Má is one of the dead. She has taken most of her secrets with her and left me with a few.

The title of her story, "War Years," refutes how Americans and perhaps people the world over usually understand the lives of immigrants and refugees, burdened by private secrets as they chase the AMERICAN DREAM™. Understanding that the AMERICAN DREAM™ is the gold-plated brand name of American colonization, I understand Má's private secrets as shaped by the open secrets of wartime, a time in which I also live. A time in which everyone who inhabits the war machine lives.

Wartime compels me to grieve, to share in more than the one grief my fellow Americans give to me, or the one grief denied me by my fellow Vietnamese in the country of my birth. These Vietnamese, after freeing themselves from the French and the Americans, repeated the brutality of their colonizers on the defeated. This brutality must not be mentioned, which is why the government will not allow the television adaptation of *The Sympathizer* to be shot on Vietnamese land. The members of the Approval Committee say that the story is

not suitable with Vietnamese standpoint when building
the image of a soldier in the revolutionary cause of
national liberation and reunification.

The story will

definitely smear the image of the Vietnamese
army and people. Because the Vietnamese people's
war is righteous, and the Vietnamese people's
treatment of prisoners is always humane, never
using savage and cruel tortures as described.

But the very existence of the Approval Committee proves that there
exist open secrets that must be denied. Cannot be approved. Spoken
out loud.

What is the greater treachery: the nation that betrays its ideals
or the person who speaks of those betrayals?

The American Revolution, waged for the freedom of all (white men),
leads to perpetual wartime and the United States taking over la mission civilisatrice in Việt Nam from the French and replacing the City
of Light with the AMERICAN DREAM™.

The Vietnamese revolution, waged for Hồ Chí Minh's sacred slogan—

NOTHING IS MORE PRECIOUS THAN
INDEPENDENCE AND FREEDOM

meaning independence and freedom are
the most important things of all

—leads to a postrevolutionary society where
nothing is more precious than independence and freedom

> meaning independence and freedom are
> worth less than nothing.

I bet Groucho would guffaw at this pun I heard in Sài Gòn in 2004, although Karl might see nothing funny. Laughter could help the Vietnamese and the Americans recognize not only the idealism and valor of their holy revolutions but the inevitable absurdity and hypocrisy, because nothing is so holy that the human species will not fuck it up. Instead of laughing about this, a good number of Vietnamese and Americans remain intent on idolizing their revolutions, nursing their wars, and fixating on their griefs.

But for the colonized or their descendants—

as well as the descendants of their colonizers—

we must not only accept our grief but also share in the grief of others.

Má is dead, but even in my lament, my cri de coeur, my need to chia buồn, I recognize that her life and death are not unique to anyone except those who love her.

> Millions of others lived lives as
> difficult, if not worse. Millions lived
> lives as courageous, if not more so.

Understanding this does not diminish my mother in any way. If anything, I understand Má better when I see her story against the backdrop of history. And so my mother's death and her memory stay with me. In "War Years," I describe Má as she appeared to me in my childhood:

Whenever she spoke in English, her voice
took on a higher pitch, as if instead of
coming from inside her, the language was
outside, squeezing her by the throat.

Or is it my language

in my hands

around her neck

making her speak?

And yet when I remember Má, I hear her speak only the mother tongue, caressing me with the love and affection she bestowed on me throughout my childhood, giving me the confidence needed to portray her. And betray her.

Now Má is silenced, but her voice remains with me.

Her mouth is open and I

cannot close it.

the end of me

After my mother's death, Lan thinks we should have another child. Má, whom Lan has come to think of as her mother, would want that. As for Ba Má, they long ago ceased calling Lan their daughter-in-law, telling Lan that they love her as a daughter.

Three hundred fifty days
after Má's death,
Simone is born.

If Ellison was named
after one great writer,
Simone is named after

Simone de Beauvoir
and
Nina Simone

strong, heroic women who faced a violent world with
philosophy, politics, writing, music, and song.

I, who never wanted to be a father, am now a father twice. I, who always distrusted the feeling of being at home, now feel at home. With my children, with Lan, in our house.

This is, perhaps, the end of me as a writer.

Or this is the beginning of me as a different kind of writer.
Fatherhood, I think, has made me a better writer.
Opened me to the care of others, to the study
of my own emotions. Made me someone
who knows how to love and to give
of myself to Lan and the children.
Made me someone who

could write this book,
which I never
wanted to
write.

The house is full of books, a precondition of happiness. And justice.
Ellison and Simone each have their own libraries, the very Extravagance
and Necessity I wished I'd had in my childhood. In giving them books,
I want them to be whatever they want to be. No need to be doctors,
lawyers, or engineers. I want them to be happy!

i.e.,
that is,
not a writer.
Or at least not
a writer like me.

What if Ellison wants to be a professional video game player? Lan asks.

Dear reader—
I hesitated.

At nine, Ellison wrote these words when asked to describe himself at
school: friend, brother, eldest child, Vietnamese boy, comic lover, artist,
writer, gamer.

So perhaps he will be a professional video game player one day.

But he is also a writer and an artist because, when he was five, after
having been exposed every day and night to the picture books and comic
books I read him in the morning and evening, and after Lan and I took
him with us to an artists' colony and writers' residency—

where one can experience what socialism probably
feels like, or should feel like, which is to say a
kinder version of capitalism, with a wealth of
resources and choices, minus the exploitation,
greed, and soul-crushing alienation, as well as a
kinder version of communism, with a commitment
to justice and collectivity, minus the paranoia,
secret police, and reeducation camps,
allowing one to be creative, playful, and free

—he wrote and drew a book of his own. I posted it on Facebook. An editor asked if this was for real, and if so, could she publish it?

I asked:
Can I make money off my son?

And so *Chicken of the Sea* was born. In the tradition of *Lester the Cat*, this gallinaceous adventure is also about animal alienation:

A flock of chickens,
bored with rural life,
abandon the farm.
And become
pirates!

I could never have imagined such a story, just as I could never now imagine *Lester the Cat*. I have lost that part of childhood, but from Ellison and now Simone, I have learned to ask the most important question of all when it comes to writing, and the imagination, and justice:

Why not?

Why not write this book in this way?
Why not tell these sad stories and
these sob stories? And then
why not crack a joke?

These children have given me a great gift, and I would have neither of
them if it were not for Lan, who believed I could be a father. And so I
feel at home, and yet I should not feel at home, when my home stands
on the land of the Hahamog'na Tribe, when so many are without homes
and when much of the world is unsettled, when the philosopher and
critic and refugee Theodor Adorno wrote

          it is part of morality not to be at home in one's home.

But as the scholar and critic and exile Edward Said, one of his inheri-
tors, who always stood with Palestinian refugees in their perpetual
homelessness, also wrote

                    what is true of all exile is not that
                home and love of home are lost, but that
              loss is inherent in the very existence of both.

And so just for now,
just for the time that I have
with these children and Lan—
I want to create a home with them,
and even if it is a home in which I can never
forget the losses of my past and the losses
of my present, it can be a home to which
one day they will want to return.
Or so I hope. And if it is not
such a home, then one day

may they write their own memoir.

đất thánh việt nam

I think he looks like a writer. As well as a father and a grandfather. Perhaps in another life he could have been a writer or a musician. But in this life he is a struggler, a survivor, a refugee, a devotee, a retiree. A widower.

Perhaps the first time Ba knows of my writerly ambitions is when I give him a Vietnamese translation of "The Other Man." The short story is about a Vietnamese refugee, a young man, who arrives in San Francisco in 1975.

And experiences sex for the first time.

With a man.

Ba never mentions the story to me. Perhaps it embarrassed him. I don't ask if he has read it. Why make a man who has sacrificed so much for me read my words? I even forget to call my father when I learn the news that changes the direction of my writing career. Why brag to a man who has been through so much, who never received any prizes for his accomplishments? But the next day he calls me and says, his voice shaking with happiness,

> The villagers in Việt Nam called—
> you won the Pulitzer Prize!

Finally. I made my father proud.
All it took was winning a Pulitzer.
The joke is on AMERICA™.
Or the joke is on me.
Time will tell.

I do not tell my father what the novel is about, especially as it is designed to offend everyone (except the Pulitzer Prize committee). Judging from this plot summary in one-star reviews, this Not So Great American Novel succeeds:

⭐☆☆☆☆ **A Divided Soul**

⭐☆☆☆☆ **A painful slog with no payoff**

⭐☆☆☆☆ **a psychological exercise in becoming conscious**

⭐☆☆☆☆ **Absurdist and repulsive**

⭐☆☆☆☆ **Absolute literary Horse Shirt**

⭐☆☆☆☆ **Bafflingly overpraised.**

⭐☆☆☆☆ **Disgusting and Hard to Follow**

⭐☆☆☆☆ **WHAT THE HECK?**

⭐☆☆☆☆ **Dark & Depressing**

⭐☆☆☆☆ **Hated it**

⭐☆☆☆☆ **Hated the book**

⭐☆☆☆☆ **Hated this book**

⭐☆☆☆☆ **If you like torture read this book**

⭐☆☆☆☆ **Pure garbage**

⭐☆☆☆☆ **Putrid**

⭐☆☆☆☆ **This book was boring. Nothing actually happene**

⭐☆☆☆☆ **Save yourself, read literally ANYTHING else.**

⭐☆☆☆☆ **Good book!**

Or perhaps my father does know how offensive the novel might be. Some Vietnamese Americans refuse to read the book because it is told from the perspective of a communist spy, even if that spy is ambivalent about communism. But if my father has heard any rumors about his son being a communist-loving, anti-American writer, he says nothing to me. We protect each other with our silences.

> While I am away at college, a disturbed man shoots two police officers to death on Fifth and Santa Clara Street, outside the SàiGòn Mới. Ba Má crouch behind the counter during the gunfire. Only decades later do I learn about this, the worst incident of police death in San José's history. Ba Má never tell me because they do not want me to worry.

Even with death, Ba does not wish to concern me or anh Tùng. He has long ago invested in his burial plot and provided us the guest list, schedule, and songs for his last Mass. Death is hard, but Ba makes it as easy for us as possible.

He was slowing down before the pandemic, but the months of isolation drastically accelerate his decline. He is, more and more, still. More and more forgetful. But, from all appearances, content, or so anh Tùng thinks. He is still the responsible eldest son and older brother, visiting every weekend, overseeing my father's care, shielding me from the worst. Assenting to this story.

When I visit and sit with Ba on the brown leather sofa, bathed in the golden light of London, he clutches my arm, pushes dollars into my pocket to pay for my gas, weeps a little in gratitude for my presence, shames me with his gratitude. I kiss his forehead. I drive him to church, where I pretend, for his sake, that I still believe.

Once I take Ba on a drive in a rented Mustang convertible. He declines
my first invitation, but when I ask again, something has shifted inside
of him. Maybe he, too, remembers the one occasion when he and Má
found the time to take a drive, just for fun, along the Monterey pen-
insula, with me in the back seat. Now I drive him slowly on the roads
that wind through the hills on the edge of San José, the top down. He
wears sunglasses and a battered black fedora, looking cool in the sun
and the breeze. We drive as we have always driven, when he was the
driver and I was the passenger, in silence, no radio, no conversation. I
get lost in the hills.

> One night, decades ago, Má asked me to go for a drive, in
> the dark, just the two of us, after a long day at the SàiGòn
> Mới. I don't recall how old I was. This was the timeless span
> of my childhood and adolescence, when I was still a part of
> Má. Something had snapped between her and Ba. I could feel
> something unspoken, something tense. I was her excuse to
> get away. My window was rolled down, the wind was
> in my face. I did not know I was sad. I knew I was
> grateful. Má wanted to spend time with me.
> She said nothing, but left me with a gift.
> This memory.

Let's go home, Ba says.
I find my way home.
I give him this memory.

Of his own fading father in his final years, Philip Roth wrote:

> To be alive, to him, is to be made of memory—
> to him if a man's not made of memory,
> he's made of nothing.

Perhaps true. But nothing is something.
Neither exists without the Other,
presence in need of absence,
positive requiring negative.

From nothing we come, and
to nothing we return.

As refugees, we came from that
terrifying void between nations
where we were cast out.

Emerging from that void of the Other,
how were we refugees to be seen by the
people of nations except as
nothing?

I am no longer a refugee and do not want to be a refugee, but I am still
a refugee who identifies with these refugees, this nothingness from
which a different future can be imagined, a future different from the
AMERICAN DREAM™ and what it compels: the desire to be somebody,
to amount to something, realized in the mythology of immigrants and
the glitter of armored citizenship. But this AMERICAN DREAM™ that
is seemingly so positive has been and is dependent on negating the
existence of so many Others. On disremembering them.

Rather than be frightened by the void of the Other, we should see
the possibility of a new world in that void, one not based on borders,
on war machines, on nation-states, all of which inevitably produce
refugees. Rather than despising the refugees who come with nothing
and are nothing, we could identify with them and their nothingness,
a blankness from which we can imagine a world free from the forces

that negate all of us—exploitation and violence, fear and terror, greed and selfishness.

I do not expect my father to agree with my negative identification, my ingratitude, my belief that we must negate this negation. For all that he has forgotten, Ba believes something and someone awaits him. He can still recite, without hesitation, the Lord's Prayer. He has not forgotten a word.

When he visits Má at the Gate of Heaven Catholic Cemetery, where she lies just beyond the shade of a Himalayan cedar, he tells her he will soon be lying next to her.

> Linda ơi! he keens.
> Anh thương em, anh
> nhớ em nhiều lắm.

The sound disorients me. Never have I seen him cry, not even when his Ba Má died in a distant land.

> Linda ơi!

Ever since Má died, he tells me whenever I visit that he, too, is preparing to depart. Neither mournful nor fearful, he is giving me a final lesson, this time in grace. If I live a life of justice in my own way, as he has done in his way, will I receive the same blessing that he is receiving? The blessing of happy forgetting?

A man of exacting attention to detail who becomes anxious when details are not planned, he has left his imprint on me. At night I check the windows and doors to make sure they are locked, as he did. I turn off the lights in unoccupied rooms and scold my son about wasting electricity, as Ba lectured me. Sometimes I hear my knees crack, as I heard the crepitus of his knees in the hallway outside the closed door of my bedroom.

A stern man whom I feared and respect, Ba never told me, when it came to his home, to love it or leave it. And for all his strictness, he did not discourage me from being a scholar or writer. He displays my books above his bed, along with the condolences that Má's friends sent for her funeral, printed on banners that were attached to lavish floral arrangements. He does not ask me what stories my books tell, only how many copies have sold. The numbers make him laugh with satisfaction.

If he loved me more than I was aware, perhaps we have loved him more than he knows. Anh Tùng and I have worn him down with our incessant repetition of con thương Ba. Now he says Ba thương con without prompting, with genuine sentiment. To his grandchildren, to Ellison and Simone, he speaks in English:

I love you.

His part of the cemetery is full of Vietnamese names. A sign proclaims this quarter of the cemetery Đất Thánh Việt Nam.

The refugees have claimed this
Muwekma Ohlone land
for themselves.
And God.

I am a part of this country, too, through my life in the war machine. The war machine's patriots cheer the Hellfire assassination of a terrorist leader in Afghanistan, standing on his balcony. I remember the ten innocent family members killed the year before, incinerated and dismembered in their courtyard by another Hellfire missile launched

by a Predator drone in the final days of the American evacuation from
Kabul. American eyes in the sky mistake a father driving his car home
for a car bomber. A righteous strike, the chairman of the Joint Chiefs
of Staff proclaims. Until it isn't.

> Zemari Ahmadi, 43. Three of his children: Zamir, 20;
> Faisal, 16; Farzad, 10. His cousin Naser, 30. Three of
> his brother Romal's children: Arwin, 7; Benyamin, 6;
> Hayat, 2. And two three-year-old girls, Malika and
> Somaya.

> The father, Zemari Ahmadi,
> worked for the Americans.

Part of me believes what
Aimé Césaire wrote in 1955:

> The hour of the barbarian is at hand. The modern barbarian.
> The American hour. Violence, excess, waste, mercantilism,
> bluff, gregariousness, stupidity, vulgarity, disorder.

It has been a long hour.
But part of me also believes what
James Baldwin wrote that same year:

> I love America more than any other country
> in the world and, exactly for this reason,
> I insist on the right to criticize her
> perpetually.

Ba Má never criticized this country. They are the grateful refugees
AMERICA™ wants. When it comes to justice, they place their faith in
God. Perhaps because I do not believe in this Catholic God, I find it

easy not to believe in the Greatest Country on Earth, unless one admits
that the greatness is inseparable from the imperialism, the conquest,
the slavery, the violence. Like many other nations, including the one
where I was born, AMERICA™ is a country of brutality and beauty, of
horror and hope. We can realize that beauty and hope only if we con-
front the brutality and the horror, only if we de-militarize, de-capitalize,
de-imperialize, de-colonize, de-carbonize. Only then might we reach
an AMERICA™ as (im)possible, as beautiful, as Ba Má's Heaven. Only
then will we see an end to refugees.

In the months after Má's death and in the great infection's early stages,
Ba came with me to visit Má. Now, I usually visit Má by myself. I enjoy
the solitude, sweeping her headstone and arranging the flowers. Geese
and deer will eat them before the dawn. No one is present to judge
my mother tongue here. I thank Má in that language for her sacrifice,
devotion, and love. I apologize for telling on her and ask for her understanding and forgiveness. I promise to tell her story to my son and
daughter, whose roots in this country are deep in this earth with Má.
And with Ba, too, eventually.

When I ask Ba if he remembers saying we are Americans now, he
laughs and shakes his head. But when I ask if he wants to be buried
in Việt Nam, he also shakes his head. This is his land now, next to Má.
But what to call this place if it is not their homeland?

Their chosen land.
Their settled land.
Their refuge.

Even so, the land is only a repository for their bodies. Their souls are
another matter. Má's headstone says that God has called her home. This
Vietnamese holy land of the cemetery, as well as the land where they
were born, is only temporary. Perhaps their conviction that the eternal

home was what really mattered helped Ba Má survive the homelessness of being refugees, just as my real home—my writing—aids me.

As for my quê, I have yet to return. That future is still to come. Perhaps
after Ba passes on. Perhaps if the members of the Approval Committee allow it. But perhaps not, because the Montagnards may see me as
just another colonizer. And even if I do return to Buôn Ma Thuột, my
origin is already lost. The forgotten beginning, the (adopted) sister, the
seed of memory, the very name, all irrevocably displaced. This, too, is
a war story, a long-delayed one, the unexploded ordnance of the past,
a mine buried in the mind. Perhaps one day I will probe and uncover
it. Perhaps one day I will write that war story even if I am sick of war
stories, because writing is the only way I know how to fight. And writing is the only way I know how to grieve.

Má's fight is over. She no longer has to go on. When I am ready to
depart, I sometimes lie down beside Má on the sheet of grass
and look up at the sky's blue screen. And there, resting
on the plot awaiting Ba, aware of how much I have
forgotten and of how I, too, will one
day be made of nothing,
I try to re member
our happy days.

for Ba
for Joseph Thanh Nguyen
for Nguyễn Ngọc Thanh
for my father

1933–

acknowledgments

This book evolved from a series of interviews and lectures that I gave from 2015 to 2022, as well as numerous essays I published during that time. The publications and venues are far too numerous to list, but I am deeply grateful to all the editors and interviewers who gave me the chance to share and develop my views, as well as all the institutions that invited me to speak. I am also deeply appreciative for the work of all those who arranged many of these opportunities: Trinity Ray, Kevin Mills, Ryan Barker, and Ariel Lewiton of the Tuesday Agency, as well as Deb Seager and John Mark Boling, my publicists at Grove Press.

I am lucky that Zoë Ruiz agreed to collect and read these interviews, lectures, and essays—altogether totaling in the hundreds—from which she produced a compilation of highlights and themes that formed the backbone of the first draft. Some of the ideas in that draft and its later revisions came from a number of graduate seminars I taught on war and memory, decolonization, and critical refugee studies. My students were valuable interlocutors who challenged me to articulate my ideas with greater clarity and depth. Not least, they made me do the reading.

I offered these seminars at the University of Southern California, which also granted research funds that were crucial to the writing of this book, including support for organizing a manuscript workshop. During this workshop of an interim draft, I benefitted greatly from critical and generous commentary by Gina Apostol, Cathy Park Hong, and Laila Lalami, who came up with the title of this book. Many of my academic colleagues also provided feedback on the manuscript-in-progress: Mei-ling Cheng, Adrian De Leon, Evyn Lê Espiritu Gandhi, Janet Hoskins, Annette Kim, Nancy Lutkehaus, Natalia Molina, Lydie Moudileno, Chris Muniz, Catherine Nguyen, Peter Redfield, and Ernest J. Wilson III. The book is much better for their insights.

My research assistant Jenny Hoang also read that draft, and, just as importantly, oversaw much of the research and administrative support I needed during the writing of the book. She was preceded and followed in that endeavor by, respectively, Rebekah Park and Titi Nguyen, whose collective managerial skill enabled me to concentrate on writing. They were helped by a team of undergraduate assistants whose enthusiasm and energy were uplifting: Christine Nguyen, Faithe Nguyen, Tommy Nguyen, Ashley Tran, and Jordan Trinh. Kathleen Hoang in particular was crucial to putting together the notes for this volume. I am forever indebted to this team for their aid.

The writer Nguyễn Phan Quế Mai helpfully clarified a few issues in Vietnamese language and culture for me. Journalist Sharon Simonson saved me a great deal of time by delving into San José's archives to figure out what happened to the SàiGòn Mới. My return to Fort Indiantown Gap was facilitated by Captain Travis Mueller and the fort's museum staff, Stephanie Olsen and Charlie Oellig, while Brad Rhen of the Pennsylvania National Guard was kind enough to document the visit with photos and an article. Superfan and friend Adiaha Spinks-Franklin read a portion of the final manuscript when I most needed it, and continually inspired me with her passionate commitment to multiracial, decolonial justice.

Writers H'Rina de Troy and Y-Danair Niehrah answered my questions about Montagnard history, politics, and culture and prompted me to reflect on the role my family played in the Central Highlands. Various members of the Vietnam Studies Group also responded to my query about Vietnamese Catholic resettlement in that region: Bradley Camp Davis, Diane Fox, Erik Harms, Lê Xuân Hy, Edward G. Miller, Nhu Miller, Michael Montesano, Paul Mooney, Phan Quang Anh, Oscar Salemink, Hue Tam Ho Tai, Philip Taylor, and Simon Toner. I thank them all for sharing their expertise, although my interpretation of Vietnamese Catholic resettlement is my own.

As always, my agents Nat Sobel and Judith Weber provided wise guidance and encouragement. I have also been able to count on the continuing support and confidence of Grove Press, beginning with my wonderful publisher Morgan Entrekin and extending to Emily Burns and Judy Hottensen. Norman E. Tuttle, Sal Destro, Gretchen Mergenthaler, and Kelly Winton did great work in designing this book and its cover. And while I owe Nancy Tan, Kathryn Jergovich, and Julia Berner-Tobin many thanks for proofreading the manuscript, any errors that remain are mine. Far from last, my brilliant editor, Peter Blackstock, made this book—as well as all my other Grove books—much better with his magical ability to suggest judicious cuts and revisions while also encouraging me to go on.

Going on was made much easier due to several years of transformative and career-changing fellowship support from the MacArthur Foundation. Its financial generosity allowed me both to write and to spend time with my family, which in the end proved as important as the act of writing itself. My children, Ellison and Simone, have taught me as much as I have taught them (or so I hope). And my partner and first reader, Lan Duong, fellow refugee, scholar, writer, and child of San José, California, brought love and a shared life's understanding to this book. She gave me the key that unlocked the final pages and brought this book to a close.

Finally, I am grateful to my brother, anh Tùng. The one who has always looked out for me, the only one who knows what we both went through, the one who knew Ba Má as well as I did, he gave the final permission for this story to be told.

notes

6   *Cluttered rooms. Bare lives:* Fae Myenne Ng, *Bone* (New York: HarperCollins, 1994), 17.

9   *It's a dumb song:* "Dionne Warwick Returns to San Jose, Named City's 'Ambassador of Goodwill,'" NBC Bay Area, August 1, 2014, https://www.nbcbayarea.com/news/local/dionne-warwick-returns-to-san-jose-to-be-named-citys-ambassador-of-goodwill/67890/.

10 *"Pentagon Admits to Civilian Casualties":* Thomas Gibbons-Neff, "Pentagon Admits to Civilian Casualties in Somalia for a Third Time," *New York Times,* July 28, 2020, https://www.nytimes.com/2020/07/28/world/africa/pentagon-somalia-civilian-casualties.html.

10 *targeting members of the Shabab:* Ibid.

10 *reported as a terrorist:* Jared Szuba, "New Evidence US Airstrike Killed Teenage Girl in Somalia, Report Says," *Defense Post,* April 1, 2020, https://www.thedefensepost.com/2020/04/01/somalia-amnesty-report-civilian-killed/.

10 *provides responsive, cost-effective engineering:* "Small Glide Munition—GBU-69/B Fact Sheet," Dynetics Corporate Communications, 2017, https://www.dynetics.com/_files/strike-systems/Dynetics%20SGM.pdf.

12 *miniature department store:* "Vietnamese Student Excels Despite Barriers," Aleta Watson, *San José Mercury,* June 25, 1981, 25.

24   *abused at the Polish border:* Jeffrey Gettleman and Monika Pronczuk, "Two Refu-
      gees, Both on Poland's Border. But Worlds Apart," *New York Times*, March 14,
      2022, https://www.nytimes.com/2022/03/14/world/europe/ukraine-refugees
      -poland-belarus.html; Monika Pronczuk and Ruth Maclean, "Africans Say
      Ukrainian Authorities Hindered Them from Fleeing," *New York Times*, March
      1, 2022, https://www.nytimes.com/2022/03/01/world/europe/ukraine-refugee
      -discrimination.html.

24   *white Ukrainians pass on through:* Miriam Jordan, Zolan Kanno-Youngs,
      and Michael D. Shear, "United States Will Welcome up to 100,000 Ukrai-
      nian Refugees," *New York Times*, March 24, 2022, https://www.nytimes
      .com/2022/03/24/us/ukrainian-refugees-biden.html; Miriam Jordan, "Ukrai-
      nians Are Trickling into the U.S. to Warm Welcomes," *New York Times*, March
      19, 2022, https://www.nytimes.com/2022/03/19/us/ukrainian-refugees
      -sponsors-us.html; Miriam Jordan, "Thousands of Migrants Have Been Wait-
      ing for Months to Enter U.S.," *New York Times*, May 19, 2022, https://www
      .nytimes.com/2022/05/19/us/migrants-border-title-42.html.

25   *smaller than Angola:* National population rankings come from Worldometer,
      https://www.worldometers.info/world-population/population-by-country/,
      accessed December 3, 2022. The forcibly displaced population has grown
      from about sixty-six million people, and the refugee population from about
      twenty-two million people, since I began consulting UNHCR figures in
      2016, so the rankings used here may be out of date by the time of this
      book's publication.

25   *The countries sending forth or forcing out:* "Refugee Data Finder," UNHCR,
      https://www.unhcr.org/refugee-statistics/.

26   *We were told to forget:* Hannah Arendt, "We Refugees," *Menorah* 31, no. 1
      (1943): 69–77.

27   *Buôn Ma Thuột is closer to Buôn Ama Thuột:* Richard Gessert pointed
      me to the Ê Đê etymology of the city's name, also found here: https://
      en.wiktionary.org/wiki/Buôn_Ma_Thuột#Vietnamese. Email to the author,
      January 13, 2021.

27   *padded barefoot:* "Ban Me Thuot before the Shells Fell: Sleepy, Charming
      Highlands Town," *New York Times*, March 12, 1975, https://www.nytimes

.com/1975/03/12/archives/ban-me-thuot-before-the-shells-fell-sleepy-charming-highlands-town.html.

28 *almost white but not quite:* This is a paraphrase of the scholar Homi Bhabha's *"almost the same but not quite. . . . Almost the same but not white"* in his essay "Of Mimicry and Man: The Ambivalence of Colonial Discourse," *October* 28 (Spring 1984): 125–33.

32 *diaspora of more than five million people:* "Overseas Vietnamese an Important Pillar in Việt Nam's Foreign Relations: Deputy PM," *Việt Nam News*, November 28, 2020, https://vietnamnews.vn/society/813937/overseas-vietnamese-an-important-pillar-in-viet-nams-foreign-relations-deputy-pm.html.

33 *828,000 square miles for $15 million:* "Lousiana Purchase Treaty (1803)," accessed January 11, 2022, https://www.archives.gov/milestone-documents/louisiana-purchase-treaty.

34 *Each barracks can house sixty soldiers:* Major General Frank H. Somer, Jr., *Back at the Gap: The History of Fort Indiantown Gap* (Fort Indiantown Gap: Pennsylvania National Guard Military Museum, 2009), 98.

35 *You got all the Vietnamese:* Richard Pryor, "New Niggers," . . . *Is It Something I Said?*, Reprise Records, 1975. Also available on YouTube, https://youtube/umpnq7QF3tc.

39 *If something is to stay:* Friedrich Nietzsche, "On the Genealogy of Morals," in *Basic Writings of Nietzsche*, trans. and ed. Walter Kaufmann (New York: Modern Library, 2000), 497.

40 *their transport plane crashes in Sài Gòn:* Rachel Martin, "Remembering the Doomed First Flight of Operation Babylift," NPR, April 26, 2015, https://www.npr.org/2015/04/26/402208267/remembering-the-doomed-first-flight-of-operation-babylift.

42 *the majority of Americans do not want:* Kevin Knodell, "America's Troubled, Contradictory Refugee Legacy," Medium, February 27, 2017, https://medium.com/war-is-boring/americas-troubled-contradictory-refugee-legacy-15c1b23c3a8.

42 *It's a terrifying device:* Andrew Lam, "Bomb Lady: Vietnamese American Makes Tools for War on Terror," Pacific News Service, December 8, 2003, https://tinyurl.com/3wyc5yxe.

43   *58 percent of the nail salon industry:* P. Sharma et al., *Nail Files: A Study of Nail Salon Workers and Industry in the United States,* UCLA Labor Center and California Healthy Nail Salon Collaborative, November 2018, https://www.labor.ucla.edu/wp-content/uploads/2018/11/NAILFILES_FINAL.pdf. Of the 79 percent of all nail salon workers who are foreign-born, 74 percent are Vietnamese, for a total of 58 percent.

44   *you will never be ignored again:* "FULL TEXT: President Donald Trump's Inauguration Speech," ABC News, January 20, 2017, http://abcn.ws/2jgVjAc.

44   *warehouses them in cages:* Nick Miroff, "'Kids in cages': It's true that Obama built the cages at the border. But Trump's 'zero tolerance' immigration policy had no precedent," *Washington Post,* October 23, 2020, https://www.washingtonpost.com/immigration/kids-in-cages-debate-trump-obama/2020/10/23/8ff96f3c-1532 -11eb-82af-864652063d61_story.html.

48   *all happy families are alike:* Leo Tolstoy, *Anna Karenina,* trans. Constance Garnett (New York: Simon & Schuster, 2010), 5.

49   *A person's home is his or her castle:* The quotations are from an August 1975 edition of *Đất Lành,* archived at the Pennsylvania National Guard Military Museum, Fort Indiantown Gap, Annville, PA.

56   *being or appearing less than perfect:* erin Khuê Ninh, *Passing for Perfect: College Impostors and Other Model Minorities* (Philadelphia: Temple University Press, 2021).

57   *"Vietnamese student excels despite barriers":* Aleta Watson, "Vietnamese student excels despite barriers," *San José Mercury,* June 25, 1981, 25.

57   *"Tongue Win":* Richard Hawkins, "Vive la Vengeance!" *San Jose High School Herald,* February 26, 1982.

58   *minor feelings:* Cathy Park Hong, *Minor Feelings: An Asian American Reckoning* (New York: One World, 2020).

62   *screens the movie in the White House:* Allyson Hobbs, "A Hundred Years Later, 'The Birth of a Nation' Hasn't Gone Away," *New Yorker,* December 13, 2015, https://www.newyorker.com/culture/culture-desk/hundred-years-later-birth -nation-hasnt-gone-away.

62   *the U.S. Marine Corps shows the movie:* Anthony Swofford, *Jarhead: A Marine's Chronicle of the Gulf War and Other Battles* (New York: Scribner, 2003), 6.

65   *But a work of art that condemns racism:* Chinua Achebe, "An Image of Africa: Racism in Conrad's *Heart of Darkness,*" *Massachusetts Review* 57, no. 1 (Spring 2016): 14–27.

65   *The white male actor who plays:* "Full Cast & Crew: *Apocalypse Now* (1979)," accessed January 13, 2023, https://m.imdb.com/title/tt0078788/fullcredits/cast.

70   *hated Vietnamese immigrants:* "Gunman 'Hated' Vietnamese," *Prescott Courier,* January 19, 1989, https://tinyurl.com/3kr7j5zk.

70   *native-born Americans:* Ibid.

70   *The damn Hindus:* Taylor Weik, "The Cleveland Elementary School Shooting in Stockton Was Forgotten by History," *Teen Vogue,* May 28, 2022, https://www.teenvogue.com/story/cleveland-elementary-school-shooting.

75   *four hundred years in a Spanish convent:* Jessica Hagedorn, *Dogeaters: A Play about the Philippines* (New York: Theatre Communications Group, 2003), Act One, Scene 2, p. 2.

75   *Mine eyes have seen:* Twain's "The Battle Hymn of the Republic (Brought Down to Date)," c. 1900, was not published in his lifetime. From Mark Twain, *Mark Twain's Civil War,* ed. David Rachels (Lexington: University Press of Kentucky, 2010), 232.

77   *2.2 million people:* Abby Budiman, "Vietnamese Population in the U.S., 2000–2019," *Pew Research,* April 29, 2021, https://www.pewresearch.org/social-trends/fact-sheet/asian-americans-vietnamese-in-the-u-s-fact-sheet/.

77   *2.7 million people:* "Military Health History Pocket Card: Vietnam," U.S. Department of Veterans Affairs, accessed December 13, 2022, https://www.va.gov/oaa/pocketcard/m-vietnam.asp.

78–79   *White folks tired of our ass, too:* Richard Pryor, "New Niggers," . . . Is It Something I Said?, Reprise Records, 1975. Also available on YouTube, https://youtube/umpnq7QF3tc.

79   *tens of thousands of Hmong:* Not surprisingly, Hmong casualty statistics are not precise or agreed on. The Minnesota Historical Society says that between 30,000 and 40,000 Hmong died in combat but provides no source:

"Hmong Timeline," *Minnesota Historical Society*, https://www.mnhs.org /hmong/hmong-timeline. The historian Sucheng Chan says, "According to one estimate, 25 percent of the Hmong who enlisted were killed. According to another estimate, seventeen thousand Hmong troops and fifty thousand Hmong civilians perished during the war," in *Hmong Means Free: Life in Laos and America* (Philadelphia: Temple University Press, 1994), 40.

79   *nine minutes and twenty-nine seconds:* Nicholas Bogel-Burroughs, "Prosecutors Say Derek Chauvin Knelt on George Floyd for 9 Minutes 29 Seconds, Longer Than Initially Reported," *New York Times*, March 20, 2021, https://www .nytimes.com/2021/03/30/us/derek-chauvin-george-floyd-kneel-9-minutes -29-seconds.html.

80   *The officer carries with him:* Ta-Nehisi Coates, *Between the World and Me* (New York: Spiegel & Grau, 2015), 103.

80   *28.3 percent for the Hmong:* "U.S. Hmong Population Living in Poverty, 2015," Pew Research Center, September 8, 2017, https://www.pewresearch.org /social-trends/chart/u-s-hmong-population-living-in-poverty/.

81   *It is not because the Indo-Chinese:* The French original is "Ce n'est pas parce que l'Indochinois a découvert une culture propre qu'il s'est révolté. C'est parce que « tout simplement » il lui devenait, à plus d'un titre, impossible de respirer," in Frantz Fanon, *Peau noire, masques blancs* (Paris: Éditions du Seuil, 1952), 183.

81   *An all-white jury acquits:* Brandt Williams, "Fong Lee's Family Angered by Verdict," MPR News, May 28, 2009, https://www.mprnews.org/story /2009/05/28/fong-lees-family-angered-by-verdict.

81   *They were the loudest voices:* Jessica Lussenhop, "George Floyd Death: 'The Same Happened to My Son,'" BBC News, June 15, 2020, https://www.bbc .com/news/world-us-canada-53023703.

82   *Go live with yourself:* Mai Der Vang, "In the Year of Permutations," poets.org, 2020, https://poets.org/poem/year-permutations.

82   *The American Dream will not save us:* Mai Der Vang, "To Hmong Americans, on Racial Justice and Patriarchy," *Margins*, June 15, 2020, https://aaww .org /to-the-hmong-community-on-racial-justice-and-patriarchy-mai-der -vang/.

82 *celebration of genocide:* Viet Thanh Nguyen, "Feeling Conflicted on Thanksgiving," *New York Times*, November 14, 2017, https://www.nytimes.com/2017/11/14/dining/viet-thanh-nguyen-thanksgiving.html.

83 *Fitzgerald says that the test:* F. Scott Fitzgerald, "The Crack-Up," *Esquire*, February, March, and April 1936. Reprinted in *Esquire*, March 7, 2017, https://www.esquire.com/lifestyle/a4310/the-crack-up/.

84 *In 1621, colonists invited Massasoit:* Tommy Orange, *There There* (New York: Knopf, 2018), 8.

84 *Gratitude is a fact of a refugee's inner life:* Dina Nayeri, *The Ungrateful Refugee: What Immigrants Never Tell You* (New York: Catapult, 2019), 344.

85 *the famous national epic:* Albert Memmi, *The Colonizer and the Colonized*, trans. Howard Greenfeld (Boston: Beacon Press, 1965), 149.

87 *Diem crushed the BAJARAKA movement:* All quotations attributed to BAJARAKA are from Degar Foundation, accessed November 30, 2022, http://www.degarfoundation.org/bajaraka.html.

88 *outsiders to the place:* "Ban Me Thuot before the Shells Fell."

91 *the Montagnards cheered for the Indians:* Gerald C. Hickey, *Window on a War: An Anthropologist in the Vietnam Conflict* (Lubbock: Texas Tech University Press, 2002), 62.

91 *This is our offspring:* Marilyn B. Young, *The Vietnam Wars, 1945–1990* (New York: HarperCollins, 1991), 59.

93 *The only good Indian is a dead Indian:* Dee Brown, *Bury My Heart at Wounded Knee: An Indian History of the American West* (New York: Holt, Rinehart & Winston, 1970), 170–72.

93 *The only good gook is a dead gook:* Richard Slotkin, *The Fatal Environment: The Myth of the Frontier in the Age of Industrialization, 1800–1890* (Norman: University of Oklahoma Press, 1998), 17.

93 *I don't go so far as to think:* Hermann Hagedorn, *Roosevelt in the Bad Lands* (New York: Houghton Mifflin Company, 1921), 355.

93 *I heard a story about:* Han Kang, *Human Acts*, trans. Deborah Smith (New York: Hogarth, 2017), 140.

94   *American-backed angel of genocide:* Don Mee Choi, *DMZ Colony* (Seattle: Wave
     Books, 2020), 121.

94   *"gook" is a variation of "goo-goo":* David Roediger, "Gook: The Short History
     of an Americanism," *Monthly Review* 43, no. 10 (March 1992): http://www
     .davidroediger.org/articles/gook-the-short-history-of-americanism.html.

95   *in the end we felt betrayed:* Dave Philipps, "'In the End We Felt Betrayed':
     Vietnamese Veterans See Echoes in Afghanistan," *New York Times*, July 7,
     2021, https://www.nytimes.com/2021/07/07/us/vietnam-war-veterans-us
     -afghanistan.html.

96   *I am an American citizen now:* Ibid.

97   *The memory stain attaches itself:* Theresa Hak Kyung Cha, *Dictee* (Berkeley:
     Third Woman Press, 1995), 131.

109 *Either of these literary allusions:* Graham Greene, *The Quiet American* (Lon-
     don: Heinemann, 1955) and Eugene Burdick and William Lederer, *The Ugly
     American* (New York: Norton, 1958).

113 *in English translation, but not in Vietnamese:* Bảo Ninh, *Hà Nội at Midnight*
     (Lubbock: Texas Tech University Press, 2023).

113 *imprisoned by the government:* Richard C. Paddock, "The Jailed Activist Left
     a Letter Behind. The Message: Keep Fighting," *New York Times*, October 14,
     2020, https://www.nytimes.com/2020/10/14/world/asia/vietnam-pham-doan
     -trang-arrest.html; "2022 Midyear Report on Vietnam's Political Prisoners,"
     88 Project for Free Speech in Vietnam, July 14, 2022, https://the88project
     .org/2022-midyear-report-on-vietnams-political-prisoners/.

117 *"Chinese Virus":* Laura Kurtzman, "Trump's 'Chinese Virus' Tweet Linked
     to Rise of Anti-Asian Hashtags on Twitter," University of California San
     Francisco, March 18, 2021, https://www.ucsf.edu/news/2021/03/420081
     /trumps-chinese-virus-tweet-linked-rise-anti-asian-hashtags-twitter.

117 *the state-sanctioned or extralegal production:* Ruth Wilson Gilmore, *Golden
     Gulag: Prisons, Surplus, Crisis, and Opposition in Globalizing California* (Berke-
     ley: University of California Press, 2007), 28.

119 *The burning of San José's Chinatown:* Kimmy Yam, "San Jose Formally Apolo-
     gizes for the Arson of Its Chinatown More Than a Century Ago," NBC

News, September 30, 2021, https://www.nbcnews.com/news/asian-america/san-jose-formally-apologizes-arson-chinatown-century-ago-rcna2478.

119   *the Chinese virus is also the Kung Flu:* David Nakamura, "With 'Kung Flu,' Trump Sparks Backlash over Racist Language—and a Rallying Cry for Supporters," *Washington Post*, June 24, 2020, https://www.washingtonpost.com/politics/with-kung-flu-trump-sparks-backlash-over-racist-language-and-a-rallying-cry-for-supporters/2020/06/24/485d151e-b620-11ea-aca5-ebb63d27e1ff_story.html.

119   *Anti-Asian violence rises:* Suyin Haynes, "'This Isn't Just a Problem for North America.' The Atlanta Shooting Highlights the Painful Reality of Rising Anti-Asian Violence around the World," *Time*, March 18, 2021, https://time.com/5947862/anti-asian-attacks-rising-worldwide/.

119   *#JeNeSuisPasUnVirus:* Vincent Coste and Sandrine Amiel, "Coronavirus: France Faces 'Epidemic' of Anti-Asian Racism," EuroNews, March 2, 2020, https://www.euronews.com/my-europe/2020/02/03/coronavirus-france-faces-epidemic-of-anti-asian-racism.

120   *We don't have coronavirus:* Cathy Park Hong, "The Slur I Never Expected to Hear in 2020," *New York Times Magazine*, April 12, 2020, https://www.nytimes.com/2020/04/12/magazine/asian-american-discrimination-coronavirus.html.

122   *In Torreón, Mexico:* Leo M. Dambourges Jacques, "The Chinese Massacre in Torreon (Coahuila) in 1911," *Arizona and the West* 16, no. 3 (Autumn 1974): 233–46.

122   *In downtown Los Angeles in 1871:* Kelly Wallace, "Forgotten Los Angeles History: The Chinese Massacre of 1871," Los Angeles Public Library, May 19, 2017, https://www.lapl.org/collections-resources/blogs/lapl/chinese-massacre-1871.

122   *the Gentlemen's Agreement of 1907:* Andrew Glass, "Theodore Roosevelt Targets Japanese Immigration, Feb. 20, 1907," This Day in Politics, *Politico*, February 20, 2019, https://www.politico.com/story/2019/02/20/theodore-roosevelt-targets-japanese-immigration-feb-20-1907-1173456.

122   *the beatings of Filipino workers:* Dennis Arguelles, "Remembering the Manongs and Story of the Filipino Farm Worker Movement," National Parks Conservation Association, May 25, 2017, https://www.npca.org/articles/1555-remembering -the-manongs-and-story-of-the-filipino-farm-worker-movement.

122   **NO DOGS AND NO FILIPINOS ALLOWED:** Deborah Kong, "Filipinos Fight to Save Calif. Enclaves," *Huron Daily Tribune*, December 24, 2002, https:// www.michigansthumb.com/news/article/Filipinos-Fight-to-Save-Calif -Enclaves-7339571.php.

123   *insultingly low prices:* Natasha Varner, "Sold, Damaged, Stolen, Gone: Japanese American Property Loss during WWII," Densho, April 4, 2017, https:// densho.org/catalyst/sold-damaged-stolen-gone-japanese-american-property -loss-wwii/.

123   *the Ku Klux Klan attacks on Vietnamese:* Laura Smith, "The War between Vietnamese Fishermen and the KKK Signaled a New Type of White Supremacy," Timeline, November 6, 2017, https://timeline.com/kkk-vietnamese-fishermen -beam-43730353df06.

123   *the social downgrading of educated Korean immigrants:* Sandy Banks, "Korean Merchants, Black Customers—Tensions Grow," *Los Angeles Times*, April 15, 1985, https://www.latimes.com/archives/la-xpm-1985-04-15-me-14008-story .html.

123   *cordons off Koreatown and lets it be burned:* Kyung Lah, "The LA Riots Were a Rude Awakening for Korean-Americans," CNN, April 29, 2017, https://www .cnn.com/2017/04/28/us/la-riots-korean-americans.

123   *Riot, says Martin Luther King Jr.:* Martin Luther King Jr., "The Other America," Grosse Pointe South High School, March 14, 1968, Grosse Pointe, MI. Transcript available at Grosse Pointe Historical Society, https://www.gphistorical .org/mlk/mlkspeech/.

130   *kill his family and himself:* Don Pendleton, *War against the Mafia*, The Executioner (New York: Pinnacle Books, 1969).

133   *I reached down to the floor:* David J. Regan, *Mourning Glory: The Making of a Marine* (Old Greenwich, CT: Devin-Adair Company, 1981), 72.

134   *It's Vietnam. It is very dangerous:* Andrew Kaczynski, "Trump, Compar-
      ing Sex to Vietnam, Said in 1998 He Should Receive the Congressional
      Medal of Honor," CNN Business, October 14, 2016, https://money.cnn
      .com/2016/10/14/media/trump-stern-vietnam-stds/index.html.

134   *an enduring myth in the American imagination:* This argument is made by
      H. Bruce Franklin, *MIA; or, Mythmaking in America* (New Brunswick, NJ:
      Rutgers University Press, 1993).

135   *its characters closely resemble:* Comment on the author's now-deleted Facebook
      author page by Paj Huab Hawj, June 2020.

144   *The Number of purely white People:* Benjamin Franklin, "Observations Concern-
      ing the Increase of Mankind, Peopling of Countries, etc.," 1751, http://www
      .columbia.edu/~lmg21/ash3002y/earlyac99/documents/observations.html.

144   *Why should Pennsylvania:* Ibid.

147   *prevent births within the group:* "Definitions: Genocide," United Nations Of-
      fice on Genocide Prevention and the Responsibility to Protect, https://www
      .un.org/en/genocideprevention/genocide.shtml.

148   *really good at killing people:* Peter Hamby, "Review: 'Double Down,' on the 2012
      Election, by Mark Halperin and John Heilemann," *Washington Post*, November
      1, 2013, https://www.washingtonpost.com/opinions/review-double-down-on-the
      -2012-election-by-mark-halperin-and-john-heilemann/2013/11/01/8bf4f050
      -3fdd-11e3-a751-f032898f2dbc_story.html.

154   *Paris police violently break up an encampment:* Aurelien Breeden, "Outcry in
      France after Police Clear Paris Migrant Camp," *New York Times*, November
      24, 2020, https://www.nytimes.com/2020/11/24/world/europe/police-paris
      -migrant-camp.html.

155   *The people we're talking about:* Associated Press, "Calling Katrina Survivors
      'Refugees' Stirs Debate," NBC News, September 6, 2005, https://www
      .nbcnews.com/id/wbna9232071.

155   *It is racist to call American citizens:* Ibid.

155   *To see them as refugees:* Joseph Darda, *How White Men Won the Culture Wars:
      A History of Veteran America* (Berkeley: University of California Press, 2021),
      161.

156   *to Europe colonialist procedures:* Aimé Césaire, *Discourse on Colonialism*, trans. Joan Pinkham (New York: Monthly Review Press, 1972), 14–15. The French original is "à l'Europe des procédés colonialistes dont ne relevaient jusqu'ici que les Arabes d'Algérie, les coolies de l'Inde et les nègres d'Afrique," from *Discours sur le colonialisme* (Paris: Éditions Présence Africaine, 1955), 88.

160   *willed to her by an aunt:* Virginia Woolf, *A Room of One's Own* (West Sussex: John Wiley & Sons), 28.

162   *One elderly Vietnamese refugee:* Anh Do, "Trump Widens a Generation Gap in Vietnamese Community: Older Hard-Liners vs. Liberal Youths," *Los Angeles Times*, February 19, 2017, https://www.latimes.com/local/california/la-me -ln-viet-refugees-20170219-story.html.

164   *did not want to accept Southeast Asian refugees:* Drew Desilver, "U.S. Pub-lic Seldom Has Welcomed Refugees into Country," Pew Research Center, November 19, 2015, https://www.pewresearch.org/fact-tank/2015/11/19 /u-s-public-seldom-has-welcomed-refugees-into-country/.

164   *As one immigrant put it:* My unreliable memory tells me that I saw the come-dian Yakov Smirnoff tell this joke in a video clip, which I can no longer find. I apologize to whoever might have said this joke for not giving them due credit.

171   *giving voice to the previously voiceless:* Philip Caputo, review of *The Sympathizer*, by Viet Thanh Nguyen, *New York Times*, April 2, 2015, https://www.nytimes .com/2015/04/05/books/review/the-sympathizer-by-viet-thanh-nguyen.html.

172   *As Arundhati Roy says:* Arundhati Roy, "Peace & the New Corporate Libera-tion Theology," City of Sydney Peace Prize Lecture, Seymour Centre, Sydney, November 3, 2004 (Sydney: Centre for Peace and Conflict Studies, University of Sydney, 2004), 1.

172   *The East is a career:* From Benjamin Disraeli's novel *Tancred*, originally pub-lished in 1847. The quotation is found on p. 141 of the 1881 edition published by Longmans, Green & Co.

173   *what we cannot not want:* Sara Danius and Stefan Jonsson, "An Interview with Gayatri Chakravorty Spivak," *boundary 2* 20, no. 2 (Summer 1993): 24–50.

174   *Harvard, where scientists invented napalm:* Robert M. Neer, *Napalm: An American Biography* (Cambridge, MA: Belknap Press of Harvard University Press, 2015).

174   *Even Winston Churchill called napalm:* "What Is Napalm and Is It Still Used in Warfare?," Forces.net, August 2, 2021, https://www.forces.net /technology/weapons-and-kit/what-napalm-and-it-still-used-warfare.

174   *Churchill, whose policies in Bengal:* Bard Wilkinson, "Churchill's Policies to Blame for Millions of Indian Famine Deaths, Study Says," CNN, March 29, 2019, https://www.cnn.com/2019/03/29/asia/churchill-bengal-famine-intl -scli-gbr.

174   *I calmed the tremor in my gut:* Viet Thanh Nguyen, *The Sympathizer* (New York: Grove Press, 2015), 241.

175   *I don't care to belong:* Groucho Marx, *The Groucho Letters: Letters from and to Groucho Marx* (New York: Simon & Schuster, 1967), 8.

175   *its ruling intellectual force:* Karl Marx and Friedrich Engels, *The German Ideology*, ed. C. J. Arthur (New York: International Publishers, 1970), 62.

184   *one to two million people in the north:* Geoffrey Gunn, "The Great Vietnamese Famine of 1944–45 Revisited," *Asia-Pacific Journal* 9, issue 5, no. 4 (January 24, 2011): https://apjjf.org/2011/9/5/Geoffrey-Gunn/3483/article.html.

184   *The total population of the north:* Maks Banens, "Vietnam: A Reconstitution of Its 20th Century Population History," HAL Open Science, 2000, 39, https:// hal.archives-ouvertes.fr/hal-00369251/document.

185   *wretched, sick, and horribly maimed:* Diana Shaw, "The Temptation of Tom Dooley: He Was the Heroic Jungle Doctor of Indochina in the 1950s. But He Had a Secret, and to Protect It, He Helped Launch the First Disinformation Campaign of the Vietnam War," *Los Angeles Times*, December 15, 1991, https:// www.latimes.com/archives/la-xpm-1991-12-15-tm-868-story.html.

185   *All in Viet Nam dream:* Ibid.

186   *the planet's biggest arms seller:* The United States sells more weapons than the next six countries combined. See "Arms Exports—Country Rankings," TheGlobalEconomy.com, accessed December 3, 2022, https://www .theglobaleconomy.com/rankings/arms_exports/.

187   *Mr. Gorbachev, tear down this wall:* Peter Robinson, "'Tear Down This Wall': How Top Advisers Opposed Reagan's Challenge to Gorbachev—but Lost," *Prologue*,

Summer 2007, https://www.archives.gov/publications/prologue/2007
/summer/berlin.html.

189   *Fellow Vietnamese refugee Lac Su:* Lac Su, *I Love Yous Are for White People: A
Memoir* (New York: Harper Perennial, 2009).

197   *seventh most common surname:* Giselle Au-Nhien Nguyen, "I Have One
of Australia's Most Common Surnames, but No-One Can Pronounce It,"
BuzzFeed, January 24, 2017, https://www.buzzfeed.com/gisellenguyen
/ng-weir-en.

197   *Your generation had Tom Vu:* Jube Shiver Jr., "Despite Florida Probe, Real
Estate Promoter Tom Vu Still Wows Crowds: Investing: Some Ex-Students
Say He Allegedly Engaged in Deceptive Trade Practices. But the Vietnam
Native Denies the Charges," *Los Angeles Times*, February 16, 1992, https://
www.latimes.com/archives/la-xpm-1992-02-16-fi-4408-story.html.

199   *Jane Fonda's son, Troy:* Steven J. Ross, *Hollywood Left and Right: How Movie
Stars Shaped American Politics* (New York: Oxford University Press, 2011),
255.

200   *executed in 1964:* "Saigon Executes Youth for Plot on McNamara," *New York
Times*, October 15, 1964, https://www.nytimes.com/1964/10/15/archives
/saigon-executes-youth-for-plot-on-mcnamara.html.

206   *What is Chinese tradition and what is the movies:* Maxine Hong Kingston, *The
Woman Warrior: Memoirs of a Girlhood among Ghosts* (New York: Vintage
International, 1989), 5–6.

206   *The Silicon Valley is L.A.:* Peter Malae, *What We Are* (New York: Grove Press,
2010), 46.

207   *in gesture and attitude:* Ibid., 64.

207   *whose Samoan father and uncle both fought:* William Ray, "'Our Story Is a Life
and Death Thing': Peter Nathaniel Malae on Reading John Steinbeck and
Writing American Literature," Steinbeck Now, October 14, 2015, http://www
.steinbecknow.com/2015/10/14/our-story-is-a-life-and-death-thing-peter
-nathaniel-malae-on-reading-john-steinbeck-and-writing-american-literature/.

207   *rising slower than the sun:* Malae, *What We Are*, 91–92.

239   *You need to have read some Shakespeare:* Valentina Rojas-Posada, "Push to Diversify Barnard English Curriculum Sparks Department-Wide Debate," *Columbia Daily Spectator,* April 19, 2018, https://www.columbiaspectator.com/news/2018/04/19/push-to-diversify-barnard-english-curriculum-sparks-department-wide-debate/#.WtvC2x6ELLc.twitter.

239   *Many professors would feel:* Ibid.

239   *slavery's profits make European modernity possible:* See, for example, Paul Gilroy's *The Black Atlantic: Modernity and Double Consciousness* (Cambridge, MA: Harvard University Press, 1993).

239   *the Americas and its Indigenous peoples:* See Anibal Quijano and Michael Ennis, "Coloniality of Power, Eurocentrism, and Latin America," *Nepantla: Views from South* 1, no. 3 (2000): 553–80.

241   *It came to me that no man:* Carlos Bulosan, *America Is in the Heart: A Personal History* (Seattle: University of Washington Press, 1973), 326–27.

248   *His habit of forgetting:* Viet Thanh Nguyen, "The Other Man," in *The Refugees* (New York: Grove Press, 2017), 42.

283   *orgy of blood:* William Carlos Williams, *In the American Grain* (Norfolk, CT: New Directions, 1925), 41.

283   *United States tested on the Marshall Islands:* "The Pacific: Atomic Bomb Testing at Bikini Atoll 1946," Nuclear Princeton, https://nuclearprinceton.princeton.edu/pacific.

284   *Muwekma Ohlone people of this land:* "Muwekma Ohlone Tribal Land Acknowledgment for the City of San Jose and Surrounding Region Thámien Ancestral Muwekma Ohlone Territory," Indian Health Center of Santa Clara Valley, https://www.indianhealthcenter.org/wp-content/uploads/2020/10/San-Jose-Muwekma-Land-Acknowledgement.pdf.

286   *I hear America singing:* Walt Whitman, *I Hear America Singing* (New York: Philomel Books, 1991).

286   *I, too, sing America:* Langston Hughes, "I, Too," in *Poems,* ed. David Roessel (New York: Knopf, 1999), 35.

286   *$3,000 to $12,000 a month in rent:* Miro, accessed December 13, 2022, https://rentmiro.com/.

294 *You must go on:* Samuel Beckett, *The Unnamable,* ed. Steven Connor (London: Faber and Faber, 2010), 133.

294 *Beckett was one:* On Beckett's refugee experiences during World War II and their impact on his writing, see Lyndsey Stonebridge, *Placeless People: Writing, Rights, and Refugees* (Oxford, UK: Oxford University Press, 2018).

309 *Asian immigrant women working in massage parlors:* Corina Knoll et al., "2 Immigrant Paths: One Led to Wealth, the Other Ended in Death in Atlanta," *New York Times,* March 24, 2021, https://www.nytimes.com/2021/03/24/us /atlanta-shooting-spa-owners.html.

312 *The killer says he is:* Teo Armus, "The Atlanta Suspect Isn't the First to Blame 'Sex Addiction' for Heinous Crimes. But Scientists Are Dubious," *Washington Post,* March 18, 2021, https://www.washingtonpost.com/nation/2021/03/18 /sex-addiction-atlanta-shooting-long/.

312 *one of George Floyd's favorites:* Robert Samuels and Toluse Olorunnipa, *His Name Is George Floyd: One Man's Life and the Struggle for Racial Justice* (New York: Viking, 2022), 74.

313 *this is for fighting, this is for fun:* "This Is My Rifle. This Is My Gun," *Full Metal Jacket,* directed by Stanley Kubrick (1987, accessed December 13, 2022), https://www.youtube.com/watch?v=4kUoXCVey_U.

313 *American soldiers gang-rape:* Larry Heinemann, *Close Quarters* (New York: Farrar, Strauss & Giroux, 1977).

314 *origins, ancestries, religions:* Laila Lalami, *Conditional Citizens: On Belonging in America* (New York: Pantheon Books, 2020).

314 *massacred 6,000 Vietnamese people:* Robert J. Hanyok, "Spartans in Darkness: American SIGINT and the Indochina War, 1945–1975" (National Security Agency: Center for Cryptologic History, 2002), 10. Accessed via https://www .nsa.gov/portals/75/documents/news-features/declassified-documents /cryptologic-histories/spartans_in_darkness.pdf.

315 *early settlers in this region:* "History," Fort Indiantown Gap Warrior Training Grounds, https://www.ftig.ng.mil/History/.

315 *a fortification was established:* "History," Fort Indiantown Gap, https:// visitlebanonvalley.com/business/fort-indiantown-gap/.

316 *More than four thousand Cherokee perish:* Four thousand dead is the commonly accepted figure. The anthropologist Russell Thornton estimates the death toll could have been as high as ten thousand in his article "Cherokee Population Losses during the Trail of Tears: A New Perspective and a New Estimate," *Ethnohistory* 31, no. 4 (Autumn 1984): 289–300.

316 *come from Paxton Township:* "The Susquehannock," Susquehannock Fire Ring, https://web.archive.org/web/20100109141308/http:/susquehannock .brokenclaw.net/susquehannock.

317 *Murdered at Conestoga Town:* Ibid.

322 *or so I imagined:* Viet Thanh Nguyen, "War Years," in *The Refugees* (New York: Grove Press, 2017), 55–56.

322 *Whereof one cannot speak:* Ludwig Wittgenstein, *Tractatus Logico-Philosophicus* (London: Harcourt, Brace & Company, 1922), 90.

322 *"happy forgetting":* Paul Ricoeur, *Memory, History, Forgetting,* trans. Kathleen Blamey and David Pellauer (Chicago: University of Chicago Press, 2004), 501.

325 *"You must not tell anyone":* Kingston, *Woman Warrior,* 3.

328 *It's difficult to look at:* ABC News (@ABC), "Pentagon press sec. John Kirby gets emotional during remarks about Pres. Putin and images of war in Ukraine," Twitter, April, 29, 2022, https://twitter.com/ABC/status /152019875092 8613377?ref_src=twsrc%5Etfw.

328 *It was a pity:* Graham Greene, *The Quiet American* (New York: Penguin, 1977), 179.

329 *Those of us who fall outside:* Rabih Alameddine, "Comforting Myths: Notes from a Purveyor," *Harper's,* June 2018, https://harpers.org/archive/2018/06 /comforting-myths/.

333 *not suitable with Vietnamese standpoint:* Memo No. 189/DA-NT from the Film Department of the Ministry of Culture, Sports and Tourism, Hanoi, March 22, 2022.

333 *definitely smear the image of the Vietnamese army:* Undated memo, no author, "SOME NOTED [sic] FROM MEMBERS OF APPROVAL COMMITTEE," received March 23, 2022.

335   *Whenever she spoke in English:* Nguyen, "War Stories," 72.

340   *Extravagance and Necessity:* Kingston, *The Woman Warrior,* 6.

342   *Hahamog'na Tribe:* "Indigenous People of San Gabriel," Discovering Pasadena, https://discoveringpasadena.com/indigenous-people-of-san-gabriel.

342   *it is part of morality:* Theodor Adorno, *Minima Moralia: Reflections from Damaged Life* (New York: Verso, 2005), 39.

342   *what is true of all exile:* Edward Said, *Reflections on Exile and Other Essays* (Cambridge, MA: Harvard University Press, 2000), 185.

348   *To be alive, to him:* Philip Roth, *Patrimony* (New York: Vintage, 2010), 124.

351   *Muwekma Ohlone land:* The Gate of Heaven Catholic Cemetery in Los Altos, California, is located within the ancestral lands and territory of the Muwekma Ohlone Tribe of the San Francisco Bay Area. See http://www.muwekma.org/.

351   *Hellfire assassination of a terrorist leader:* Bernd Debusmann Jr. and Chris Partridge, "Ayman al-Zawahiri: How US Strike Could Kill al-Qaeda Leader—but Not His Family," BBC, August 3, 2022, https://www.bbc.com/news/world-us-canada-62400923.

352   *A righteous strike:* Vanessa Romo, "No U.S. Troops behind a Drone Strike That Killed Afghan Civilians Will Be Punished," NPR, December 13, 2021, https://www.npr.org/2021/12/13/1063880137/no-punishment-troops-afghanistan-kabul-strike-civilians.

352   *worked for the Americans:* Matthieu Aikins et al., "Times Investigation: In U.S. Drone Strike, Evidence Suggests No ISIS Bomb," *New York Times,* September 10, 2021, https://www.nytimes.com/2021/09/10/world/asia/us-air-strike-drone-kabul-afghanistan-isis.html.

352   *The hour of the barbarian is at hand:* Aimé Césaire, *Discourse on Colonialism* (New York: Monthly Review Press, 1972), 59. The French original from Éditions Présence Africaine, 1955: "L'heure est arrivée du Barbare. Du Barbare moderne. L'heure américaine. Violence, démesure, gaspillage, mercantilisme, bluff, grégarisme, la bêtise, la vulgarité, le désordre" (*Discours sur le colonialisme,* 70–72).

352   *I love America more than:* James Baldwin, "Autobiographical Notes," in *Notes of a Native Son* (Boston: Beacon Press, 1955), 9.